820.8.

The Literature of Terror

The Literature of Terror

A HISTORY OF GOTHIC FICTIONS
from 1765 to the present day

David Punter

VOLUME 1

THE GOTHIC TRADITION

Longman

An imprint of **Pearson Education**

Harlow, England · London · New York · Reading, Massachusetts · San Francisco
Toronto · Don Mills, Ontario · Sydney · Tokyo · Singapore · Hong Kong · Seoul
Taipei · Cape Town · Madrid · Mexico City · Amsterdam · Munich · Paris · Milan

Pearson Education Limited
Edinburgh Gate, Harlow,
Essex CM20 2JE, England
and Associated Companies throughout the world

Visit us on the World Wide Web at:
www.pearsoned.co.uk

First published in 1996

ISBN 0 582 237149 PPR

British Library Cataloguing-in-Publication Data

A catalogue record for this book is available from the British Library

Library of Congress Cataloging-in-Publication Data
Punter, David.
The literature of terror : a history of gothic fictions from 1765
to the present day / David Punter.
p. cm.
Previous ed. published in 1 v.
Includes bibliographical references (p.   ) and index.
Contents: v. 1. The gothic tradition
ISBN 0–582–23714–9 (v. 1)
1. English literature—History and criticism.   2. Gothic revival
(Literature) 3. Horror tales, English—History and criticism.
4. Horror tales, American—History and criticism.   5. American
literature—History and criticism.   I. Title.
PS408.G68P8   1966
823′.0872909—dc20
                                                        95–30686
                                                           CIP

10 9   8   7   6
06 05

Typeset by 20 in Baskerville 10/12 pt

Printed in Malaysia, GPS

Contents

COLEG POWYS

BRECON

Preface to the First Edition

This book has grown out of a combination of interests. First and most important is my fascination with much of the literature, which has been considerably increased by experiences of teaching it to students, at Cambridge, but with far more interesting results over the last five years at the University of East Anglia. Associated with this has been a growing dissatisfaction with the adequacy of available approaches to Gothic, a point to which I address myself several times in the course of the text. Behind this, however, there lurks a more general dissatisfaction, which can be summed up like this: it has seemed to me that the most valuable general approaches to literary criticism, which I take to be grounded in Marxist and sociological ways of thinking, have acquired the habit of falsely restricting themselves (with one or two honourable exceptions) to examining literary material which we can broadly term 'realist'. I hope this book can be seen as a contribution to a dialogue about this persistent tendency.

I want to use this brief Preface to make a few methodological points, some large and some small. First, I assume that the consequence of my remark above is that the best literary criticism is written from a standpoint which is at least implicitly interdisciplinary. However, I have found the task of fulfilling this demand while attending to an enormous range of material difficult. It seems to me that the main orientation of the book has therefore remained 'critical'; on the other hand, I hope that it suggests lines of argument which could be borne out by the proper processes of cultural research, even where considerations of space and time have prevented me from filling out the relevant connections.

Second, I have planned this book as an introduction to Gothic fictions for the student and for the interested general reader, and have adopted one or two devices in furtherance of this end. In terms of quotations and references, I have varied procedure. With fiction which is currently available, I have cited the most readily obtainable version, even where this might be a paperback reprint. With fiction which is unavailable outside central libraries, I have reverted to the usual scholarly procedure, citing the original text. With poetry, where textual variation is of greater consequence, I have relied on standard editions of complete works where possible. There are various points in the text where I have had to take a choice as to whether to support my argument with esoteric quotations, or with those which are more frequently referred to in the critical literature. I have consistently tended towards the latter, as conducive to furthering a continuing and focused *debate* about the nature of Gothic.

Third, I am aware that some of these comments may make the reader suppose that he or she will find much reference in the text to Marx and to Marxists. This is not the case. On the other hand, there is a good deal of specific reference to Freud. It would be ponderous to attempt an explanation of this here; I hope the reasons emerge in the course of reading. It is, however, perhaps worth pointing out the obvious, that Marx had little to say about literature in general, and nothing whatever about Gothic fictions, whereas Freud's theory both contains an implicit aesthetic dimension and centres upon an analysis of fear; the uses to which I have put this configuration seem to me at no point incompatible with an underlying historical materialism.

I began to write this book in 1976. Since then there has been a sizeable increase in the quantity of criticism of Gothic. I have rarely included explicit reference to this very recent critical material in the text (although I am aware that some arguments, about, for instance, the relations of women to and in Gothic and about the formal nature of Gothic, have crept in anyway). This is because this material is as yet largely unavailable to the student or general reader. There are, however, relevant references in the Bibliography.

Finally, I should point out that the chapter divisions are not based on a simple historical sequence. My principle of organisation has been based on historical progression, but has also taken into account other considerations. Each chapter is centred on what I take to be, in one way or another, a coherent body of literary work; and most of the chapters also specialise in one of a series of linked critical approaches to the material.

D.G.P.
University of East Anglia
December 1978

vii

Preface to the Second Edition

In producing a second, revised edition of *The Literature of Terror*, I initially found myself confronting a well-nigh impossible task. The original version was begun in 1976, completed in 1978, and published in 1980. Since those years, a flood of critical material on the Gothic has appeared; furthermore, whole sets of assumptions about critical thinking have been modified or overturned, and my own conception of the nature of criticism and interpretation has inevitably altered in explicit and implicit ways. Perhaps even more important, there is a whole history of writing over these last fifteen or so years which has not merely added to but *changed* the notion of what Gothic might be seen to be about, what it might be conceived to be; if there was a 'canon' in the late 1970s, then that canon, or more correctly those coordinates of canon-formation, can now only be radically different.

While trying to think about these difficulties, I found myself reading the Preface to the second, revised edition of an entirely different book, *Imagined Communities* by Benedict Anderson, and what he says there seems so sensible that I would like to quote it here as part of a signature to my own efforts: to adapt his book, he says, 'to the demands of these vast changes in the world and in the text is a task beyond my present means. It seemed better, therefore, to leave it largely as an 'unrestored' period piece, with its own characteristic style, silhouette, and mood'.

Some restorations, however, I have attempted. In both volumes, I have updated the Bibliography. In the first volume I have also added a brief 'Appendix on Criticism', which attempts to offer some guidance about recent criticism of the 'classic' Gothic canon. And in the second volume, in the most significant additions, I have added a further chapter on the contemporary Gothic and have also substantially revised the chapter originally entitled 'Towards a theory of the Gothic'. I am not at all sure I have managed these changes seamlessly; but I hope that at least they provide, along with the separation of the book into two volumes, some further starting-points for considering the Gothic not only in its historical formation but also as a contemporary phenomenon, and one with considerable implications for the wider cultural and social sphere.

D.G.P.
University of Stirling
January 1995

CHAPTER 1

Introductory: dimensions of Gothic

In a book on Gothic fictions, it seems reasonable to begin with a brief examination of the word 'Gothic' itself. It is a word which has, even now, a wide variety of meanings, and which has had in the past even more. It is used in a number of different fields: as a literary term, as a historical term, as an artistic term, as an architectural term. And as a literary term in contemporary usage, it has a range of different applications.

In a literary context, 'Gothic' is most usually applied to a group of novels written between the 1760s and the 1820s. Their authors are now, with few exceptions, not the object of much critical attention, although some names still stand out: Horace Walpole, Ann Radcliffe, Matthew Lewis, C. R. Maturin, Mary Shelley. As we shall see, there are important differences between the better-known Gothic novels; nonetheless, literary history has tended to group them together into a homogeneous body of fiction. When thinking of the Gothic novel, a set of characteristics springs readily to mind: an emphasis on portraying the terrifying, a common insistence on archaic settings, a prominent use of the supernatural, the presence of highly stereotyped characters and the attempt to deploy and perfect techniques of literary suspense are the most significant. Used in this sense, 'Gothic' fiction is the fiction of the haunted castle, of heroines preyed on by unspeakable terrors, of the blackly lowering villain, of ghosts, vampires, monsters and werewolves.

And indeed, if this were the only literary meaning of Gothic, the term would be reasonably easy to describe and define. But it is not: over the last two centuries, it has acquired a number of other usages, some of them apparently only tangentially related to the 'original Gothic', and it is now a term which crops up continually both in academic discourse and also in more popular reviews of fiction. For instance, 'Gothic' is the term which publishers still use to sell a particular genre of paperback historical romance. The genre can be conveniently identified from the blurb on the back of *The Spectral Bride* by 'Margaret Campbell', published by Sphere as a 'QueenSize Gothic':

> James Daintry, Lord Manton, was the heir of a noble line. And like his father before him he brooded on the ancient crime that marred so hideously his family's history. It was said that the ghost of the murdered Harriet Bond haunted the grave, seeking revenge, seeking to become James's spectral bride. The arrival of the lovely young Adelaide Fenton and her sister Caroline drew James from his brooding, until a vengeful ghost arose to possess the young lord in search of awful justice for an ancient crime.

Inside the covers is a turgidly-written medley of slightly perverse romance and tame supernaturalism, a *Woman's Own* story set precariously in the 1870s. The elements which seem most universal in the genre are the apparent presence of a ghost, often finally explained away by non-supernatural means; the very real presence of one or more members of the aristocracy, with castles and other props to match; and a dominant love-plot, generally set in the past but with very little attempt at real historical distancing beyond, perhaps, occasional vocabulary and sometimes the interpolation of references to actual historical events. The novels show the marks of being written for a largely captive audience: the same themes are repeated with only the slightest of variations, and assumptions are frequently made which point to a readership already thoroughly familiar with a certain set of narrative and stylistic conventions.

And there are other contemporary uses of the term 'Gothic': a cardinal example is its reappearance as a description of a certain kind of American fiction of which the main practitioners are usually taken to be James Purdy, Joyce Carol Oates, John Hawkes and Flannery O'Connor. At first glance, it is not easy to see what these writers have in common, but what the critics seem to have in mind is a literature of psychic grotesquerie. This 'New American Gothic' is said to deal in landscapes of the mind, settings which are distorted by the pressure of the principal characters' psychological obsessions. We are given little or no access to an 'objective' world; instead we are immersed in the psyche of the protagonist, often through sophisticated use of first-person narrative. It may or may not be coincidence that writers and settings alike have connections with the American South; in one way or another, feelings of degeneracy abound. The worlds portrayed are ones infested with psychic and social decay, and coloured with the heightened hues of putrescence. Violence, rape and breakdown are the key motifs; the crucial tone is one of desensitised acquiescence in the horror of obsession and prevalent insanity.

And 'Gothic' is also used in a less tendentious sense to refer to horror fiction itself, in the common form of the ghost story. Here there is a clear historical element in the usage: many of the best-known masters of supernatural fiction – Algernon Blackwood, M. R. James, H. P. Lovecraft – derive their techniques of suspense and their sense of the archaic directly from the original Gothic fiction, and many of their crucial symbols of the supernatural were previously the property of these older writers. This is not, of course, to say that all twentieth-century horror fiction has its roots in the Gothic: but it is remarkable how much of it does, how much it relies on themes and styles which, by rights, would seem to be more than a century out of date.

A crucial example here, and one to which we shall return, is the horror film. These, clearly, come in all shapes and sizes, but several of the major sub-genres – for instance, the American films of the 1930s and the products of England's Hammer Studios – deal constantly in settings and characters taken from the late eighteenth and early nineteenth centuries. The reasons for this are difficult to see: there are many films of terror, Alfred Hitchcock's and Roman Polanski's among them, which ably demonstrate that fear is at its fiercest when it is seen to invade the everyday contemporary world, yet alongside these films Hammer has turned out further versions of the staple Gothic fictions, with every appearance of continuing commercial success.

And then again, there are many contemporary and near-contemporary writers who have nothing to do with any of these genres, and yet who in one way or another regard themselves as personally indebted to the Gothic tradition. One of the most notable was Mervyn Peake, who created in his *Gormenghast* trilogy (1946–59) a fantasy world entirely out of the elements of early Gothic fiction.

> The while, beneath the downpour and the sunbeams, the Castle hollow as a tongueless bell, its corroded shell dripping or gleaming with the ephemeral weather, arose in immemorial defiance of the changing airs, and skies. . . . Stone after grey stone climbed. Windows yawned: shields, scrolls, and legendary mottoes, melancholy in their ruin, protruded in worn relief over arches or doorways; along the sills of casements, in the walls of towers or carved in buttresses. Storm-nibbled

3

heads, their shallow faces striated with bad green and draped with creepers, stared blindly through the four quarters, from between broken eyelids.

Stone after grey stone; and a sense of the heaving skywards of great blocks, one upon another in a climbing weight, ponderous and yet alive with the labour of dead days.[1]

The resonances here force us back to the castles of Ann Radcliffe and Matthew Lewis, to the angry and potent ruins from which the first Gothic novelists built their literary dreams and nightmares. Another type of interpretation of Gothic is suggested by Angela Carter in the Afterword to her collection of tales, *Fireworks* (1974), where she discusses her own debt to the 'Gothic tradition' as represented by Edgar Allan Poe and E. T. A. Hoffmann:

> The Gothic tradition in which Poe writes grandly ignores the value systems of our institutions; it deals entirely with the profane. Its great themes are incest and cannibalism. Character and events are exaggerated beyond reality, to become symbols, ideas, passions. Its style will tend to be ornate, unnatural – and thus operate against the perennial human desire to believe the word as fact. Its only humour is black humour. It retains a singular moral function – that of provoking unease.[2]

A particular attitude towards the recapture of history; a particular kind of literary style; a version of self-conscious un-realism; a mode of revealing the unconscious; connections with the primitive, the barbaric, the tabooed – all of these meanings have attached themselves in one way or another to the idea of Gothic fiction, and our present apprehension of the term is usually an uneasy concatenation of them, in which there is a complicated interplay of direct historical connections and ever variable metaphor.

To see the reasons for this flexibility, we have, however, to look back beyond Gothic *fiction* and into the history of the word 'Gothic' itself, which is not of course exclusively or even primarily a literary term; we need particularly to mention a set of cultural and linguistic changes during the eighteenth century which largely conditioned later uses of the word. The original meaning, not unnaturally, was literally 'to do with the Goths', or with the barbarian northern tribes who played so somewhat unfairly reviled a part in the collapse of the Roman empire, although even this apparently literal meaning was less simple than it appears, because the seventeenth- and early eighteenth-century writers who used the term in this sense had very little idea of who the Goths were or what they were like. One thing that was known was that they came from northern Europe, and thus the term had a tendency to broaden out, to become virtually a synonym for 'Teutonic' or 'Germanic', while retaining its connotations of barbarity.

During the course of the eighteenth century, however, this was to change. In the first place, less weight came to be placed on the geographical significance of the word and correspondingly more on the historical. Here again the problem occurred that very little was known about the history of the Dark Ages, or even about medieval history; it is well known that the eighteenth century possessed a somewhat foreshortened sense of past chronology, and from being a term suggestive of more or less unknown features of the Dark Ages, 'Gothic' became descriptive of things medieval – in fact, of all things preceding about the middle of the seventeenth century. Another connotation naturally accompanied this: if 'Gothic' meant to do with post-Roman barbarism and to do with the medieval world, it followed that it was a term which could be used in opposition to 'classical'. Where the classical was well-ordered, the Gothic was chaotic; where simple and pure, Gothic was ornate and convoluted; where the classics offered a set of cultural models to be followed, Gothic represented excess and exaggeration, the product of the wild and the uncivilised.

These extensions in meaning have a perceptible logic; but what started to happen in the middle of the eighteenth century had more to do with a shift in cultural values. For while the word 'Gothic' retained this stock of meanings, the value placed upon them began to alter radically. It is not possible to put a precise date on this change, but it was one of huge dimensions which affected whole areas of eighteenth-century culture – architectural, artistic and literary; for what happened was that the medieval, the primitive, the wild, became invested with positive value in and for itself.

Gothic stood for the old-fashioned as opposed to the modern; the barbaric as opposed to the civilised; crudity as opposed to elegance; old English barons as opposed to the cosmopolitan gentry; indeed, often for the English and provincial as opposed to the European or Frenchified. Gothic was the archaic, the pagan, that which was prior to, or was opposed to, or resisted the establishment of civilised values and a well-regulated society. And various writers, starting from this point, began to make out a case for the importance of these Gothic qualities and to claim, specifically, that the fruits of primitivism and barbarism possessed a fire, a vigour, a sense of grandeur which was sorely needed in English culture. Furthermore, they began to argue that there were whole areas of English cultural history which were being ignored, and that the way to breathe life into the culture was by re-establishing relations with this forgotten, 'Gothic' past.

Many of the crucial texts which made this point were written in the 1760s; perhaps the most important of all was Bishop Hurd's *Letters on Chivalry and Romance* (1762). Hurd was a littérateur and no historical scholar, but he summarised a very widespread flow of thought in his enquiry into the nature and value of the Gothic:

> The greatest geniuses of our own and foreign countries, such as Ariosto and Tasso in Italy, and Spenser and Milton in England, were seduced by these barbarities of their forefathers; were even charmed by the Gothic Romances. Was this caprice and absurdity in them? Or, may there not be something in the Gothic Romance peculiarly suited to the views of a genius, and to the ends of poetry?[3]

The arts of our ancient forefathers and the folk traditions on which they drew, Hurd is saying, may have been rude and may indeed not have conformed to rules which we have since come to regard as constitutive of aesthetic success and propriety; but may not this very rudeness and wildness be itself a source of power – a power which Spenser and Milton saw and which we may not be able to reclaim by any other means?

It is not simple to pin down precisely who the 'forefathers' were to whom Hurd refers, but one can point to four principal areas of past literature which were brought back into cultural prominence under the aegis of the 'revival of the Gothic'. First, there was the truly ancient British heritage, insofar as any of it was available in the eighteenth century. The poet Thomas Gray regarded himself as well read in old Welsh poetry; James Macpherson, the celebrated forger, was referring back to an ancient British 'tradition' in his 'translations' of the imaginary Gaelic poet 'Ossian'; Thomas Percy's translation in 1770 of P. H. Mallet's *Northern Antiquities* was designed to reacquaint its readers with the ancient history of northern Europe. Second, there were the ballads. Percy's crucial collection, *Reliques of Ancient English Poetry*, was published in 1765, and it was the re-establishment of the credentials of this form of 'folk-poetry' which led on, through poems like Blake's 'Gwin, King of Norway', written in the 1770s, to Coleridge's 'Ancient Mariner' (1797–8) and then to Keats's 'La Belle Dame sans Merci' and Shelley's *Mask of Anarchy*, both written in 1819.

Third, Gothic was taken to include English medieval poetry, pre-eminently the works of Chaucer, which were given a scholarly edition by Thomas Tyrwhitt in 1775–8. And fourthly, it included, at least for some critics and writers, the major work of Spenser and of the Elizabethans which, it now came to be thought, had been buried under the reputation of the achievements of the mid-seventeenth century. This shift of value was probably complete by the 1780s: not, that is, in that Gothic ever became a universal standard of taste, but in that by that time the arguments which supported it had received their fullest articulation and the stage was set for Gothic to flow into romantic poetry which, apart from the fiction itself, was to prove its major cultural influence.

As we have said, however, the literary effects of this change in values were by no means the whole of the picture; the other principal application of the term 'Gothic' was, as it still is, in the field of architecture, where it was used to refer to medieval architecture, principally ecclesiastical, from about the twelfth to the sixteenth centuries. Alongside its taste for 'ancient' literature, the late eighteenth century acquired a pronounced taste for medieval buildings, and the wealthy even went to the extent of building Gothic ruins, ready-made; perhaps the most famous example of Gothic building in the period was Horace Walpole's Strawberry Hill, a Gothic castle in miniature, although much the most impressive was William Beckford's Fonthill, which collapsed under the weight of its own grandiosity. The inheritor of this taste, of course, was to be the 'Gothicising' mania of the Victorians.

However, the principal issue which confronts us here is that of Gothic fiction, and here the situation is somewhat complicated. Like any other genre, it appears at first glance to be a relatively homogeneous body of writing, linked stylistically, thematically and ideologically, but on closer inspection the illusion falls away, revealing a very disparate collection of works. What one can do, however, is say a little about what Gothic fiction appeared to be during its first heyday, from the 1760s to the 1820s. In the first place, it is necessary to emphasise that, within the circumscribed limits of the reading public of the time, it was an extremely copious and popular form of fiction; during the 1790s at least, it virtually dominated the novel market.[4] Its relationship to the general Gothic revival was in fact rather tangential, but nonetheless there were some important points of contact. Many of the novels were set in the past, sometimes only nominally, sometimes with considerable effort. Many of them used castles, ruins, convents, as settings. And many of them deliberately set out to portray precisely those manifestations of the wild and the barbaric which appeared to appeal to the taste of the day. But they had other, less acceptable, features too, which had a less

7

obvious relation to Gothic in general; many of them were more or less crudely sensationalist, in that they tended to derive their force from the portrayal of extreme situations, mostly situations of terror. It is partly for this reason that Gothic has not been well treated by literary critics; it has been said that it was crude, exploitative, even sadistic, and that it pandered to the worst in the popular taste of its time. In 1800, Wordsworth appended to the second edition of *Lyrical Ballads* a lengthy Preface, the main purpose of which was to justify the use of 'natural diction' rather than ornament and artifice, and included these comments, with the taste for Gothic fiction very much in mind:

> the human mind is capable of excitement without the application of gross and violent stimulants; and he must have a very faint perception of its beauty and dignity who does not know this, and who does not further know that one being is elevated above another in proportion as he possesses this capability. . . . The invaluable works of . . . Shakespeare and Milton, are driven into neglect by frantic novels, sickly and stupid German Tragedies, and deluges of idle and extravagant stories in verse.[5]

As can be seen from this, the public taste for Gothic was not restricted to the novel, but it was here that it was at its most significant. For Wordsworth, literature should be morally and spiritually uplifting, and of course the revival of Shakespeare and Milton was admissible on these grounds; Gothic fiction frequently depicted, and sometimes appeared to revel in, vice and violence. For Wordsworth, the writer had a vital social role to play in elevating the minds and morals of his audience and returning them to communion with the natural bases of life; the Gothic writers appeared to give themselves no such tasks and to be quite content to pander to the minds and morals of their readers as they found them, and to portray unnaturalness in all its most lurid colours. Already we can see the extent to which Gothic fiction was moving beyond the more general Gothic revival in its devotion to the barbaric and the violent.

Eighteen years later Jane Austen, in *Northanger Abbey*, wrote a parody of Gothic fiction of which this is the opening:

> No one who had ever seen Catherine Morland in her infancy, would have supposed her born to be an heroine. Her situation in life, the character of her father and mother, her own person and disposition, were all equally against her. Her father was a clergyman, without being neglected, or poor, and a very respectable man, though his name was Richard – and he had never been handsome. He had a considerable independence, besides two good livings – and he was not in the least addicted to locking up his daughters. Her mother was a woman of

useful plain sense, with a good temper, and, what is more remarkable, with a good constitution. She had three sons before Catherine was born; and instead of dying in bringing the latter into the world, as any body might expect, she still lived on – lived to have six children more – to see them growing up around her, and to enjoy excellent health herself.[6]

What can be derived from this is a picture, by negation, of the conventions by which the Gothic novel was supposed to operate, and, however unfair this might be to the more important works, it undoubtedly represents reasonably a mass of the lesser fiction. The world of this lesser fiction was one which dealt in simple moral and social oppositions; one in which there was always a central heroine, abandoned by her parents and cast adrift on the mercies of a savage world; one in which one could reasonably assume any clergyman to be neglected and poor, unless he was one of the unrespectable and malevolent monks and confessors who similarly abounded in the world of the Gothic; one in which men were never called Richard because names of Italian or German extraction were the rule; one in which harsh treatment by fathers and the early death of mothers were to be expected as a matter of course; a world, in short, at a considerable distance from the contemporary world of the eighteenth-century realist novel and ruled over by simple, primitive laws and conventions.

If the violent subject-matter and the simplified and exaggerated characterisation of Gothic fiction earned it enemies, so did its prevalent style, which, again in the less important works, was much given to ornateness, hyperbole, violent exclamation – in fact, to most of the stylistic features which were later to appear on the stage in the form of melodrama. It strove above all, albeit with variable success, to eschew the contemporary world, the world of commerce and the middle class, and so it strove also to avoid the language of the everyday, although in most cases the writers were signally unable to achieve any real simulation of linguistic archaism. The world in which it did deal was peopled with stock characters, who discoursed in predictable ways: the shy, nervous, retiring heroine, who was nevertheless usually possessed of a remarkable ability to survive hideously dangerous situations; the heavy-handed, tyrannical father; the cast of comic extras and servants who, like many of the other characters, often seem to be lifted wholesale out of Jacobean drama; and above all the villain. The villain was always the most complex and interesting character in Gothic fiction, even when drawn with a clumsy hand: awe-inspiring, endlessly resourceful in pursuit of his often opaquely evil ends, and yet possessed of a mysterious attractiveness, he stalks from the pages of one Gothic novel to another, manipulating the doom of others while the knowledge of his own eventual fate surrounds him like the monastic habit and cowl which he so often wore.

To contemporaries, however, it was usually a different feature of Gothic fiction which appeared to be the most significant and around which critical controversy raged, namely, the element of the super-natural. It is a commonplace of literary history that, through the earlier part of the eighteenth century, the ghosts and phantoms which had played so important a part in earlier literature seemed to disappear, because there was no room for them in the supremely rational world of the Augustans. But they started to reappear with the Gothic revival, occurring often in the old ballads, and from there they moved into Gothic fiction. The ways in which they were presented were manifold: in some works, there are any number of genuinely supernatural occurrences, in others only events which prove after all to have reasonable and natural explanation. It is important, however, to point out that in one sense this makes very little difference: even if the ghosts are eventually explained away, this does not mean that their actual presence within the text can be forgotten, and almost all the Gothic writers used the fear of the supernatural for one purpose or another.

For a sample of the kind of writing which Wordsworth condemns and on which Austen looks with an amused and half-affectionate condescension, we can turn to a Gothic tale written roughly halfway between the time of the *Lyrical Ballads* and that of *Northanger Abbey*. All we need to know is that the character named Verezzi has been captured by three villains called Zastrozzi, Bernardo and Ugo, who clearly intend some unspeakable deed:

> At last they stopped – they lifted their victim from the chariot, and bore him to a cavern, which yawned in a dell close by.
>
> Not long did the hapless victim of unmerited persecution enjoy an oblivion which deprived him of a knowledge of his horrible situation. He awoke – and overcome by excess of terror, started violently from the ruffians' arms.
>
> They had now entered the cavern; Verezzi supported himself against a fragment of rock which jutted out.
>
> 'Resistance is useless,' exclaimed Zastrozzi. 'Following us in submissive silence can alone procure the slightest mitigation of your punishment.'
>
> Verezzi followed as fast as his frame, weakened by unnatural sleep, and enfeebled by recent illness, would permit; yet, scarcely believing that he was awake, and not thoroughly convinced of the reality of the

scene before him, he viewed everything with that kind of inexplicable horror which a terrible dream is wont to incite.

After winding down the rugged descent for some time, they arrived at an iron door, which at first sight appeared to be part of the rock itself. Everything had till now been obscured by total darkness; and Verezzi, for the first time, saw the masked faces of his persecutors, which a torch brought by Bernardo rendered visible.

The massy door flew open.

The torches from without rendered the darkness which reigned within still more horrible; and Verezzi beheld the interior of this cavern as a place whence he was never again about to emerge – as his grave.

The repetition of 'horror' and 'horrible'; the 'total darkness' and the 'masked faces' of the villains; the black-and-white tone of 'unmerited persecution'; the insistence on the potential finality of the imprisonment; the note of half-gasping, half-gloating voyeurism – all are commonplaces of the genre. And yet this is not from a text by an unknown writer, but from the short novel *Zastrozzi*, written by Shelley in 1810.[7] It is, of course, the work of a schoolboy; but it is no worse and no better than much of the popular Gothic fiction of its day.

And this is one of the most interesting features of the Gothic, that it influenced most of the greatest writers of its time. One critic has remarked that 'the horror novel . . . affects all the great romantics without exception';[8] Scott thought Matthew Lewis, author of *The Monk*, the most scandalous of all the early Gothic works, one of the greatest of novelists; Coleridge, Keats and Byron all show strong traces of Gothic interests and concerns, not only derived from the harmless historicism of the Gothic revival but also owing a great deal to the apparent excesses of Gothic fiction. Lewis and, more particularly, Ann Radcliffe, were acclaimed by a wide variety of contemporary reviewers. Shelley liked to claim on occasion that his Gothic enthusiasm had passed off in later life; as he says in 'Hymn to Intellectual Beauty' (1816):

> *While yet a boy I sought for ghosts, and sped*
> *Thro' many a listening chamber, cave, and ruin,*
> *And starlight wood, with fearful steps pursuing*
> *Hopes of high talk with the departed dead.*[9]

Those impressionable times, he goes on to claim, are over, but even in 1821, when describing the death of Gherardi in 'Ginevra', he has recourse to a panoply of imagery made available and popular by the Gothic novelists:

Some melted into tears without a sob,
And some with hearts that might be heard to throb
Leant on the table, and at intervals
Shuddered to hear through the deserted halls
And corridors the thrilling shrieks which came
Upon the breeze of night, that shook the flame
Of every torch and taper as it swept
From out the chamber where the women kept; –
Their tears fell on the dear companion cold
Of pleasures now departed; then was knolled
The bell of death, and soon the priests arrived,
And finding death their penitent had shrived,
Returned like ravens from a corpse whereon
A vulture has just feasted to the bone.

(*Works*, IV, 109–10)

There are many other features of Gothic which could be mentioned, but these will emerge more clearly from an examination of
the texts themselves. For the moment, it is more important to
pose the question of what *happened* to Gothic fiction and its influence. It is a kind of question which is intrinsically difficult to answer,
like the old question of what happened to epic, or the more modern
doubts about the fate of tragedy. Any answer to it depends on how
we identify and define Gothic fiction, either as a historically
delimited genre or as a more wide-ranging and persistent tendency
within fiction as a whole. Were we to assume the former, it could be
said that Gothic fiction disappeared in the middle of the nineteenth
century, and that the last writers to use anything like the full range
of Gothic imagery and effects were figures like William Harrison
Ainsworth, Bulwer Lytton and G. W. M. Reynolds. But to answer the
question in this way would be to ignore the real cultural problem
posed by Gothic. Why, in that case, does 'Gothic' still continue to
be a term which writers and critics invoke? Why has so much nine-
teenth- and twentieth-century writing found conscious inspiration
in the original Gothic works? Why is the term still used as an
approximate equivalent for the barbaric, the primitivist, that which
deals directly in the symbolism of the unconscious? A satisfactory
answer to these questions can only be found through a dialectical
analysis, which on the one hand seeks to establish the cultural
significance of Walpole, Radcliffe, Lewis and their followers, while
on the other extrapolating the relation between Gothic and the
later and quite diffferent social and cultural formations within which
it has, in some sense, continued to survive. The beginning of such
an enterprise has to rest on perceiving the Gothic as a way of
relating to the real, to historical and psychological facts, which will

clearly contain a moment of variation as other aspects of cultural life vary, but which nonetheless has forms of continuity which we can trace right through from the eighteenth-century writers to the contemporary world. Part of the justification for such an approach is that Gothic fiction has, above all, to do with terror; and where we find terror in the literature of the last two centuries, in Britain and in America, from Lewis to Conan Doyle, from Mary Shelley to Ambrose Bierce, from Dickens to J. G. Ballard, we almost always find traces of the Gothic. The concepts of 'Gothic' and 'terror' have become intertwined in literary history, and what is needed is an investigation of how and why that has become the case.

Previous critics of the Gothic, however, have almost always restricted themselves to Gothic as a historically circumscribed phenomenon, and at this point it is worth noting one or two features of that criticism. Although in recent years academic activity in this area has increased and a number of important and stimulating articles have been published, there are still very few large-scale studies, and those that do exist are of a rather special kind. Since Gothic fiction was for so long held to be disreputable, a number of the critics who have ventured into the field have either been impelled by a particular and tendentious thesis, or have tended to be overdefensive about their interest. The earliest important study, however, Edith Birkhead's *The Tale of Terror* (1921), is mercifully free from these difficulties. It is a poised and often witty book, and still the best introduction to the major texts. Birkhead has no specific thesis to prove; she is not particularly concerned with the problematic popularity of the genre, or with studying its lesser manifestations, but simply with providing access to those books which have survived the onslaught of history. One of the most important points she makes, however, and one to which we shall return, is that although the supernatural was largely absent from the earlier eighteenth-century *novel*, it was eminently present in the form of chapbooks and translated tales, and Gothic needs to be seen in the context of this provenance.[10]

In 1927, Michael Sadleir published *The Northanger Novels: A Footnote to Jane Austen*, which is basically an account of the Gothic novels mentioned by name in *Northanger Abbey*, which had previously been supposed to be Austen's inventions. But he also makes some general comments on the social significance of Gothic fiction; one fruitful approach which he suggests is to see in it a gesture of defiance, albeit unsystematic and often abortive, in the face of the established conventions of eighteenth-century social life and literature. 'A ruin', he claims,

> expresses the triumph of chaos over order . . . Creepers and weeds, as year by year they riot over sill and paving-stone, defy a broken despotism; every coping-stone that crashes from a castle-battlement into the undergrowth beneath is a small victory for liberty, a snap of the fingers in the face of autocratic power. (*Northanger Novels*, p. 7)

It is from these statements that the vexed controversy about the political implications of Gothic began, a controversy which still underlies much of the criticism, albeit often in a singularly uncomprehended and undeveloped form.

Eino Railo's *The Haunted Castle* appeared in the same year, and took a very different approach to the problems of describing Gothic fiction. Railo's study is basically a catalogue of themes and settings: he takes various specific examples – the motif of the criminal monk, the pact with the devil, the haunted castle itself – and lists instances indefatigably but to very little general effect. One fundamental question which is prompted by this approach is why many of these features should be regarded as characteristic of the Gothic in particular, since most of them occur with equal frequency in, at least, Jacobean drama; Railo virtually ignores questions of literary technique and cultural significance.

J. M. S. Tompkins's *The Popular Novel in England, 1770–1800* appeared in 1932 and made a very important contribution to the study of the Gothic. Tompkins's book is a model of meticulous research; she studies the entire range of fiction produced in England during those three decades, without either condescension or excessive tolerance, and isolates some extremely interesting features. Most importantly, she makes the point that the mass of the sentimental fiction of the age was substantially without plot; that is to say, the novels concentrated on providing a series of very loosely linked episodes and events, connected only by their common bearing on a central moral argument. It is to the Gothic, she claims, that we owe the entire apparatus of novelistic suspense; it is only for the Gothic writers that complexity of plotting was necessary, because it was only for them that the process of suspense and release was an essential fictional mechanism.[11] It is with Tompkins's work that one begins to glimpse the possibility of describing Gothic not only in sociocultural and thematic terms but also in terms of specific developments of form.

In 1938, Montague Summers published *The Gothic Quest*, the most considerable of his several contributions to the criticism of the Gothic, and amply demonstrated the worst of the dangers into which that criticism is liable to fall. Essentially, Summers was a bibliophile, and the book degenerates into a catalogue of obscure Gothic texts, many of which Summers himself appears to have possessed the only extant copy. The notion of Gothic as a widespread and popular form was still comparatively novel at the time, but Summers, trying to avoid describing it merely as a series of 'major works', ends up with far too much material to handle. *The Gothic Quest* is also seriously marred by tendentiousness, both in connection with the worth of certain individual writers, and more importantly in political terms: in his zeal to prove Sadleir and André Breton wrong in their assertion of the subversive tendencies of Gothic, he tries to turn it into an ideally conservative form, referring to it at one point as the 'aristocrat of literature' (Summers, p. 397). *The Gothic Quest*, like Railo's book, is at its best on the life and works of Lewis; when Summers ventures to generalise, he falls constantly into the trap of special pleading, making the book all but useless as an introduction to Gothic.

Although *The Gothic Quest* is now over fifty years old, there have been only two other books of significance. The first of these is Devendra Varma's *The Gothic Flame* (1957), a strange and irritating book which is in fact largely a collation of the earlier critics, sometimes with attributions, sometimes not. Almost all that is interesting in it comes from Birkhead, sometimes even in whole paragraphs, and where Varma tries to formulate a general argument of his own he ends up by merely saying that Gothic fiction marked some kind of rebirth of the 'spiritual'. One comment, however, is worth bearing in mind, because it opens up further possibilities about the relation between Gothic and its age: Varma defines the 'fantastic' in literature as 'the surrealistic expression of those historical and social factors which the ordinary chronicle of events in history does not consider significant' (Varma, p. 217). The importance of this is that it suggests the possibility that Gothic, precisely insofar as because of its historical and geographical distancing it does not appear to represent a 'real' world, may in fact be delivering that world in an inverted form, or representing those areas of the world and of consciousness which are, for one reason or another, not available to the normal processes of representation.

Finally, in *The Romantic Novel in England* (1972), Robert Kiely takes a group of novels written between 1760 and 1840, which naturally includes a number of the major Gothics, and subjects them to a largely formalist analysis. His chief contention is summed up when he claims that in the romantic novel 'confrontation and breakdown are not merely fictional themes but structural and stylistic problems. . . . Romantic novels thrive like parasites on structures whose ruin is the source of their life' (Kiely, pp. 1–2). In other words, the 'romantic novel' in the historical sense is an intrinsically flawed form, which tries to convey in novelistic shape a vision of the world which is not truly assimilable to that shape; it is a familiar argument, but Kiely is one of its best exponents. This, again, is a view which needs to be considered in describing the Gothic, and it serves as a salutary reminder that many of the traditions out of which Gothic fiction grew were in themselves not novelistic but poetic and dramatic.

The established body of criticism, then, takes the form of a set of attempts to isolate and define a historically limited entity, and that definition is cast in a number of forms: sociocultural, thematic, formal, psychological. We find a similar profusion of projects when examining the various ways in which critics have tried to divide Gothic internally, to establish sub-genres within it. If one places four of these categorisations alongside each other – those of Railo, Summers, Varma and Maurice Heine[12] – one finds that almost every permutation of grouping is covered by the available terms. 'Sentimental-Gothic', 'terror-Gothic', 'gothique noir', 'réalisme noir', 'Schauer-Romantik' swim around in dizzying disarray. But this is obviously only a secondary critical problem, which merely follows from the first: how are we to define Gothic?

That is the problem of this book as a whole, and it would be wrong to attempt a definition before studying the texts themselves; but it is worthwhile extrapolating from the existing criticism of Gothic, five principal approaches to a possible definition. Having examined the texts, we can then return to them in order to establish the extent to which they seem sufficiently flexible and precise. First, there is the approach via the Gothic revival as a recognisable movement in the history of culture, with recognisable sociopsychological causes, according to which Gothic fiction is a specific outcropping of a general flow of ideas and attitudes. Within this approach there is the possibility of developing the important analogue with architecture: this is the line adopted most fully by the French critic Maurice Lévy, who takes architecture as the essential model for Gothic and lays stress on the symbolic meaning of the Gothic building, the ideas of aspiration towards the divine which are expressed by it.[13]

Second, there is the suggestion made by Tompkins and developed later by other critics that Gothic fiction can be defined in terms of the nature of plot: not, of course, that Gothic has a monopoly on plot, but that the original Gothic achieved certain specific advances in this area which might be seen as accounting for later traces of Gothic in other fields of fiction. Kiely's argument, which we can take third, is significantly different from this, and it actually appears at first glance rather difficult to square them; the implication of his work is that, far from defining Gothic in terms of narrative achievement, one might be better advised to do so in terms of narrative difficulty.

There are, of course, ways of bringing these two arguments into line, and one which is worth mentioning is by way of Freud's arguments on the nature of language;[14] one might suggest that if it is true that Gothic fiction is marked by narrative complexity, and by its tendency to raise technical problems which it often fails to resolve, then this complexity might precisely be an evasive response to a difficulty, and this difficulty might reside in the taboo quality of many of the themes to which Gothic addresses itself – incest, rape, various kinds of transgression of the boundaries between the natural and the human, the human and the divine. And if this is so, it could well connect with a fourth approach to the Gothic, summarised by Herbert Read, namely the definition of Gothic as the representative of a particular antagonistic attitude towards realism. 'It is proper', says Read, 'for a work of the imagination to be fictitious, and for characters to be typical rather than realistic. Realism is a bourgeois prejudice – what is there of realism in the characters of Sophocles or Racine, Dostoevsky or Sartre?'[15]

Many issues are raised here. The attempt of Gothic fiction to deal with the tabooed and its opposition to realism can obviously be connected. We have already mentioned the popularity of Gothic during the period from the beginnings to the 1820s, and one feature which is characteristic of most really popular art-forms is precisely that they are not realistic. Then again, it needs to be borne in mind that the popularity which Gothic fiction had was of a highly specific kind: it was popular with a new reading public which was itself predominantly bourgeois – popular, in fact, with a middle class who had only twenty years earlier been reading a vastly different kind of novel. The social relations of Gothic appear to be more complex than Read suggests, and this again is a point to which we will return in later chapters.

The last definitional parameter is thematic: Railo and Varma both subscribe to the idea that there are particular themes which are distinctively Gothic, but, on the basis of what we have suggested above, this must be taken in conjunction with other elements. Possibly all themes prescribe a style; but whether they do or not, Gothic themes do because of their uneasy social and psychological situation. In dealing with terror, Gothic deals with the unadmitted, and it is not possible to do that in modes which have already been appropriated for other purposes. A definition of Gothic will have to take into account both theme and style, and other features as well.

This does not, of course, exhaust the possible approaches; on the contrary, this is only the beginning. At the moment, however, before turning to the texts themselves, it is enough to point out that in studying Gothic fiction almost nothing can be assumed, not even the limits of the field; and so I shall hope to evolve a set of descriptions at the same time as attending to the texts, a set of descriptions which will both help to identify the historical Gothic while suggesting reasons for its survival and for the multifarious forms in which it has survived. In the following chapters, I shall bring together examples of writing across two centuries which have been considered 'Gothic', and shall attempt to offer some conclusions on the basis of this material. There is, however, one element which, albeit in a vast variety of forms, crops up in all the relevant fiction, and that is fear. Fear is not merely a theme or an attitude, it also has consequences in terms of form, style and the social relations of the texts; and exploring Gothic is also exploring fear and seeing the various ways in which terror breaks through the surfaces of literature, differently in every case, but also establishing for itself certain distinct continuities of language and symbol.

Notes and references

1. **Mervyn Peake**, *Titus Groan*, introd. Anthony Burgess (Harmondsworth, Middx., 1968), p. 497.
2. **Angela Carter**, *Fireworks: Nine Profane Pieces* (London, 1974), p. 122.
3. **Richard Hurd**, *Letters on Chivalry and Romance*, ed. Hoyt Trowbridge (Los Angeles, 1963), p. 4.
4. See **Montague Summers**, *A Gothic Bibliography* (London, 1941); and, on the popularity of Gothic, **J. M. S. Tompkins**, *The Popular Novel in England, 1770–1800* (London, 1932), pp. 243 ff.
5. **William Wordsworth** and **S. T. Coleridge**, *Lyrical Ballads*, ed. R. L. Brett and A. R. Jones (London, 1968), pp. 248–9.
6. **Jane Austen**, *Northanger Abbey*, ed. A. H. Ehrenpreis (Harmondsworth, Middx., 1972), p. 37.
7. **P. B. Shelley**, *Zastrozzi*, introd. Phyllis Hartnoll (London, 1955), pp. 12–13.
8. **Allan Rodway**, *The Romantic Conflict* (London, 1963), p. 59.

9. *The Complete Works of Percy Bysshe Shelley*, ed. Roger Ingpen and Walter E. Peck (10 vols, New York, 1965), II, 61.
10. See Birkhead, pp. 1–15.
11. See, e. g. Tompkins, pp. 249–50, 346.
12. See Railo, pp. 324–5; Summers, pp. 28–31; Varma, p. 206; and **Maurice Heine**, 'Promenade à travers le Roman noir', *Minotaure*, No. 5 (May 1934), 1–4. This and subsequent references to 'Summers' are to *The Gothic Quest*.
13. See **Maurice Lévy**, *Le roman gothique anglais, 1764–1824* (Toulouse, 1968), pp. 9 ff.
14. See **Sigmund Freud**, *Jokes and Their Relation to the Unconscious* (1905), in *The Standard Edition of the Complete Psychological Works of Sigmund Freud*, ed. James Strachey (24 vols, London, 1953–74), VIII, for the basis of this argument.
15. **Herbert Read**, Foreword, in Varma, p. vii.

CHAPTER 2

The origins of Gothic fiction

Sentimentalism, Graveyard Poetry, The Sublime, Smollett, Horace Walpole, Clara Reeve, Sophia Lee

The origin of Gothic fiction cannot be separated from the origin of the novel form itself. As we are all now well aware, the eighteenth century was the era of the rise of the novel. There had, of course, been many forms of literary prose prior to the eighteenth century, some of them well developed, particularly the prose romance; but the works of Richardson and Fielding in the 1740s nevertheless marked an enormous change in prose writing – specifically, the abandonment of the fanciful in the name of a realistic depiction of contemporary life. This statement would need much amplification and qualification if we were concerned here with attempting to define the novel: but for our purposes it is sufficient to bear in mind the new realism which appeared in the writings of the mid-eighteenth century, a realism of course in some ways prefigured by the semifictional narratives of Defoe. Where the romance-writers of the sixteenth and seventeenth centuries had chosen archaic, mythic or fanciful settings, events in *Clarissa Harlowe* (1748) and *Tom Jones* (1749) occurred in the midst of a contemporary world, and were related to the production and vindication of a contemporary morality. The question of the relation between Gothic and the rise of the novel in general is related to that of how it was possible for a new literary *form* to emerge in this way; and what occasioned such a massive change in the panorama of literary production.

The principal point here is the eighteenth-century change in English social structure and the associated development of the reading public. Where the writer in the mid-seventeenth century had usually perforce produced within the system of patronage and for the benefit of a closed aristocratic circle, increasingly the appearance of a trading middle class and the growth of urban centres combined to produce other potential readers. Raymond Williams notes the growth in the number of printing-houses in London, from sixty at the Restoration, to seventy-five in 1724, and to between 150 and 200 by 1757.[1] Of course, the printing-houses were concerned with all kinds of different work, but Ian Watt's tentative figures on the appearance of works of fiction show us that, at least from the 1740s on, increase in this area would have been a significant factor in the growth of the houses: 'the annual production of works of fiction', he writes, 'which had averaged only about seven in the years between 1700 and 1740, rose to an average of about twenty in the three decades following 1740, and the output was doubled in the period from 1770 to 1800'.[2] Watt emphasises that these figures are only approximate, but the growth is nonetheless obvious; and the middle-class reading public clearly developed in these years a taste for a kind of reading which, while dealing in unreal incident, nonetheless located such incident in a readily recognisable world, rather than in the idealised and remote countries of the Elizabethan romancers.

Under these conditions, the sales of individual works of fiction increased markedly. Williams again quotes some figures: Fielding's *Joseph Andrews* (1742) sold 6,500 copies in thirteen months, Smollett's *Roderick Random* (1748) 5,000 copies in a year, Richardson's *Sir Charles Grandison* (1754) 6,500 in a few months (*Long Revolution*, p. 161). It is, in passing, interesting to note that, although to a certain extent things changed later, the best-sellers then were very much those books which we still read now. The real take-off point, in terms of both the expansion of printing-houses and the sales of individual novels, seems to have been around 1740; and it is precisely in this decade that we can locate another major alteration in reading habits, the sudden growth of the circulating libraries, libraries, that is, which lent out books for a membership fee, generally of some 10*s.* or £1 a year. The importance of the circulating libraries is twofold: first, price thereby ceased to be as much of a barrier to varied reading by the middle classes as it had been; and second, books could now percolate through to some extent to those classes of society who were literate but who could never have dreamed of buying books of their own, principally the domestic servants.[3]

But despite all these things – the composition of the reading public, the increase in sales figures, the rise of the circulating libraries – despite these factors, it is very important not to overemphasise the changes which the eighteenth century saw. The price of books was in general prohibitive. In the late seventeenth century, duodecimo novellas cost 1*s.* each; examples would have been Aphra Behn's *Oroonoko* (1688) and Congreve's *Incognita* (1693). And during the eighteenth century, these prices increased considerably: in the case of the Gothics in particular, Ann Radcliffe's *The Castles of Athlin and Dunbayne*, published in 1789, cost 3*s.*; her *Mysteries of Udolpho*, published five years later, cost £1.5*s.* for the full four volumes; while Lewis's *Monk*, published in 1796, cost half a guinea for three volumes.

In the 1740s, most labourers and domestic servants earned around 2*s.* to 3*s.* a week. Regardless of questions of literacy, to buy a book would have been financially unthinkable. Later in the century, this income might have increased to around 8*s.*; the matter remained unthinkable. And, perhaps more significantly, the skilled craftsmen, shopowners, small tradesmen were in a scarcely better position: throughout the century, a one-volume book would probably have cost at least half their weekly income, while to buy a four-volume novel could have involved up to a year's saving. Money, then, was one principal constraint on the public: the other was literacy, but here we are in a field which is even more difficult to assess. It is far from clear what literacy means, and no reliable statistics from the time are available; but from what little we know of attempts at self-education and of the abilities of domestic servants, it seems fair to hazard a guess that there were more literate people than there were people financially able to buy books, although these former could never have amounted to more than one-third of the population, on the most liberal scale of measurement. It would, of course, be this situation which would account for the success of the circulating libraries. Taking both constraints together, we are enabled to place the changes in perspective. If, in a population of between six and seven million, book sales rarely exceeded a few thousand copies, it seems profoundly unlikely that novels were reaching any kind of mass audience, no matter what their content. Richard Altick doubts that the audience for books ran as high as Edmund Burke's contemporary guess of 80,000.[4] It is for this reason that Gothic fiction should not be characterised as a popular literature in the sense which we would now recognise. Labourers and domestic servants might be in a position, rarely, to acquire small penny romances, or certain kinds of ephemeral and periodical literature; they would never have been able to afford the novels of

Radcliffe or Lewis. And although a small number of domestic servants might have found themselves with access to their mistresses' copies of such books, it is highly improbable, as we shall see when we move on to look at the novels themselves, that they would have been able to make head or tail of them; for they are not written in anything remotely resembling a popular style. Walpole and Radcliffe write within a complex web of classical and Shakespearean allusions. Lewis writes an admittedly dramatic but very complicated prose. Mary Shelley's work is packed with elaborate and erudite social argument. Radcliffe, it is true, received the then colossal sums of £500 for *Udolpho* and £600 for *The Italian*; but it could not have come, directly or indirectly, from the lower classes. Indeed, the evidence seems to point quite clearly to the hypothesis that, despite the differences between the realistic novel and the Gothic, and despite the attacks mounted on Gothic fiction by various arbiters of middle-class taste, the readership for the two genres must have been pretty much the same. In some way, the middle-class audience for whom Fielding had catered must have changed its tastes quite radically during the third quarter of the eighteenth century, as well as developing in size; contemporary settings were again in part supplanted by settings inherited from the old romances, and the exotic was drawn into the realm of the novel itself, and this was largely at the implicit behest of the bourgeoisie.

Part of the explanation for this shift might lie in a specific contradiction in the history of eighteenth-century ideas, a contradiction between 'official culture' and actual taste. On the official side, the eighteenth century was the great era of rationalism and Enlightenment. Associated principally with the French thinkers Diderot and Voltaire, but also in different ways affecting English thinkers from David Hume to William Godwin, the Enlightenment saw itself as the bearer of a radically progressive philosophy. Eschewing all reliance on faith and revealed religion, it declared itself in favour of scientific progress towards knowledge. Perhaps its most typical product was the *Encyclopédie* (1751–80), which professed to be a systematic account of all human knowledge; perhaps its most persistent claim was that man was potentially all-powerful, that there were no secrets of the universe which would remain unrevealed to him if he were only to pursue the paths of science and reason. The human reason was the only guide to truth; if there was a God, his only function had been to create the universe, and he had no further role to play.

But it is, of course, possible to interpret this eighteenth-century reliance on reason in several different ways. Although the removal or distancing of the divine and the insistence on human knowledge can be seen as progressive, the reduction of the human to the rational can also be seen as circular and sterile; this, for instance, is how Blake saw it.[5] Reliance on reason may appear to remove mystery, but only at the expense of outlawing large expanses of actual experience, the experience of the emotions, the passions. This is the view of Enlightenment as 'mythic fear turned radical. The pure immanence of positivism, its ultimate product, is no more than a, so to speak, universal taboo. Nothing at all may remain outside, because the mere idea of outsideness is the very source of fear.'[6] According to such an interpretation, fear is both the root and the product of the attempt to bring all things under rational control, and rationalism will be a self-defeating system because that which cannot be thus assimilated will therefore become all the more taboo; reason will create its own enemies. To consider the passions and the emotions as mere subject faculties to be brought under the sway of an all-dominant reason, as the Enlightenment thinkers did, will render those faculties all the more incomprehensible, and in some ways eighteenth-century fiction shows an increasing awareness of this problem.

In any case, at a simpler level, the principles of the Enlightenment never came into easy relationship with the novel form, in its realistic or any other manifestation. In more abstract literary genres like the meditative poem, it may be possible to support such an over-consistent view of man; but the panoramic nature of the novel, its ability to sustain the contradictions of actual behaviour, meant from the beginning that it never bore the full burden of rationalism, and, presumably, also that this was not what its readers demanded. In Defoe, rationalism becomes submerged under a set of arguments about the nature of self-interest, and a novel like *Moll Flanders* (1722) ironically suggests the severity of the circumstantial limitations on reasonable behaviour. In Fielding, nominal acquiescence in rational principles is set against an awareness of complexity and simple messiness that again turns Enlightenment against itself, again to the apparent delight of his readers. In fact, the noted irony of the eighteenth-century novelists appears to stem in large part from their awareness that the official account of human behaviour and motivation could not stand much scrutiny from the point of view of everyday life.

One major eighteenth-century novelist did not share this irony, and that was Richardson: not by any means because he accepted the official canons of Enlightenment, but because he was barely concerned with them at all. Richardson's whole project was founded on an investigation into the emotions, into the strength of those feelings which the rationalist tried to suppress; and it is Richardson who is by far the most important progenitor of the kinds of fiction being written in the final three decades of the century.

We have already mentioned that much of that fiction was Gothic; but there is another, more general term, which covers quite a lot of the Gothic itself and almost everything else that was popular between 1770 and 1800, and that is sentimentalism. 'Between Richardson and Jane Austen', a critic writes, 'sentimentalism gave the prevailing tone to fiction; few writers were untouched by its stigma';[7] and the only relation between sentimentalism and rationalism is negative. The same critic defines sentimentalism as the 'cult or creed of sentimentality', which is 'not merely high emotionality; it is a stimulated consciousness of emotion, and even a certain vanity in that consciousness. Needless to say, when self-conscious emotionality becomes a test of fineness of nature, it can, like any other mental trait, become a part of social education. It can likewise become a fad' (Steeves, p. 161). And, indeed, a fad is what it became. The sentimental novel was one which dwelt upon the fine emotions of its characters, tracing their feelings minutely, choosing situations to bring out their heightened self-consciousness, situations filled with pathos and anguish. Preeminently, sentimentalism was a tone: an example can be taken from the model of the genre, Henry MacKenzie's *The Man of Feeling* (1771). The scene is a visit to a sick-bed by an erstwhile benefactor of the invalid:

> On something like a bed lay a man, with a face seemingly emaciated with sickness, and a look of patient dejection; a bundle of dirty shreds served him for a pillow; but he had a better support – the arm of a female who kneeled beside him, beautiful as an angel, but with a fading languor in her countenance, the still life of melancholy, that seemed to borrow its shade from the object on which it gazed. There was a tear in her eye! the sick man kissed it off in its bud, smiling through the dimness of his own! – when she saw Mountford, she crawled forward on the ground and clasped his knees; he raised her from the floor; she threw her arms round his neck, and sobbed out a speech of thankfulness, eloquent beyond the power of language.
> 'Compose yourself, my love,' said the man on the bed; 'but he, whose goodness has caused that emotion, will pardon its effects.'[8]

It is a tone which it is very difficult for us now to appreciate, and we shall come across it again in the early Gothic novels, particularly those of Radcliffe and her school. Its universality at the time was remarkable, and we can even sense it lingering in some of the bleaker passages of Dickens. It rests partly on a number of stylistic conventions: the reference to the speech which transcends language; the oddly well-formed discourse delivered by the sick man; the exclamation marks placed to point out to the reader those moments at which his sentimental appreciation is to be particularly delighted – by the well-placed tear in the girl's eye, by the emotionally correct reaction of the invalid. The angelic beauty, the fading languor, the excess of thankfulness have nothing to do with the reasonable, and very little to do with the real: they are designed to angle the scene towards the demonstration of the moral and aesthetic lesson which it so obviously preaches.

The strength of sentimentalism, the aspect of the real which nevertheless underlies all this conventional paraphernalia, was the minute and detailed observation of emotions, as we can see from a further passage from MacKenzie, where the protagonist is in the presence of the recently deceased Man of Feeling himself:

> I entered the room where his body lay; I approached it with reverence, not fear: I looked; the recollection of the past crowded upon me. I saw that form, which, but a little before, was animated with a soul which did honour to humanity, stretched without sense or feeling before me. 'Tis a connection we cannot easily forget: – I took his hand in mine; I repeated his name involuntarily: – I felt a pulse in every vein at the sound. I looked earnestly in his face; his eye was closed, his lip pale and motionless. There is an enthusiasm in sorrow that forgets impossibility; I wondered that it was so. The sight drew a prayer from my heart; it was the voice of frailty and of man! the confusion of my mind began to subside into thought; I had time to weep!
>
> (*Man of Feeling*, p. 131)

The Gothic could not have come into being without a style of this kind, for it is in this style that we begin to glimpse the possibility of the balance and reason of the Enlightenment being crushed beneath the weight of feeling and passion. Despite the chronic indulgence which vitiates sentimentalism, there is a kind of precision to passages like this, almost a stream-of-consciousness precision, a precision in the attempt to cope with psychological facts for which no rational explanation exists. There is also a movement, a movement of excitement: the sentence is broken, distorted by the pressure which feelings exert on the ordering of the mind. The specificity of 'reverence, not fear' may appear merely self-congratulatory, but it also economically effects a real discrimination; again, the interjection of 'I wondered that it was so' is gauche, but it also shows MacKenzie's discontent with the neat picture of the interplay of separate faculties which had passed in earlier years for psychology. The argument is perhaps best evidenced from Sterne's *Sentimental Journey* (1768), where, in the very act of parodying sentimentalism, Sterne simultaneously provides a fine example of the absurd richness of the mode.

The popularity of the sentimental novel demonstrates the contradictions in taste of the eighteenth-century bourgeoisie. It also shows, more precisely, the area in which these contradictions were most strongly felt: the area of the passions, of the emotional life. Of course the emotions presented by the sentimentalists seem odd, distorted, artificial; but this is hardly surprising at a time when for generations social and cultural life had been dominated by a set of ideas which attempted to reduce the power and practical effectiveness of these emotions and, in the end, deny them. In sentimentalism, the middle classes are gropingly moving back towards the notion of psychological depth which the bland superficialities of the Enlightenment had tried to obliterate, towards the important perception that an account of behaviour cannot substitute for an account of motivation. The connection which needs to be made in terms of the novels of the period 1770–1800 is that this project, which itself penetrates deeply into Gothic fiction, is closely allied with another more obvious Gothic project, the recapture of history.

This is not, of course, by any means the prerogative of the Gothic novel as such; it is, as we have seen, the essence of the Gothic cultural emphasis. The catalogue of works of the later eighteenth century which contribute to the reappropriation of the past would be endless: Hurd's *Letters*; Percy's *Reliques*; the work of 'Ossian'; Thomas Chatterton's Rowley poems; John Carter's *Specimens of Ancient Sculpture and Painting* (1780–94); Joseph Ritson's scholarly collections of ancient poetry: these are only the outstanding works. What they all have in common is a questioning of assumptions about what constitutes the civilised. The thinking which the scholarly antiquarians and Gothics were questioning was Augustanism; and without some understanding of Augustan principles and their role in eighteenth-century thought it is difficult to understand the real purposes of the Gothic revival, either in terms of history, or in terms of the way in which it purported to offer a new conception of the relations between the human, the natural and the divine.

Augustanism took its name from the Augustan period of the Roman empire. The Augustans saw their period of national history as analogous to this past age, in that it too seemed to them a silver age: that is, it seemed poised between golden achievements in the past and possible future collapse into a barbarian age of bronze. In Augustan thinking, the barbarians are forever at the gates; the writer's role is to maintain the defensive fires of culture. In this sense, Augustanism was perforce conservative; reason was again the dominant mental faculty, and was the main barricade against invasion and the death of civilisation. It is tempting to see in Augustanism the doctrine of a small cultural élite holding on to power and status under increasing pressure, and that pressure as precisely that exerted by the new reading public on the homogeneity of the old literary establishment.

As with all large terms, it is difficult to find particular figures whom the term 'Augustanism' entirely fits. Fielding was undoubtedly Augustan in his belief in the stability of social roles and in the necessity of social and psychological compromise, but his mocking, half-amused attitude towards the doctrine of literary kinds shows his detachment from the more rigid Augustan formulae. Johnson, on the other hand, was a firm believer in these literary rules, and yet it was his view of Shakespeare which became the first significant breach in them. To find the ideas in their purest form it is necessary to stay early in the century, with essayists like Addison and Steele and with the master of Augustan poetry, Pope; and to see how Augustan cultural ideals were translated into literary terms, to look at Pope's own work of critical theory, the *Essay on Criticism* (1711):

> *First follow Nature, and your Judgment frame*
> *By her just Standard, which is still the same:*
> *Unerring Nature, still divinely bright,*
> *One clear, unchang'd, and Universal Light,*
> *Life, Force, and Beauty, must to all impart,*
> *At once the Source, and End, and Test of Art.*
> *Art from that Fund each just Supply provides,*
> *Works without Show, and without Pomp presides:*
> *In some fair Body thus th'informing Soul*
> *With Spirits feeds, with Vigour fills the whole,*
> *Each Motion guides, and ev'ry Nerve sustains;*
> *It self unseen, but in th'Effects, remains.*
> *Some, to whom Heav'n in Wit has been profuse,*
> *Want as much more, to turn it to its use;*
> *For Wit and Judgment often are at strife,*
> *Tho' meant each other's Aid, like Man and Wife.*
> *'Tis more to guide than spur the Muses' Steed;*
> *Restrain his Fury, than provoke his Speed;*
> *The winged Courser, like a gen'rous Horse,*
> *Shows most true Mettle when you check his Course.*
> * Those Rules of old discover'd, not devis'd,*
> *Are Nature still, but Nature Methodis'd;*

Nature, like Liberty, is but restrain'd
By the same Laws which first herself ordain'd.[9]

The outstanding feature here is the image of the 'Muses' Steed'; Pope claims that restraint and control are more important than the 'spur'. The Augustan critical attitude despised spontaneity and wildness and argued instead for a controlled, reasonable poetry marked by balance and closed structure. The argument is not that poetry has nothing to do with emotion or passion, but that these must accept the dominion of reason; the 'winged courser' must accept the bit.

The relations which Pope depicts between the faculties are in fact ambiguous: on the one hand, wit and judgement should be 'like Man and Wife', which we might naïvely suppose to imply an equality of partnership, but restraint is also valued more highly than speed and flight. The balance is not really an equal one: rather, the function of balance itself is being vindicated at the expense of any sign of rebellion against the rational mind. Pope's argument about freedom and poetry has a similar shape in claiming that to be bound by laws of your own devising is not to be bound at all. These laws, he says, have been 'discover'd, not devis'd': that is, they are not man-made impositions, but discoveries about how nature works. And these discoveries were made by the classical poets, primarily Homer.

The notion that the classical poets discovered nature's secrets is very convenient, in that it enables one to identify on good authority not only the rules of nature but also the rules of literary form. Poetry, the argument runs, must stay close to nature – that is, it must avoid the improbable or fanciful – but it best achieves this end by drawing on the classics. This produces a strange paradox: a poetry which claims proximity to nature while demonstrating a full use of the resources of literary artifice.

The laws of nature are, for Pope, permanent and all-embracing, and the task of the poet is therefore not to attempt presumptuously to discover novelty but to continue to express old truths in increasingly perspicuous and beautiful forms; such was the central tenet of Augustanism, but its hold on English poetry was brief. We have already seen the 1740s as the decade of Fielding and Richardson; but in poetry it was also an important decade, the decade which saw the growth of a kind of poetry which was radically different from anything Pope had advocated, and which came to be called 'graveyard poetry'. At this point, it is worth going into graveyard poetry in some detail for several reasons: because its involvement with death and suffering prefigures the Gothic novel; because it marks an early stage of the renewed desire for literary 'novelty' which characterised the later part of the century; because it challenges rationalism and vaunts extremity of feeling; and because its actual influence on Gothic fiction was considerable, although in a rather curious way: it exerted an enormous influence on German writers of terror-fiction, and through them retained an influence in Britain well into the 1790s and beyond.

Edward Young's *Night Thoughts* came out between 1742 and 1745; Robert Blair's *The Grave* in 1743; James Hervey's major work, *Meditations among the Tombs*, between 1745 and 1747; Thomas Warton's work *On the Pleasures of Melancholy* in 1747; and Gray's famous *Elegy* in 1751. We can best appreciate the difference between Augustan and graveyard poetry, and at the same time perceive the continuity of tone and feeling between graveyard and Gothic, by comparing a further passage from Pope with two of the most impressive pieces of graveyard writing, Thomas Parnell's early 'Night-Piece on Death' (1722) and the notorious *Night Thoughts*. Parnell's poem was written before the intensive Gothic revival of Miltonic and pre-Miltonic poetry was properly under way, Young's at the heart of this revival.

Pope's *Essay on Man* (1733) was the most important single statement of Augustan philosophical and social ideas, and it also exemplifies in its form the cultural criteria and attitudes which it sets out to justify. A passage on man's place in the world provides a particularly apt comparison with Parnell and Young:

> *Go, wiser thou! and in thy scale of sense*
> *Weigh thy Opinion against Providence;*
> *Call Imperfection what thou fancy'st such,*
> *Say, here he gives too little, there too much;*
> *Destroy all creatures for thy sport or gust,*
> *Yet cry, If Man's unhappy, God's unjust;*
> *If Man alone ingross not Heav'n's high care,*
> *Alone made perfect here; immortal there:*
> *Snatch from his hand the balance and the rod,*
> *Re-judge his justice, be the God of God!*
>
> *In Pride, in reas'ning Pride, our error lies;*
> *All quit their sphere, and rush into the skies.*
> *Pride still is aiming at the blest abodes,*
> *Men would be Angels, Angels would be Gods.*
> *Aspiring to be Gods, if Angels fell,*
> *Aspiring to be Angels, Men rebel;*
> *And who but wishes to invert the laws*

Of Order, sins against th'Eternal Cause.

Ask for what end the heav'nly bodies shine,
Earth for whose use? Pride answers, "Tis for mine:
For me kind Nature wakes her genial pow'r,
Suckles each herb, and spreads out ev'ry flow'r;
Annual for me, the grape, the rose renew
The juice nectareous, and the balmy dew;
For me, the mine a thousand treasures brings;
For me, health gushes from a thousand springs;
Seas roll to waft me, suns to light me rise;
My foot-stool earth, my canopy the skies.'

But errs not Nature from this gracious end,
From burning suns when livid deaths descend,
When earthquakes swallow, or when tempests sweep
Towns to one grave, whole nations to the deep?
'No ('tis reply'd) the first Almighty Cause
Acts not by partial, but by gen'ral laws;
Th'exceptions few; some change since all began,
And what created perfect?' – Why then Man?
If the great end be human Happiness,
Then Nature deviates; and can Man do less?
                    (Poems, III i, 129–34)*

The most prominent stylistic feature here is, of course, a balance, the variety of which is astonishing. In its simplest form, there is the internal rhythmic balance which gives strength to 'When earthquakes swallow, or when tempests sweep/Towns to one grave, whole nations to the deep'. In the couplet 'For me, the mine a thousand treasures brings;/For me, health gushes from a thousand springs', both rhyme and the displaced repetition of 'thousand' work together with the rhythm. In the line 'Re-judge his justice, be the God of God', parellelism and balance are not working in a void, but point the paradox which Pope is exposing: the very simplicity of the structure is supposed to replicate the paucity of the argument. Again, the placing of the words 'Of Order', precisely dis-ordered *vis-à-vis* the rest of the line, is rhetorical evidence of the disorganisation – and hence, naturally, the incorrectness – of the beliefs under attack.

For this passage is fundamentally an attack, on those who claim that nature's purpose is merely to serve man's needs. To Pope, this is the sin of pride, which makes men out to be gods, and it is in this context that the references to the rebellion of the angels have their meaning. The condemnation is dual: not only of the proud, but also of any literature which displays pride by attempting a task outside its orbit. The failure of Satan's rebellion is also the failure of Milton's epic poem, which attempted a task beyond human means. The form of the passage, the arrangement of the couplets, the marshalling of the verse-paragraphs, all are signs of the limitations which the poet should accept. For Pope, there is licit and illicit knowledge: to suppose that one can fully interpret the laws of nature is illicit, and will incur that punishment reserved for the unnaturally aspiring.

Parnell's 'Night-Piece'[10] is a blend of Augustan and non-Augustan ideas; it opens with a comparison of different kinds and sources of knowledge:

> *By the blue taper's trembling light,*
> *No more I waste the wakeful night,*
> *Intent with endless view to pore*
> *The schoolmen and the sages o'er:*
> *Their books from wisdom widely stray,*
> *Or point at best the longest way.*
> *I'll seek a readier path, and go*
> *Where wisdom's surely taught below.*

Subdued though his language is, Parnell is saying something quite startling. Unlike Pope, he is not impressed with the attempts made by reason to define the limits of human understanding; like Wordsworth later, he claims that nothing can be learnt from books, from abstracted experience. To learn aright, one must take the quicker path, which is the path of intense feeling; one can best learn the secrets of life from meditation on its extreme limit, death. One has to ask why this should be a 'readier' path: whether it will convey wisdom seems doubtful, but then it seems rather to be excitement which Parnell is seeking, that thrill of entering forbidden realms which was to become so all-pervasive in the Gothic novel.

Parnell recounts his explorations 'among the livid gleams of night', and sees the tombs of the poor and forgotten, and of the vanished mighty. Then the dead come forth:

> *Hah! while I gaze, pale Cynthia fades,*
> *The bursting earth unveils the shades!*
> *All slow, and wan, and wrapp'd with shrouds,*
> *They rise in visionary crowds,*
> *And all with sober accents cry,*
> *'Think, mortal, what it is to die'.*
>
> *Now from yon black and funeral yew,*
> *That bathes the charnel-house with dew,*
> *Methinks I hear a voice begin;*

(Ye ravens, cease your croaking din,
Ye tolling clocks, no time resound
O'er the long lake and midnight ground!)
It sends a peal of hollow groans,
Thus speaking from among the bones.

The first paragraph is straightforwardly Virgilian, but in the second a more febrile and indulgent tone creeps in. Most obviously, the lines are already containing an array of Gothic props: charnel-house, ravens, tolling clocks, hollow groans. But it is not just that: the actual flow of the lines is different. The couplet structure is momentarily dissolved, and replaced by a more extended, incantatory flow, as the voice – the voice of Death – takes over from the discourse of the poet. This replicates the holding back of time, the perpetuation of a moment of ghastly revelation in which reason reels before the onset of the irrational. Death's message is, in the first instance, reassuring:

'*When men my scythe and darts supply,*
How great a king of fears am I!
They view me like the last of things:
They make, and then they dread, my stings.
Fools! if you less provok'd your fears,
No more my spectre form appears.
Death's but a path which must be trod,
If man would ever pass to God;
A port of calms, a state of ease
From the rough rage of swelling seas.

'*Why then thy flowing sable stoles,*
Deep pendant cypress, mourning poles,
Loose scarfs to fall athwart thy weeds,
Long palls, drawn hearses, cover'd steeds.
And plumes of black, that, as they tread,
Nod o'er the scutcheons of the dead?'

In other words, man's fear of death is self-created: if he ceased to adorn it with the *symbols* of fear, he would lose the fear itself. The message is rational; the moment of dread has passed and the poet has been taught the mistake of abandoning himself to a reverie of feeling. And yet the ending of the poem is still surprising:

'*As men who long in prison dwell,*
With lamps that glimmer round the cell,
Whene'er their suffering years are run,
Spring forth to greet the glittering sun:
Such joy, though far transcending sense,
Have pious souls at parting hence.
On earth, and in the body plac'd,

> A few, and evil years they waste;
> But when their chains are cast aside,
> See the glad scene unfolding wide,
> Clap the glad wing, and tower away,
> And mingle with the blaze of day.'

The poet has received the knowledge which should make him feel at peace with the human condition, yet the final word of the message is that life is made up of 'a few, and evil years'. The voice of Death is positively seductive as it portrays the grandeur which awaits, not specifically in heaven, but beyond the bounds of the 'prison' of life.

What is proposed in the last four lines is precisely the conversion of men into angels against which Pope rails. The knowledge which the poet has gained is one calculated to make him dissatisfied with his destined place in the great chain of being, to encourage him towards a 'rush into the skies', a divine consummation, albeit beyond the bounds of death. The 'Night-Piece' is an uneasy poem in that it alternates between moral prudence and recklessness, seeming to subjugate the demands of feeling to the dictates of reason while suggesting an apotheosis to be attained through abandonment to the deathly impulse.

Some passages from Young suggest other problems of the transition from the 'peace of the Augustans' to the restlessness of the later eighteenth century:

> Silence and darkness! solemn sisters! twins
> From ancient night, who nurse the tender thought
> To reason, and on reason build resolve,
> (That column of true majesty in man)
> Assist me: I will thank you in the grave;
> The grave, your kingdom: there this frame shall fall
> A victim sacred to your dreary shrine.
> But what are ye? Thou, who didst put to flight
> Primeval silence, when the morning stars,
> Exulting, shouted o'er the rising ball;
> O Thou! whose word from solid darkness struck
> That spark, the sun; strike wisdom from my soul;
> My soul, which flies to Thee, her trust, her treasure,
> As misers to their gold, while others rest.[11]

One is immediately struck by Young's cosmic perspective: the soul of the poet, not bounded by earthly chains, invokes the powers of darkness to assist his journey, but this journey is not a hesitant probing among tombs but a visionary voyage embracing the earth, the stars, the whole universe. Formally, Young rejects Augustanism for the sonorous lines of Milton; 'ancient night' is also familiar to us from association with Milton's Satan, whose aspiration and descent among the stars are continually invoked. The poet's soul, much like the persona of Keats's 'Ode on Melancholy', is passive yet exalted; it is not that which *achieves* wisdom, but that from which wisdom can be struck, yet, with assistance, it is able to mingle with the angels.

Young is self-consciously an orator, and *Night Thoughts* is an attempt at epic, despite its largely mental landscape, an epic in tone and in the implications for human status which that tone carries. But alongside the exaltation of the poet's stance and vision lies an intense and related dependence on images of death, guilt and repression:

> Tho' nature's terrors, thus, may be represt;
> Still frowns grim Death; guilt points the tyrant's spear.
> And whence all human guilt? From death forgot.
> Ah me! too long I set at nought the swarm
> Of friendly warnings, which around me flew;
> And smil'd, unsmitten: small my cause to smile!
> Death's admonitions, like shafts upwards shot,
> More dreadful by delay, the longer ere
> They strike our hearts, the deeper is their wound;
> O think how deep, Lorenzo! here it stings:
> Who can appease its anguish? How it burns!
> What hand the barb'd, invenom'd thought can draw?
> What healing hand can pour the balm of peace?
> And turn my sight undaunted on the tomb?
>
> (*Works*, I, 57)

Where Parnell was content to say that he as an individual had derived a lesson from thinking on death, Young is far more insistent, ascribing all human guilt to forgetfulness of the fact of mortality. And where Parnell's gaze upon death was untroubled once the first shock of the vision had worn off, Young advises a tortured and self-torturing concentration, turning the 'invenom'd thought' in the everlasting wound. He concentrates on death not to acquire peace of mind but to experience the ultimate anguish, and at points in the poem this becomes a morbid indulgence which strongly pre-figures the meditations of writers like Lewis and Maturin:

> What awful joy! what mental liberty!
> I am not pent in darkness; rather say
> (If not too bold) in darkness I'm embower'd.
> Delightful gloom! the clust'ring thoughts around
> Spontaneous rise, and blossom in the shade;
> But droop by day, and sicken in the sun.

> *Thought borrows light elsewhere; from that first fire,*
> *Fountain of animation! whence descends*
> *Urania, my celestial guest! who deigns*
> *Nightly to visit me, so mean; and now,*
> *Conscious how needful discipline to man,*
> *From pleasing dalliance with the charms of night*
> *My wand'ring thought recalls, to what excites*
> *Far other beat of heart! Narcissa's tomb!*
> *Or is it feeble nature calls me back,*
> *And breaks my spirit into grief again?*
> *Is it a Stygian vapour in my blood?*
> *A cold, slow puddle, creeping thro' my veins?*
> *Or is it thus with all men? – Thus with all.*
>
> (*Works*, I, 83–4)

A reversal of values is signified by the darkness in which one is not 'pent' but 'embower'd'; 'gloom' which is 'delightful'; thoughts which 'blossom' by night, 'droop' and 'sicken' by day. Young is, of course, meditating on recent death, but this is a slight occasion for the obsessive seeking after things of the night which we find here. Like the Augustans, Young regards day as the time of reason, night as escape, but for him reason is mere 'discipline', and darkness and death are thus mysteriously alluring.

For night has to do with fear, and fear has a positive place in Young's cosmic scheme. He asks why, in the end, death proves so elusive to thought; is it judgement, he asks, which prevents us from capturing its essence:

> *Or is it fear turns startled reason back,*
> *From looking down a precipice so steep?*
> *'Tis dreadful; and the dread is wisely plac'd*
> *By nature, conscious of the make of man.*
> *A dreadful friend it is, a terror kind,*
> *A flaming sword to guard the tree of life.*
>
> (*Works*, I, 90)

If this seems a mere tissue of paradoxes, it is nonetheless one which possessed a considerable cultural force: again, it is a blend of indulgence and moral rectitude which we shall find throughout Gothic writing. Essentially, it is a justification for a literature of terror, on the grounds that terror guards our sanity.

But alongside the dark side of Young's vision there is also a celebration of man, but of a very different kind from Pope's:

> *How poor, how rich, how abject, how august,*
> *How complicate, how wonderful, is man!*
> *How passing wonder He, who made him such!*
> *Who centred in our make such strange extremes!*

From diff'rent natures marvellously mixt,
Connection exquisite of distant worlds!
Distinguish'd link in being's endless chain!
Midway from nothing to the deity!
A beam ethereal, sullied, and absorpt!
Tho' sullied, and dishonour'd, still divine!
Dim miniature of greatness absolute!
An heir of glory! a frail child of dust!
Helpless immortal! insect infinite!
A worm! a god! – I tremble at myself,
And in myself am lost! at home a stranger,
Thought wanders up and down, surpris'd, aghast,
And wond'ring at her own: how reason reels!
O what a miracle to man is man,
Triumphantly distress'd! what joy, what dread!
Alternately transported, and alarm'd!
What can preserve my life? or what destroy?
An angel's arm can't snatch me from the grave;
Legions of angels can't confine me there.
                              (Works, I, 3–4)

The fact of man's mixed being is to Young a source of grandeur, and the most impressive passages of *Night Thoughts* are those in which the reader soars with the poet into the boundless reaches of the universe, man's natural home, and aspires to divinity. For Young, no knowledge is illicit, and already here we can see the beginnings of the myth of Frankenstein, partly in the figure of Prometheus which he invokes, partly in the relevance of Milton's Satan, of whose rebellion *Night Thoughts* can be read as a sustained vindication.

The revival of interest in antiquity and the emergence of a poetry of defiance and divine aspiration were thus two roots of Gothic fiction; a third which needs to be mentioned is the development in the mid-eighteenth century of the theory of the sublime. The major influence here was the classical critic Longinus, of whose work this is a typical passage:

> Now I am well aware that the greatest natures are least immaculate.
> Perfect precision runs the risk of triviality, whereas in great writing
> as in great wealth there must needs be something overlooked. Perhaps
> it is inevitable that the humble, mediocre natures, because they never
> run any risks, never aim at the heights, should remain to a large extent
> safe from error, while in great natures their very greatness spells
> danger.[12]

In place of 'precision', Longinus advocated a literature of sublimity, by which he means that which does not 'persuade' but 'entrances', a literature not of the limited but of the limitless, a kind of writing which 'masters' its audience with its grandeur and scope and which resists false and imposed constraints:

> In dealing, then, with writers of genius, whose grandeur is of a kind that comes within the limits of use and profit, we must at the outset form the conclusion that, while they are far from unerring, yet they are all more than human. Other qualities prove their possessors men, sublimity lifts them near the mighty mind of God. (Fyfe, p. 227)

To the Longinian, all the pettier Augustan virtues were merely ways of attaining to eminence in the second-rate. True grandeur was reserved for those who made the 'rush into the skies', of whom Longinus' favourite example was Demosthenes. He claims that Demosthenes' audacity of conception 'far exceeds the limits of mere persuasion .... our attention is drawn from the reasoning to the enthralling effect of the imagination, and the technique is concealed in a halo of brilliance' (Fyfe, p. 179). It was true, of course, that Augustan theory had allowed for the cooperation of reason and the imagination, of the suasive and the pleasurable, but what it did not allow for was a situation in which reason is swamped amid the glories and splendours of sublimity. Longinus asserts the superiority of flawed sublimity to flawless mediocrity, and thus encourages the poet to undertake the grand and the extreme rather than concentrating on the trivialities of technical perfection.

Clearly the Longinian influence on *Night Thoughts* is strong, and we can also see in the poem a specific conjunction of Longinian theory and Miltonic practice: the 'Gothic' revival of earlier poetry, poetry unaffected by the rigorous rules of Augustanism, required alternative justification and it was often Longinus who was taken to provide it. Milton was, after all, the example of flawed sublimity; but where the model of Virgil, interpreted according to a theory of the decline of culture, had encouraged Pope and others towards a poetry which, they assumed, could only be inferior to the original, the model of Miltonic striving, interpreted according to the Longinian theory of the paramountcy of genius, encouraged a wholly different attitude, which Young expressed:

> What glory to come near, what glory to reach, what glory (presumptuous thought) to surpass, our predecessors! And is that then in nature absolutely impossible? Or is it not, rather, contrary to nature to fail in it? Nature herself sets the ladder, all wanting is our ambition to climb. For by the bounty of nature we are as strong as our predecessors; and by the favour of time (which is but another round in nature's scale) we stand on higher ground.[13]

The association of Young's aspiration with Satan's is underlined by the word 'ambition', the key motivation of the Gothic hero; and many of the Gothic writers were heavily influenced by the cult of sublimity as represented by Longinus, Young and Edmund Burke's *Origin of our Ideas of the Sublime and Beautiful* (1756). No matter how Young chooses to dilute it, the central claim which he makes is the claim of self-divinity, the conviction of being potentially a God:

> Therefore dive deep into thy bosom; learn the depth, extent, bias and full fort of thy mind; contract full intimacy with the stranger within thee; excite and cherish every spark of intellectual light and heat, however smothered under former negligence, or scattered through the dull, dark mass of common thoughts; and collecting them into a body, let thy genius rise (if a genius thou hast) as the sun from chaos; and if I should say then, like an Indian, *Worship it,* (though too bold) yet should I say little more than my second rule enjoins, (viz.) *Reverence thyself.* (*Conjectures*, p. 24)

The importance of Burke's treatise to Gothic writing was equally central, for it was here that the first attempt was made to systematise a connection between sublimity and terror. 'Whatever is fitted in any sort to excite the idea of pain, and danger, that is to say, whatever is in any sort terrible, or is conversant about terrible subjects, or operates in a manner analogous to terror, is a source of the *sublime;* that is, it is productive of the strongest emotion which the mind is capable of feeling.'[14] In these celebrated words, Burke announces the development of what had in Longinus been a matter of rhetorical theory, and what was in the graveyard poets becoming a matter of rising taste, into a whole new field of psychological speculation. There were, of course, many faulty areas in his work, in particular his doomed attempt to ground his psychological ideas in the physiological and his insistent production of examples, which tend sometimes towards the ludicrous; nonetheless, an entire new dimension to the relation between literature and fear is out-lined in passages like this:

> The passion caused by the great and sublime in nature, when those causes operate most powerfully, is Astonishment; and astonishment is that state of the soul, in which all its motions are suspended, with some degree of horror. In this case the mind is so entirely filled with its object, that it cannot entertain any other, nor by consequence reason on that object which employs it. Hence arises the great power of the sublime, that far from being produced by them, it anticipates our reasonings, and hurries us on by an irresistible force. (*Enquiry*, p. 57)

Thus the excitation of fear becomes one of the most significant enterprises a writer can undertake; thus also fear is recognised as the primary means by which the dictates of reason can be bypassed. Many of the details of Burke's analysis have relevance to the Gothic writers – in particular his emphasis on obscurity, vastness, magnificence as constitutive elements of the sublime – but his most important contribution was to confer on terror a major and worthwhile literary role.

The background against which the emergence of Gothic fiction needs to be seen, then, is a complex one, in which intellectual, technical and commercial developments all play a part. It is a background which includes the appearance and early growth of the novel form itself; the attendant emphasis on realism, and the complicated relationship which that bears to rationalist philosophy; Augustan cultural thinking and the view of human psychology which it entails; the emergence of an emphasis on extreme emotionality which produces sentimental fiction; rival views of the relevance to contemporary writing of immediate and distant history; and the developments in poetic practice and theory in the mid-eighteenth century. Under such circumstances, it is not surprising that the elements of Gothic fiction first begin to emerge, in a hesitant way, within the mainstream of the realist novel itself. Watt claims that *Tom Jones* contains 'the first Gothic mansion in the history of the novel' (Watt, p. 29), and that the end of Richardson's *Clarissa Harlowe* should be regarded as graveyard literature (Watt, pp. 225–6); Varma mentions Fielding's description of the Palace of Death in *Journey from this World to the Next* (1741–2) (Varma, p. 11). In these instances, certainly, we see the gathering together of props; but the first important eighteenth-century work to propose terror as a subject for novelistic writing was Smollett's *Ferdinand Count Fathom* (1753). *Fathom* is, in many ways, conventional enough: it is a satirical novel about the abominable exploits of an international confidence trickster who finds temporary success and eventual failure in duping a wide variety of people in settings spread across Europe; it is a variation of picaresque fiction, although written without the sympathy for the rogue hero which characterises many other examples of the genre, and with a particularly bitter and savage awareness of the hypocrisy and violence of 'elegant' society. Smollett justifies his topic thus:

> Almost all the heroes of this kind, who have hitherto succeeded on the English stage, are characters of transcendent worth, conducted through the vicissitudes of fortune, to that goal of happiness, which ever ought to be the repose of extraordinary desert. – Yet the same principle by which we rejoice at the remuneration of merit, will teach

us to relish the disgrace and discomfiture of vice, which is always an
example of extensive use and influence, because it leaves a deep
impression of terror upon the minds of those who are not confirmed
in the pursuit of morality and virtue, and while the balance wavers,
enables the right scale to preponderate.[15]

This is a remarkably cynical claim, and Smollett was probably aware
of that, but it does give him a chance to probe the emotions of
fear. Most of the relevant scenes occur in relation to Fathom's
treatment of a lady called Monimia (the name crops up again in
Charlotte Smith's *The Old Manor House* (1793)), on whom he preys
because of her wealth, and whom he subjects to long imprisonment
and the depths of misery and terror. At one point, Monimia reflects
poignantly on the fate which has placed her in Fathom's hands:

> Common affliction was an agreeable reverie to what she suffered,
> deprived of her parents, exiled from her friends and country, reduced
> to the brink of wanting the most indispensable necessaries of life, in a
> foreign land, where she knew not one person to whose protection
> she could have recourse, from the inexpressible woes that environed
> her: she complained to heaven, that her life was protracted for the
> augmentation of that misery which was already too severe to be
> endured; for she shuddered at the prospect of being utterly
> abandoned in the last stage of mortality, without one friend to close
> her eyes, or do the last offices of humanity to her breathless corse.
> These were dreadful reflections to a young lady who had been born
> to affluence and splendor, trained up in all the elegance of education,
> by nature fraught with that sensibility which refines the sentiment and
> taste, and so tenderly cherished by her indulgent parents, that 'they
> suffered not the winds of heaven to visit her face too roughly'.
>
> (*Fathom*, pp. 237–8)

The situation and description owe a great deal to Richardson, arch-
portrayer of virtue in distress; but the emphasis Smollett lays on the
contrast between the elegant treatment which Monimia is accus-
tomed to expect and the brutality which she receives further extends
Richardsonian practice in a direction already implicit in it: towards
a kind of sadistic pornography. The essential features which Smollett
is trying to convey are isolation, deprivation, vulnerability; that 'sensibility which refines the sentiment and taste' may well be necessary
equipment for behaviour *in society*, but what happens to 'trained
up', indulged young ladies when they find themselves outside social
norms? In theory, Smollett is maximising his and the reader's condemnation of Fathom; actually, he is exploiting the threat of rape
and violence, although in doing so he is also demonstrating the
practical uselessness of sentimentalism when social conventions
break down. This uselessness is emphasised even more strongly in

the person of Monimia's ineffectual lover, Melvile, who, being informed that she is dead (which is untrue), falls into a state worthy of a man of sentiment: 'he became so enamoured of her tomb [falsely so designated by Fathom], that he could no longer resist the desire which compelled him to make a pilgrimage to the dear hallowed spot, where all his once gay hopes lay buried; that he might nightly visit the silent habitation of his ruined love, embrace the sacred earth with which she was now compounded, moisten it with his tears, and bid the turf lie easy on her breast' (*Fathom*, p. 306). Smollett refers to this practice rather dismissively as a 'gloomy enjoyment', again making much of the psychological reversals caused by Melvile's inability to cope with a sudden and disastrous change in his fortunes. And alongside Melvile, to point at the contrast between superficial civilisation and deep savagery which primarily concerns him, Smollett introduces a further figure 'enamoured' of death, Don Diego the Castilian, who believes he has murdered his wife and daughter, and thus laments his situation:

> Count Melvile has reason to grieve; Don Diego to despair: his misfortunes flow from the villainy of mankind; mine are the fruit of my own madness: he laments the loss of a mistress, who fell a sacrifice to the perfidious arts of a crafty traitor . . . nightly he visits the dreary vault where she now lies at rest; her solitary grave is his couch; he converses with darkness and the dead, until each lonely aisle re-echoes his distress. What would be his penance, had he my cause? were he conscious of having murthered a beloved wife and darling daughter! ah wretch! ah cruel homicide! what had those dear victims done to merit such a fate? (*Fathom*, p. 329)

Diego is a forerunner of the Wandering Jew, Cain, Melmoth – all those Gothic characters doomed to live with the consciousness of extreme guilt in a world from which forgiveness has been banished. 'My heart was bursting', he says, 'while I dismissed them to the shades of death: I was maddened with revenge! . . . O! I am doomed to never-ceasing horror and remorse!' (*Fathom*, pp. 329–30). The roots of this meditation are, plainly, in the Jacobean debate about the value of extreme honour; and as in Jacobean drama and much Gothic fiction, southern European characters and settings are being used to heighten the implications of the concept of honour. And from the same root also springs Smollett's ambiguous attitude towards the homage Melvile pays to the dead; in Smollett's hands, this kind of honourable behaviour is dangerously close to necrophilia.

In the end, the terrors which Fathom has inflicted on Monimia

and Melvile are revisited on him; he is discovered, in a passage
which bears comparison with MacKenzie, on a sick-bed and near to
death:

> The young countess, whose tender heart could not bear the shock of
> such a spectacle, retired to the coach with madame Clement and the
> Jew, while Renaldo, accompanied by the rest, entered a dismal
> apartment, altogether void of furniture and convenience, where they
> beheld the wretched hero of these memoirs, stretched almost naked
> upon straw, insensible, convulsed, and seemingly in the grasp of
> death. He was worn to the bone either by famine or distemper; his
> face was overshadowed with hair and filth; his eyes were sunk, glazed
> and distorted; his nostrils dilated; his lips covered with a black
> slough, and his complexion faded into a pale clay-colour, tending to
> a yellow hue: in a word, the extremity of indigence, squalor and distress,
> could not be more feelingly represented.   (*Fathom*, p. 353)

What is most striking here is the overwhelming physicality by means
of which Smollett extends and undercuts sentimental conventions by
placing them alongside the reality of disease and suffering. Fathom's
reward for dehumanising others has been his own dehumanisation,
his reduction to a mere object of loathing and disgust.

The Gothic quality of *Fathom* rests on a number of points: the
attempt to embody a theory of the social purposes of terror;
the portrayal of the misery of separation from civilised norms, and
the inadequacy of most of the characters to deal with extreme
situations; the interest in the perverse tendencies of sensibility; the
insistence on the power of guilt; the physical treatment of loathing
and disgust. And it is interesting that these are features which could
be grafted on to a literary form which was largely realist in form
and socially critical in intention. For although one may doubt that
Smollett's purposes were as positive or pure as he claims, nonetheless he *had* purposes, and they were mostly to do with exposing
the flimsiness and hypocrisy of civilisation. Summers echoes other
opinions of the eighteenth century when he calls it 'the century of
systematised licentiousness ... corrupt to the core' and asserts that
'all social life was concentrated on the elegant accomplishment of
the sexual act'[16]; this is the vision of Smollett's most vicious novel,
a vision of the violence and sexual rapacity which underpins civilised
norms and Enlightenment thinking.

Eleven years later, Horace Walpole published *The Castle of Otranto*,
which has since been regarded as the originator of Gothic fiction.
It is worth pointing out, however, that *Fathom* and *Otranto* have very
little in common, representing as they do different ends of the
'Gothic' spectrum, and that the Gothic novels of the 1790s were, in

a sense, *facilitated* by *Otranto*, but in order to express a set of *attitudes* which have much more in common with *Fathom*. To put it simply, *Fathom* and the works of Radcliffe and Lewis are dark books, heavy books, where *Otranto* is light and airy, a fairy-tale rather than a nightmare, even when it strives for the horrific. What is vital about *Otranto*, though, is the fact that it was the earliest and most important manifestation of the late eighteenth-century revival of romance, that is, of the older traditions of prose literature which had apparently been supplanted by the rise of the novel. Walpole himself spoke of his book as an attempt to combine features of both:

> It was an attempt to blend the two kinds of romance, the ancient and the modern. In the former all was imagination and improbability: in the latter, nature is always intended to be, and sometimes has been, copied with success. Invention has not been wanting; but the great resources of fancy have been dammed up, by a strict adherence to common life. But if in the latter species Nature has cramped imagination, she did but take her revenge, having been totally excluded from old romances. The actions, sentiments, conversations, of the heroes and heroines of ancient days were as unnatural as the machines employed to put them in motion.[17]

But if *Otranto* was really supposed to be a combination of fantasy and realism, it is the former which stands out now and which stood out at the time. *Otranto* is set approximately in the twelfth century, in and around a castle clearly modelled on Walpole's own Strawberry Hill, and the plot is a joyous compilation of absurdities, including a host of romance ingredients: a tyrannical baron and his machinations, complicated revelations about paternity, and most important of all a panoply of supernatural portents and appearances. It was certainly not the only work in which such romance traditions were revived – other important examples were William Beckford's *Vathek* (1786) and James While's *Earl Strongbow* (1789) – but it was the earliest, and it was the one which made the most unashamed use of the supernatural.

Otranto was vastly popular; it is said to have gone through more than 115 editions since it first appeared, and in 1781 it was dramatised by Robert Jephson as *The Count of Narbonne*. Critical reaction to Walpole's book was understandably mixed: Tompkins summarises it well in saying that 'the demand for colour and sublimity', which the critics were willing to concede, 'brought with it the demand for the marvellous, and the critical world, which approved the first two qualities in measure, looked askance at the third' (Tompkins, p. 209). And *Otranto*, if nothing else, is 'marvellous': from the outset,

Walpole deliberately sets out to flout realist conventions, not only in terms of the supernatural but also in his depiction of the setting and in the casual slightness of his character portrayal. Beneath the glittering surface there are some parallels, if not similarities, with the sombre world of *Fathom*: Walpole, like Smollett, believes in the power of terror to awaken and sustain interest and, again like Smollett, plans his book as an assault on Enlightenment norms. His characters are neither lifelike nor reasonable in themselves: they are posturing puppets. Walpole himself makes a great deal of the connections between his work and Shakespearean tragedy, but this needs to be taken in part ironically. He appeals to the example of Shakespeare in precisely the area which the Augustans condemned, that is, in his mixing of kinds and genres; in *Otranto* he uses and deliberately exaggerates several devices of which the Augustans could not approve, notably the interspersal of 'low scenes' with scenes of 'high life', and the presentation of buffoon and servant figures in the same continuum as their betters and masters.

This is not to say that Walpole's affinities with Elizabethan writing are not real: they are real, not in the sense that Walpole was trying to write like them, but in that he wanted to use their example to give himself licence, and this, of course, was particularly necessary in the matter of the supernatural. Here Walpole combines devices from folklore with Elizabethan motifs to produce an armoury of magical helmets, speaking pictures, ghostly giants, but the tone in which they are described is unique: a good example comes when Manfred, tired of his wife, attempts to seduce his daughter-in-law Isabella. He apprises her of his intentions, whereupon she shrieks and runs:

> Manfred rose to pursue her; when the moon, which was now up, and gleamed in at the opposite casement, presented to his sight the plumes of the fatal helmet, which rose to the height of the windows, waving backwards and forwards in a tempestuous manner, and accompanied with a hollow and rustling sound. Isabella, who gathered courage from her situation, and who dreaded nothing so much as Manfred's pursuit of his declaration, cried, Look, my lord! see heaven itself declares against your impious intentions! – Heaven nor hell shall impede my designs, said Manfred, advancing again to seize the princess. At that instant the portrait of his grandfather, which hung over the bench where they had been sitting, uttered a deep sigh and heaved its breast. Isabella, whose back was turned to the picture, saw not the motion, nor knew whence the sound came, but started and said, Hark my lord! what sound was that? and at the same time made towards the door. Manfred, distracted between the flight of Isabella, who had now reached the stairs, and his inability to keep his eyes from the picture,

which began to move, had however advanced some steps after her, still looking backwards on the portrait, when he saw it quit its pannel, and descend on the floor with a grave and melancholy air. Do I dream? cried Manfred returning, or are the devils themselves in league against me? Speak, infernal spectre! Or, if thou art my grandsire, why dost thou too conspire against thy wretched descendant, who too dearly pays for – Ere he could finish the sentence the vision sighed again, and made a sign for Manfred to follow him. Lead on! cried Manfred; I will follow thee to the gulph of perdition. The spectre marched sedately, but dejected, to the end of the gallery, and turned into a chamber on the right hand. Manfred accompanied him at a little distance, full of anxiety and horror, but resolved. As he would have entered the chamber, the door was clapped-to with violence by an invisible hand. The prince, collecting courage from this delay, would have forcibly burst open the door with his foot, but found that it resisted his utmost efforts. Since hell will not satisfy my curiosity, said Manfred, I will use the human means in my power for preserving my race; Isabella shall not escape me.   (*Otranto*, pp. 23–4)

This is obviously not a use of the supernatural which is intended to terrify, but an ironic use which is meant to interest and amuse us by its self-conscious quaintness. Manfred's behaviour reminds us of Hamlet's only so that we can smile at its comparative inadequacy and, indeed, the insignificance of the ghost. Whether Walpole's constant descents into the matter-of-fact are equally deliberate is more doubtful: at all events, they too have the effect of distancing us, of making us look upon the book as a virtuoso performance in novelty and the exotic rather than as a serious attempt at psychological probing.

And the same is partly true of the historical content of *Otranto*. Walpole is quite unconcerned with the details of life in the Middle Ages; what he is concerned with is conjuring a general sense of 'past-ness' by the occasional insertion of costume detail or its equivalent. And yet, in another sense, *Otranto* is serious about history. For whatever its shortcomings and infelicities, it does give evidence of an eighteenth-century view of feudalism and the aristocracy, and in doing so originates what was to become perhaps the most prevalent theme in Gothic fiction: the revisiting of the sins of the fathers upon their children. When this is placed in a contemporaneous setting, it is a simple theme; but it becomes altogether more complex when the very location of crime and disorder is thrust back into the past. The figure of Manfred, laden with primal crime, is considerably larger than *Otranto* itself: his violence, his bullying, his impatience with convention and sensibility mark him out not only as the caricature of a feudal baron, but also as the irrepressible villain who merely mocks at society, who remains unassimilable.

What is interesting is the conjunction in Manfred, and after him in so many other Gothic villains, of the feudal baron and the figure of antisocial power. If, as seems likely, the widespread appearance of these figures signifies a social anxiety, then that anxiety clearly had a historical dimension: threat to convention was seen as coming partly from the past, out of the memory of previous social and psychological orders. In other words, it came from the atrophying aristocracy; and if one thing can be said of all the different kinds of fiction which were popular in the later eighteenth century, it is that they consistently played upon the remarkably clear urge of the middle classes to read about aristocrats. *Otranto's* strength and resonance derive largely from the fact that in it Walpole evolved a primitive symbolic structure in which to represent uncertainties about the past: its attitude to feudalism is a remarkable blend of admiration, fear and curiosity.

If realistic depiction of everyday life and a rational approach to nature were linked in the novels of the mid-century, Walpole originates a genre in which the attractions of the past and of the supernatural become similarly connected, and, further, in which the supernatural itself becomes a symbol of our past rising against us, whether it be the psychological past – the realm of those primitive desires repressed by the demands of closely organised society – or the historical past, the realm of a social order characterised by absolute power and servitude. But although in this sense *Otranto* originated a genre, it was another thirteen years before a successor appeared, Clara Reeve's *The Old English Baron* (1777), which in some ways followed Walpole's example in the field of romance, but in others attempted to divert the stream of the revival.

Reeve's book was partly an attempt to combine features of *Otranto* with a rather different but related area of fiction, which included books like Thomas Leland's *Longsword* (1762) and William Hutchinson's *The Hermitage: A British Story* (1772). These were straightforward historical novels, although they suffered greatly from an equally straightforward historical ignorance. Reeve's purpose, essentially, was to use the supernatural devices of Walpole, to a limited extent, and the historical settings of Leland and others to give narrative interest and attractiveness to a tale with a didactic purpose. She objected to *Otranto* on two counts: it did not appear to have such a purpose, but set itself out merely to amuse, and it used the supernatural in such a way as to sacrifice narrative probability. Reeve thought that there was a way in which the supernatural could be used without entirely sacrificing probability; not surprisingly, this drew down upon her a rebuke from Walpole, who commented that her novel was 'so probable, that any trial for murder at the Old Bailey would make a more interesting story'.[18]

The Old English Baron has a very simple plot, in which a young man of uncertain origins but with great talents is taken into a noble household, where he earns the envy and enmity of the sons of the house. They visit various evils upon him, but with the help of highly placed friends he is enabled at length to discover the secret of his birth, which, of course, is as noble as that of his rivals. As a story, it is hardly worthy of attention, and its use of the supernatural is tamer and more incompetent than Walpole's; what is interesting about *The Old English Baron* is the way in which it differs in intention and tone from *Otranto*. Summers, a great admirer of Walpole, is extremely severe on Reeve, and the reasons are not difficult to see: for Summers, Gothic is, as we have said, an 'aristocratic' genre, and it looks to him as though Reeve is deliberately trying to take it outside this category. Her greatest fault in Summers's eyes is revealed by Varma when he says that she was a 'disciple of Richardson, and a friend of his daughter' (Varma, p. 79); the complaint behind this is that the world of *The Old English Baron* is, despite appearances, the world of the eighteenth-century middle class. Walpole, admittedly, found it very difficult to conjure up an alternative world, but at least he tried 'pour épater le bourgeois', if only by producing strangeness and exoticism: Reeve merely takes the conventional behaviour and motivations of her contemporaries and dresses them in knightly costumes. Tompkins comments that 'it is this homely and practical streak that differentiates *The Old English Baron* from any other Gothic story whatever; nowhere else do we find knights regaling on eggs and bacon and suffering from the toochache' (Tompkins, pp. 229–30).

The past is not a source of fear and wonder to Reeve, but a source of comfort; one feels that she is encouraging a constant sense of relief at the comparative normalcy of our ancestors. Far from being dangerous villains with megalomaniac tendencies, our forefathers were susceptible to much the same feelings and reasonings as we are: her text, in her later *Memoirs of Sir Roger de Clarendon* (1793) was 'Let us now praise famous men, even our fathers who begat us',[19] which could scarcely be farther from the attitude to the past which Walpole bequeathed to Radcliffe and Lewis. Similarly, the supernatural is not truly terrifying; to be frightened by it is merely a mark of superstition. At one point the hero, Edmund, is conferring with friends, when 'at the hour of twelve they heard the same groans as the night before in the lower apartment; but, being somewhat familiarised to it, they were not so strongly affected'.[20]

It has been said of the Gothic that 'no self-respecting ghost ever troubles the middle classes' (Birkhead, p. 78), although the reasons for this are much more contradictory than they appear, but Reeve does set out to bring the supernatural within the fold of bourgeois feelings and responses. Indeed, although Walpole may not in fact have achieved the reconciliation of romance and novel which he claimed to be attempting, Reeve comes much closer, and in doing so brings out a considerable problem. For to treat ghosts in a matter-of-fact way is in itself to demystify them; even to make them 'appear' on the page requires a certain development of narrative techniques, as Radcliffe was to realise. Walpole and Reeve share an inability to get round this problem: they try to tackle it head-on rather than obliquely. The results, however, are very different: Walpole's sheer bravado, and his comparative freedom from moral purpose, enable him to create something which is strange even in its failures, whereas Reeve's commonsensicality, her acquiescence in a fundamentally rationalist ideology, mean that her ghosts do nothing to differentiate her book from the mainstream of eighteenth-century literature. Already in these two texts a curiously paradoxical situation is emerging about the social relations and emphases of Gothic.

The technical problem in Gothic fiction remained substantially unchanged until the advent of Radcliffe: but there is a specific continuity between Walpole and Reeve which we need to note. Both *The Castle of Otranto* and *The Old English Baron* are 'framed' narratives; that is to say, both writers present their texts as manuscripts which they have discovered, and of which they are, so to speak, the 'editors'. The most obvious reason for this is defensiveness; it was not until the second edition of *Otranto* that Walpole dared admit to his authorship, and Reeve was similarly and conventionally modest about her efforts. Again, the manuscript device helps with verisimilitude: if archaism of setting is difficult to achieve, it is not difficult to describe gaps and hiatuses in a manuscript, and it may indeed be very useful, in order to pass over tedious parts of the narrative. The increasing complexity of the concept of the discovered manuscript is a significant part of the history of the Gothic novel; and one of the most interesting books in this respect is *The Recess* (1783–5) by Sophia Lee, which is very much more sophisticated than its predecessors. In form it derives from the epistolary novel, and intersperses letters and portions of manuscript with considerable abandon. Sometimes Lee is able to retain character cogency within this format, sometimes not, but at least she clearly shows that she is aware of the difficulty of designing an inserted letter which will both reflect the persona of its supposed author and carry out the actual author's narrative purposes. *The Recess* is a remarkably rich and complex book, set in the reign of Elizabeth, and recounting the adventures of two imaginary sisters, illegitimate daughters of Mary Queen of Scots; in the course of the book, Lee brings in almost every major event and personage of Elizabeth's reign, connecting them in with her narrative with great ingenuity and confidence. The sheer range of the book, in terms of setting and character, and the dense texture of the story place it much closer to Radcliffe than to Walpole or Reeve; however, what is remarkable about it formally is that Lee is able to use her modified epistolary technique to give us conflicting viewpoints on events. This, of course, had always been the strength of the novel in letters: but in, say, Richardson, the reader is left in little doubt, except perhaps temporarily, about the standpoint he or she is supposed to take about various characters' protestations. In *The Recess*, the case is different: the central portion of the book is taken up by two long letters, one by each sister, recounting their different perspectives on substantially the same events. One sister is enamoured of the Earl of Leicester, the other of the Earl of Essex, and their versions of the machinations of Elizabeth and her favourites are quite different. Lee makes no attempt to resolve this conflict, and we are left with a text embodying attitudinal contradictions and allowing the reader more freedom of realisation, it is fair to say, than any other novel of the period.

Essentially, *The Recess* allows us to make up our own minds about history, and to help us with this task it supplies a wealth of historical detail quite foreign to anything in Walpole or Reeve. In respect of this historical realism, as with her narrative techniques, Lee owed a great deal to the French historical romance, and particularly to the abbé Prévost and Baculard d'Arnaud, but her development of a specific period of *British* history has few contemporary rivals. Furthermore, the particular historical themes on which she concentrates prefigure those which were to claim the special attention of the majority of Gothic writers; unlike contemporary German authors, the English writers of the 1790s and after were not on the whole to follow Walpole's lead and concern themselves with things medieval; they were primarily interested in a different period, the sixteenth and seventeenth centuries, and certain themes within that period recur: the problem of Catholicism, the meaning of Jacobitism and, often centrally, the reign of Elizabeth herself. Lee originates a trend in treating Elizabeth as a persecutor, for despite the fundamental anti-Catholicism of most Gothic fiction she is rarely treated well; in *The Recess*, it seems that she figures principally as 'unnatural'. Clearly the notion of the Virgin Queen was not an easy one for Lee and her contemporaries to assimilate.

The whole question of the emergence of the 'historical novel' and its relation to Gothic is a vexed one. As Summers points out, there had been plenty of historical romances in England in the seventeenth and early eighteenth centuries. Leland's *Longsword*, often hailed as the first historical novel, is hardly really distinct from these romances, and certainly Reeve added little in terms of historical information to the tradition. Against this background, *The Recess* does stand out as innovative, although it is a matter of degree rather than of kind. Partly it is that Lee simply *knows* more; but more importantly, it is a question of breadth. Most of her predecessors had tended to treat history as an excuse for biography, and individual biography at that: Lee's interest goes two ways. Tompkins points out quite rightly that in *The Recess* 'private loves and vengeances replace political motives, and love . . . accounts in Miss Lee's eyes for Essex' behaviour in Ireland and Sidney's death at Zutphen' (Tompkins, pp. 227–8), and of course this results in historical distortion, but Lee's project was not to use events to demonstrate the greatness of great men but rather the other way round, to use personalisation of motive as a way of coming to understand history itself. This is most aptly described as a process of ideological naturalisation, by which the distant is familiarised, and in this respect Lee follows Reeve and not Walpole. Where Walpole inflates, makes strange, creates a structure of symbols, Reeve and Lee deflate, bring history within the purview and understanding of contemporary norms. Yet where Reeve's interest is moral and didactic, Lee's is historical and interpretative: she does not set out to create her own truth, but to mould a cogent set of truths out of the elements history has left her. The result is unwieldy, with that distinctive unwieldiness which is to become characteristic of so much long Gothic fiction: but this is because Lee does not shirk the intractable nature of much of her material, and is content to allow mystery and contradiction to stand.

Thus far, it might be said that *The Recess* is, after all, not a Gothic but a historical novel, in so far as such a line can be drawn; but within the frame of history, the themes which attract Lee's attention are those which are going to become peculiarly the property of the Gothics. The whole plot is based on persecution, on the danger which the existence of Mary's daughters presents to the state and on the various attempts made to suppress that danger. The nature and extent of this persecution remains ambiguous, for the simple reason that *The Recess* is a first-person narrative. The fears of the narrator are, presumably, partly justified; but they are also partly irrational fears. The world of *The Recess*, even more explicitly than the world of Radcliffe's novels, is one in which women are in constant danger, almost regardless of their rank and historical importance, a world in which men as protectors pass almost naturally from kindness to rape. The heroines themselves are equally sources of danger to others: 'I was born the fate of all I ever loved',[21] says one of the sisters, prefiguring doom-laden protagonists from Coleridge to Oscar Wilde. The end-point of these interlocking dangers is madness, and one of the sisters eventually passes over the line, broken and deranged by the strains of the world of violence to which she is exposed. Much is made of the emotional power of gloomy surroundings; passages detailing the effects of exposure to the insignia of death show clear traces of the influence of Parnell and the other graveyard writers. And, above all, *The Recess* is Gothic in being a novel of suspense, a suspense sustained through four volumes at an intensity which would have been inconceivable a mere ten years earlier.

But the crucial feature of these first Gothic novels is to do with their relation to history; it is only later, in the 1790s, that Smollett's preoccupation with terror as such returns and becomes substantially connected with historical interest. And the reason why it is so difficult to draw a line between Gothic fiction and historical fiction is that Gothic itself seems to have *been* a mode of history, a way of perceiving an obscure past and interpreting it. In the 1770s and 1780s, several different kinds of new fiction arose to challenge the realist tradition, but what they all had in common was a drive to come to terms with the barbaric, with those realms excluded from the Augustan synthesis, and the primary focus of that drive was the past itself.

Notes and references

1. **Raymond Williams**, *The Long Revolution* (London, 1961), p. 161.
2. **Ian Watt**, *The Rise of the Novel* (London, 1957), p. 330.
3. On the circulating libraries, see particularly Tompkins, pp. 1–10.
4. **Richard Altick**, *The English Common Reader: A Social History of the Mass Reading Public, 1800–1900* (Chicago, 1957), p. 49.
5. See, for instance, 'The Marriage of Heaven and Hell', *The Poetry and Prose of William Blake*, ed. David V. Erdman (New York, 1965), p. 34. All subsequent Blake references are to 'Erdman'.
6. **Max Horkheimer** and **T. W. Adorno**, *Dialectic of Enlightenment*, trans. John Cumming (London, 1973), p. 16.
7. **Harrison R. Steeves**, *Before Jane Austen: The Shaping of the English Novel in the Eighteenth Century* (London, 1966), pp. 164–5.
8. **Henry MacKenzie**, *The Man of Feeling*, ed. Brian Vickers (London, 1970), pp. 121–2.
9. *The Poems of Alexander Pope*, ed. John Butt (10 vols, London, 1939–67), I, 246–9.
10. In *The Poetical Works of Thomas Parnell* (London, 1833). pp. 93–6.
11. **Edward Young**, *The Complaint, or, Night Thoughts*, in *The Poetical Works of Edward Young* (2 vols, London, 1834), I. 2.
12. **Longinus**, *On the Sublime*, trans. W. Hamilton Fyfe, in *Aristotle, Longinus, Demetrius* (London, 1927), p. 219.
13. **Edward Young**, *Conjectures on Original Composition*, ed. Edith J. Morley (Manchester, 1918), p. 12.
14. **Edmund Burke**, *A Philosophical Enquiry into the Origin of our Ideas of the Sublime and Beautiful*, ed. J. T. Boulton (London 1958), p. 39.
15. **Tobias Smollett**, *The Adventures of Ferdinand Count Fathom*, ed. Damian Grant (London, 1971), p. 3.
16. See Varma, p. 224.
17. **Horace Walpole**, *The Castle of Otranto; A Gothic Story*, ed. W. S. Lewis (London, 1969), p. 7.
18. *Horace Walpole's Correspondence*, ed. W. S. Lewis (34 vols, New Haven and London, 1937–71), XXVIII, 381–2.
19. On this point, see Tompkins, p. 231.
20. **Clara Reeve**, *The Old English Baron; A Gothic Story*, ed. James Trainer (London, 1967), p. 69.
21. **Sophia Lee**, *The Recess, or, A Tale of Other Times* (3 vols, London, 1785), II, 70.

CHAPTER 3

The classic Gothic novels

Ann Radcliffe and Matthew Lewis

The Gothic novel reached its first peak, in terms of quantity and popularity, in the mid-1790s; it is an exaggeration to say that 'this body of fiction may well have established the popularity of the novel-form' (Varma, p. 3), but certainly it was the dominant genre of the decade, and part of the explanation for this is that it was now beginning to gain critical acclaim on the grounds that 'it gives great scope for the portrayal of violent emotion, and by the middle 'ninet-ies it was sometimes allowed that vigour and boldness may compen-sate for the lack of probability, while the younger critics were speaking as if it were, at all events, some merit to spurn the common bounds' (Tompkins, p. 217). The merit of Gothic seen thus is as a kind of transgression – which, of course, is by no means the same as an escape. The 1790s were chaotic years in which domestic unrest and fears of invasion from abroad shaped political and cultural life, and the literary market was flooded with a mass of fiction which rejected direct engagement with the activities of contemporary life in favour of geographically and historically remote actions and set-tings; but these two facts must be positively connected. As Tompkins again points out, 'a natural reaction from a long period of sobriety in literature combined with revolutionary excitement and the growth of the reading habit in the lower middle classes to intensify the appeal of the terrible and increase the opportunities of gratify-ing it' (Tompkins, p. 221). Within the Gothic we can find a very intense, if displaced, engagement with political and social problems, the difficulty of negotiating those problems being precisely reflected in the Gothic's central stylistic conventions.

From this mass of fiction, three works stood out even then and were greeted by reviewers with an uneasy mixture of highbrow disapproval, puritanical doubts and awkward admiration: Ann Radcliffe's two major novels, *The Mysteries of Udolpho* (1794) and *The Italian* (1797), and Matthew Lewis's *The Monk* (1796). The three are interconnected in a complex web of influence, disagreement and rejection: Lewis claimed to have been largely inspired by the success of *Udolpho*, while *The Italian* was Radcliffe's rather shocked response to the sensationalism and sexual explicitness of *The Monk*. Radcliffe and Lewis have traditionally been seen as the protagonists of two distinct types of Gothic, but in fact alongside the stylistic differences lies a considerable and, in a sense, embarrassing identity of thematic preoccupation.

When *Udolpho* was published, Ann Radcliffe was thirty, the wife of a reasonably prosperous lawyer and littérateur. We know little about her life except that it seems to have been secure and uneventful, and all the interesting stories which grew up around her are now known to have been untrue. She was personally shy and fond of privacy, preferring to avoid the literary world which would have been only too willing to welcome her, partly initially as a curiosity but also as a considerable market success. Up to and including *The Italian* she wrote five novels, beginning with *The Castles of Athlin and Dunbayne* (1789), which owed a great deal to *The Recess*; they all show considerable involvement with the work of Lee and of Charlotte Smith.[1] The remaining twenty-nine years of her life were passed in literary silence; a final book, *Gaston de Blondeville*, a historical romance, was published in 1826 after her death, and was rather different from the others largely because of the growing influence of Scott and a consequent increased involvement with 'real' history.

Other relevant information can only be found in the novels themselves, and these at least give us a good picture of her education and literary taste, for Radcliffe was a deeply 'literary' writer and her works are steeped in quotations and allusions which indicate a wide range of reading. By far the strongest influences were Shakespeare and Milton: not only do quotations abound, but in *The Italian*, for example, the entire closing section reads as a modulation of a Shakespearean comic finale, while the character of Schedoni, the hero/villain, owes a vast debt to Milton's portrayal of Satan. Her taste in 'modern' eighteenth-century writers extended in two principal directions: towards Richardson, Prévost and the sentimental novel, and towards the 'poets of landscape and the night', particularly Gray, Macpherson, Young and James Thomson. There is, however, an important distinction to be drawn here: while the kinds of feeling and structures of characterisation on which Radcliffe draws are deeply rooted in the sentimental tradition, it is to Shakespeare and to the poets that she looks to substantiate the truth of her depiction, often with apt and summarising quotations. She seems to have seen her debt to Richardson and Prévost as largely one of method: the overall vision of life which she strives to embody clearly seemed to her poetic, and there is good reason for this, for the nexus of feelings and moods which she tries to present in her writing – sublimity, melancholy, tragic aspiration and downfall – had not previously fallen within the domain of prose fiction, and it is from this fact that some of her creative problems arise. Scott comments that 'Fielding, Richardson, Smollett, even Walpole, though writing upon an imaginative subject are decidedly prose authors. Mrs Radcliffe has a title to be considered as the first poetess of romantic fiction, that is, if actual rhythm shall not be deemed essential to poetry.'[2]

Matthew Lewis wrote *The Monk*, in a remarkably short space of time, at the age of twenty in the intervals of embarking on a political and diplomatic career for which he had been destined by reason of birth and wealth. He belonged to a *nouveau riche* family which had made money out of colonial estates, and where with Radcliffe we have a dearth of biographical information, with Lewis we have all too much, for he was an avid seeker of publicity. Abandoning politics out of boredom, he went on to become a prominent literary figure chiefly by reason of the eighteen plays, of varying quality, which he wrote or translated out of the German, some of which were great contemporary successes. It is very difficult now to comprehend the success of any of these plays, which appear crude and derivative, or of the short novel *The Bravo of Venice* (1804), which Lewis translated from the German of the terror-writer Heinrich Zschokke, yet the *Critical Review* found, albeit somewhat condescendingly, that 'the history of the Bravo of Venice is interesting, the language glows with animation, and the "denouement" is rapid and surprising'.[3] Summers comments that Zschokke's 'pronounced political opinions . . . were hardly acceptable to the government' (Summers, p. 269), for Zschokke was in a recognisable German tradition, of which the chief exponent was Schiller, in using terror-fiction as an advocate of individual freedom from social constraints; but Lewis appears to have purged much of this emphasis from the book. Summers, with characteristically partisan exaggeration, refers to Lewis's play *The Castle Spectre* (1797) as 'the most famous and the most typical specimen of all Gothic melodramas' (Summers, p. 254), and to *Alfonso, King of Castile* (1801) as 'very near being a great tragedy' (Summers, p. 262), but while one cannot dissent from at least the fame and typicality of the former, *Alfonso* is much closer to being a monumental disaster, a wooden imitation of the worst of Jacobean melodrama.

But although Lewis never wrote another novel, and despite the embarrassing unoriginality of many of his minor works, *The Monk* was sufficiently notorious to ensure that he was not forgotten in his lifetime, and other writers, Scott and Byron in particular, looked up to him with awe and respect. He fathered a host of derivative works, and significant traces of *The Monk's* influence can be found, for instance, in Charlotte Dacre's novels, in E. T. A. Hoffmann, and in such later writers as G. W. M. Reynolds and T. P. Prest.[4]

Much has been made of Lewis's familiarity with German literature, which was undoubtedly great: he was an accomplished translator, was well read in the works of Goethe, Schiller and C. M. Wieland, and was in addition conversant with the wave of terror-fiction which flourished in Germany in the 1790s. But a word needs to be said about the nature and history of this influence. The translation of German terror-fiction actually began in 1794 with the appearance of an English version of Benedikte Naubert's *Hermann von Unna* (1788), and proceeded apace for the next decade: but although there are affinities between the German writing and English Gothic, there is also a very important difference. The typical German work 'is often susceptible of political meaning; not only is its anti-clericalism more virulent than the picturesque iniquities evolved by English authors, but it is strongly marked by idealism of the feudal past and the Holy Roman Empire' (Tompkins, p. 244). The involvement of English Gothic with political advocacy was principally the reserve of the poets, of Shelley above all; the English Gothic *novel* on the whole tended to transmute immediate social comment into the substance of metaphysical tragedy.

And this was not difficult to do, because the German fiction itself had arisen largely as a result of English influence. In the eighteenth century, Germany was unprecedentedly fond of English literature, probably for reasons connected with the German interest in the problems of national identity. F. G. Klopstock, C. F. Gellert and Wieland all claimed strong influences from Richardson; Shakespeare and Milton were very widely read and edited, and acclaimed as among the greatest of writers. Yet the overall choice of British writers by the Germans was not on the whole what we might expect. In 1817, Coleridge drew attention in *Biographia Literaria* to three figures whom he regarded – from experience – as particularly influential in Germany: one of them is Richardson, but the other two are Young and his fellow graveyard-writer, James Hervey.[5] Goethe, indeed, went so far as to bracket Young's name with Milton's. And the German terror-novel may justly be said to have been inspired by Young and Hervey and, a little later, by Walpole, who was also extensively read. In the 1790s, these novels began to circulate in England, novels by such writers as C. A. Vulpius, whose very popular *Rinaldo Rinaldini* (1798) was translated in 1800, Leonhard Wächter, C. H. Spiess and others. The translation of Schiller's *Die Räuber* (1777–80) in 1792 was particularly important, for *Die Räuber* was the fountain-head of this type of 'political Gothic', and its hero, Karl von Moor, was as popular a symbol of the aspiration towards freedom as Byron's heroes were to become. Even Radcliffe was influenced by Schiller, particularly, in *Udolpho*, by *Der Geisterseher* (1789).

But although Lewis's work shows definite traces of German influence in terms of the amount of licence he permits himself in the description of violence and lust, it shows no serious involvement with the radical content of the terror-novel. He was also a reader and writer of ballads, and knew about the German collections as well as English ones; but German writing, of whatever kind, was only one source of *The Monk*, and it needs to be remembered that most of the German material was extraordinarily crude, even by comparison with the worst of Lewis; for like Radcliffe, Lewis also looks back to Shakespeare and Milton, although his use of them is both less obtrusive and less skilful than Radcliffe's.

What is interesting about that central area of tradition which Radcliffe and Lewis share is that it is not a tradition of prose fiction: it offers a range of feelings and moods, but almost no help with the problems of narrative. Both writers prided themselves, rather unreasonably, on their poetry, and Lewis was to go on to become almost exclusively a playwright, and the combination of skills and ineptitudes which their novels display owes much to this problem of genre. Radcliffe and Lewis attempted an even more ambitious synthesis than Walpole's, in which prose equivalents were sought for poetic and dramatic conventions, and could sometimes only be found at the price of narrative distortion; and much that is curious about all three texts derives from this kind of uncertainty.

The Mysteries of Udolpho is by far the longest of the three, and it relates the simplest narrative, fundamentally a single story structured round the experience of a single character. Emily St Aubert lives in idyllic peace at the chateau of La Vallée in Gascony with her parents.

In the year 1584, Emily's mother dies, and, after a sudden decline and a lengthy journey made for recuperative purposes, her father follows, leaving Emily in distressing financial circumstances and at the mercy of her father's unprepossessing sister, Madame Cheron. Emily has met a youth named Valancourt, with whom she has fallen in love, and while at Tholouse under Cheron's care their courtship is, for purely economic reasons, encouraged; however, Cheron herself marries a sinister Italian nobleman called Montoni, and Emily is whisked away from happiness, first to Venice, where she is almost married against her wishes to one Count Morano, and then to Montoni's decaying castle in the Apennines, Udolpho, in which she is effectually imprisoned during the central and most memorable part of the book.

It is a mark of Radcliffe's skill that the many and terrifying dangers which threaten Emily while at Udolpho are never clear. At one moment, it seems to be forced marriage, at another rape, at another the theft of her remaining estates, at another supernatural terrors, but none of these come to pass. Eventually, after many nights of horror and after her aunt has been done to death, Emily escapes to the chateau of Le Blanc, which proves to have sinister connections with her own family and an assembly of ghosts of its own. These, however, are duly exposed, as were the phantoms of Udolpho, and Emily rediscovers Valancourt; he repents of the moral decline which has overtaken him since their parting, and the lovers are married.

Despite the brilliant and much-praised use of suspense techniques, there are certain problems in the narrative. The incidents at Le Blanc are pallid beside the richly coloured and terrifying Udolpho scenes, and Radcliffe fails in her apparent design of using them to show how Emily has recovered from the over-credulity which has caused her such misery earlier. The removal of Montoni from the action and his subsequent death leave a regrettable space which is never filled; and the attempt to introduce the Villefort family as a further centre of narrative interest is too cursory to succeed. But the strengths of *Udolpho* lie less in narrative than in other areas: character psychology, symbolic intensification, and an extraordinary use of suspense and doubt which constantly blurs the boundaries of reality and fantasy. In terms of character, not only is Montoni an excellent and sometimes subtle version of the attractively cruel villain, but Emily herself, although she emerges as a highly conventional eighteenth-century heroine, is given to us clearly and in enormous, moment-by-moment detail. Her fearful plight is continually referred back to the other stories and legends of cruelty and murder which lurk, half-told and threatening, in the background: the mysterious disappearance of the former owner of Udolpho, the murder of the Marchioness de Villeroi, the fate of Madame Cheron herself, are interesting not in themselves but for the terrifying parallels they offer of the various dooms which Emily barely avoids. This kind of symbolism reaches a high point in the scene at Le Blanc where the servant Ludovico, locked for a night in a haunted room, reads a ghost story which eventually shades into reality; the celebrated fact that Radcliffe in the end explains all her apparently supernatural machinery in no way removes the power which her ghosts have over Emily or over the reader.

There is a significant point, halfway through the second book, when Emily is on the eve of being married to the undesirable Morano: alone, friendless, fearful of the malignity of Montoni, 'her mind, long harassed by distress, now yielded to imaginary terrors; she trembled to look into the obscurity of her spacious chamber, and feared she knew not what'.[6] It is possible to read the whole of the rest of the work as the nightmare which follows that eve of terror, as the poetic and symbolic correlative of the state of Emily's over-wrought imagination; and no explanation can destroy the potency of dreams. The inhabitants of Udolpho may be ghosts, bandits or devils: to Emily they are the incarnation of evil, and their reality can only be read through the medium offered by her dislocated mind.

The Monk is two stories in one, and although there seems little narrative connection between them, their co-presence allows Lewis scope for the dramatic alternations which give the book a pace and energy quite foreign to the languorous, opiated mood of Radcliffe. The major story concerns the monk Ambrosio, a paragon of virtue and famous throughout Madrid for his powerful, 'sublime' sermons. His closest associate in the abbey, a young and virtuous novice, reveals himself to be a woman, Matilda by name, and proceeds to seduce him, a deed which releases Ambrosio's pent-up passions and sets him on a course of violence and self-destruction. Dissatisfied with Matilda, he sets about seducing the young and naïve Antonia, whereupon Matilda rather surprisingly offers him supernatural assistance, which he accepts with initial reluctance. The scheme goes wrong, and Ambrosio murders the girl's mother to prevent her from publicly revealing his true character. With further demonic help, however, Ambrosio is enabled to carry Antonia off, apparently dead, to a crypt where, on her awakening, he savagely rapes her.

Meanwhile we are being told the story of two lovers, Raymond and Agnes: Agnes is destined from birth for the convent, although she increasingly dislikes the idea, and by various stratagems her relatives manage to discourage her from her plans of eloping with Raymond and persuade her to take the veil. Raymond finds her in Madrid, in the convent adjoining Ambrosio's, and convinces her that he has been misrepresented; in the course of the surreptitious meetings they hold to discuss the possibility of her escape, she becomes pregnant. The Abbess – abetted by Ambrosio, whom she is concerned to impress – determines to make an example of her and subjects her to a hideous imprisonment, Raymond finds her, and she is rescued amid a bloodbath of popular anticlerical violence during which the abbess is torn to pieces and her convent sacked. The rescuers of Agnes also find Ambrosio in the vaults with the corpse of his victim, whom he has now murdered, and he is captured and brought before the Inquisition. Matilda, who has been captured with him, succeeds in tempting him to complete his transactions with the devil by selling his soul in exchange for freedom, where-upon Satan, with predictable jocularity, cheats him and brings him to a horrible end.

Unlike Radcliffe, Lewis makes no excuses for the supernatural, and indeed near the end of the book he even suggests that Matilda has been a demon all along, although this would make nonsense of much of the earlier part. Interwoven with the main stories are elements of many of the fearsome legends most dear to the roman-tics: the Wandering Jew, Faustus, the Water-King, the pact with the devil. There are also lesser-known legends, like that of the Bleeding Nun, which Lewis found in the German writers and happily wove into his fabric. But although these are materials which Radcliffe would have found sensationalist and implausible, they contribute in *The Monk* to a textual density not unlike that of *Udolpho*: the suffer-ings of Agnes and of Antonia are situated against a background of legend which both substantiates and intensifies their plight. Lewis, in fact, manages to take materials far more arcane and improbable than Radcliffe's and, by a terseness of style which sometimes approaches naturalism, to make them seem oppressively solid. We are not really required to *believe* in the supernatural by Lewis – this is assumed: rather, we are required to *see* it before us, lurid and gory as a stage ghost.

Although Lewis's methods are sometimes crude, *The Monk* is a very self-conscious book, much more so than *Udolpho*, and delights in complications of narrative. The reader is made to move through a series of stories, and stories within stories: we experience Raymond's history as told by himself to his friend Lorenzo, and within it is a further tale of banditry. Also within Raymond's narration, Agnes relates the tale of the Bleeding Nun, 'in a tone of burlesqued gravity'.[7] But a little later, the story of the Bleeding Nun is told again, all too seriously, by the Wandering Jew, who has come to exorcise her; and the Nun herself gives a brief account of her plight, which is basically the same as the Provençal Tale in *Udolpho*. Agnes eventually gets round to completing her own history; and, as if Lewis were precociously determined to show us how conscious his methods were, the servant Theodore is made to spend a couple of happy hours frightening the nuns of the convent with ridiculous tales and songs. In *Udolpho*, the boundaries of reality and fantasy were blurred and softened: Lewis, taking the antirealist process a step further, begins the essentially Gothic construction of a world of mutually self-validating fictions which are texturally more 'real' than reality itself.

Seen in these terms, *The Italian* is a cogent response to the decadence which Lewis's procedure suggests; it is at least partly a kind of deparodisation of *The Monk*, especially, for instance, in the opening scene in the church of San Lorenzo. It is a far more complex book than either of the others, for Radcliffe has become, rather unexpectedly and perhaps partly because of further reading in French and German (Baculard d'Arnaud, Schiller, Naubert, Karl Grosse), able to handle sophisticated alternations, not only between scenes but, more significantly, between different characters as centres of interest and feeling; but it is also far more insistent in its bending of a typically Gothic multiplicity of tales and half-remembered details towards a complex central plot. The statutory pair of lovers are Ellena and Vivaldi; their wishes are frustrated by Vivaldi's aristocratic parents, in particular his mother, who conspires with her confessor, a monk named Schedoni, to remove the genteel but poverty-stricken Ellena to the appalling convent of San Stefano, where she undergoes predictable rigours. She is rescued by Vivaldi, who manages to persuade her of the necessity of a clandestine marriage; but this is again frustrated, at the last moment, by the complicated and only gradually revealed machinations of Schedoni, who arranges, in a single master-stroke, that Vivaldi be consigned to the Inquisition while Ellena is sent off to be murdered in a sinister house on the shores of the Adriatic.

Thereafter scenes alternate and develop rapidly: Schedoni, on the point of killing Ellena, finds that she seems to be his long-lost daughter and has to change his plans, realising that liaison with the Vivaldi family would now be the best way of fulfilling his inordinate ambition, which he had previously hoped to gratify by putting the Marchesa in his debt. But Vivaldi himself has meanwhile encountered in the chambers of the Inquisition an even more bizarre ecclesiastic, Nicola di Zampari, whose often unintelligible behaviour turns out to be designed as a betrayal of Schedoni, his former associate. Schedoni is arrested, and a mass of complicated information about his former life comes to light from various sources, including the fact that he is not Ellena's father but her uncle and the murderer of his own brother. He manages to evade punishment by poisoning both himself and Nicola, whereupon Vivaldi and Ellena are enabled to reunite.

Ellena and Vivaldi are no more interesting in themselves than were Emily and Valancourt, but Radcliffe seems to realise this, and instead of describing them exhaustively gives most of her attention to Schedoni and the Marchesa; the conversations between them are masterpieces of mutual guilt and hypocrisy, cast in veiled utterance and half-confidences. The investigation of their psychology is thorough and convincing, largely because we are in no doubt about their overall purposes and motives, which, although changeable, are always clear and brutal. The scenes in the Inquisition, partly derived from Lewis but described largely in terms of dialogue, are almost impressionistic in their manner: mysterious voices in the gloom, flitting figures and unknown instruments of torture create a picture of fear which reduces Udolpho to a toy castle. Radcliffe responds to the blatancy of Lewis and the earlier Gothic writers with a virtuoso demonstration of the imaginative power of the half-seen and half-explained, as if to show that there are kinds of vividness which depend less on concrete authorial depiction than on releasing the springs of the reader's fantasy.

Again, *The Italian* is a work which, like many other Gothic works, plays with story. Like *Otranto, The Old English Baron* and *The Recess* it is 'framed', as a book read by later English visitors to Naples, the scene of most of the action; and the revelations at the end rely on the piecing together of further stories, each of which contains a different aspect of the essential information. Radcliffe even throws in tales which turn out to be totally irrelevant, including one about a Baróne di Cambrusca, whom we are supposed to conceive as an earlier incarnation of Schedoni but who turns out not to be. The high point of Radcliffe's manipulative technique comes in the third book, when Schedoni encounters a peasant who may or may not know facts about the past which the monk wants concealed: on the one hand, he needs to know the peasant's story in case it threatens him with exposure, while on the other he does not want the peasant to think he is interested. The story is thus thwarted at every turn by Schedoni's interruptions and anticipations, but the peasant struggles through, adhering to his determination to tell what he knows clearly and in the right order, while Schedoni continually tries to claim that it is all nonsense, even saying towards the end that 'the narrative resembles a delirious dream, more than a reality',[8] which opens up a whole range of speculations about Radcliffe's opinions of her own art. The episode is a masterly parody of the twists and turns of Gothic fiction itself, reminiscent of a similar awareness in an episode of *The Old English Baron*: ' "Tis a long story", said she, "and cannot be told in a few words." – "It will never be told at this rate," said he; "sit down and begin it instantly" ' (*Old English Baron*, p. 58).

Seen – as Radcliffe and Lewis certainly saw them – as a series, these books show important developments in scope and consciousness of narrative technique. Various attempts have been made to draw a clear distinction between the two writers: the most usual one is that between 'explained' and 'unexplained' supernatural, but the supernatural, in either form, is by no means at the heart of the books. Like Coleridge, Radcliffe and Lewis were both interested, from different perspectives, in phantasm and illusion; but again like Coleridge, it was for them principally an apt metaphor in which to convey wider thematic concerns. For all three of the books are, like so many other romantic works, thematically centred on the complex relations between solitude, society and the imagination, between the individual's internal liberation into the worlds of 'fancy' and his or her outward subservience to the bonds of convention and repression. Thus they are essentially explorations of the relation between the individual and the environment, which is, of course, the subject with which other writers of Gothic like Godwin and Shelley were to be concerned from a more overtly political point of view. Radcliffe and Lewis were not writing, as Fielding and his followers had been, behavioural histories of individuals, but fables about those points of vision and obsession where individuals blur into their own fantasies; and they perforce questioned the boundaries on which individual identity depends. And this becomes essentially a question of form: what poets from Young to Coleridge could explore, free from the bondage of narrative, becomes problematic in Radcliffe and Lewis precisely at the point of the relation between character development and thematic cogency. Although both writers can incidentally provide us with reasonably well-realised characters, their special strength, which owes more than a little to Sophia Lee, is in the detailed and often poeticised depiction of states of mind.

Their novels thus have in common an investigation into certain recognisable sociopsychological traits, and offer symbolic suggestions, sometimes conscious and sometimes apparently unconscious, about their causes and consequences. Outstandingly, they are concerned with the concept of sensibility and the problems inherent in it. Emily, Antonia and Vivaldi are all people endowed with an undue amount of it, and to this fact their griefs and sufferings are directly related. In *Udolpho*, Radcliffe points out very early that Emily is possessed of 'a degree of susceptibility too exquisite to admit of lasting peace' (*Udolpho*, p. 5), and it is this quivering sensitivity which continually prostrates her before spectres of her own imagining. Antonia's 'sensibility of countenance' (*Monk*, p. 8) betokens an unworldly faith in other people's goodness and sensitivity, and Lewis has her abducted, poisoned, raped and murdered as a savage indication of the inadequacy of this faith. Vivaldi, who is also 'susceptible', is accused both of being 'romantic' – by his father – and of Quixotism (*Italian*, pp. 29, 30), and it is finally, and rather unfairly, suggested that everything would have been all right were it not for his impressionable nature. This is not to say that either Radcliffe or Lewis portray sensibility as a worthless quality; Radcliffe, at least, takes great pains to point out that it is preferable to the hardness of heart which is the peculiar prerogative of villains like Montoni and Schedoni. But it is an extreme, and as such it is bound to produce conflict with what we might term the 'reality-principle'; essentially, the aspect of sensibility which concerns the Gothic writers is its incompatibility with the general fabric of social activity – it deals, as it did in *The Man of Feeling*, with impressions and feelings in a manner too subtle and too lengthily indulgent to be socially useful. A typical scene occurs in *Udolpho*: Emily, treated to a harangue by Madame Cheron, decides by means of her acute perceptions that Cheron's 'misfortunes did not admit of real consolation', and does not bother to reply. Cheron, perhaps understandably piqued by this lack of response, becomes even angrier: 'O! I suspected what all this boasted sensibility would prove to be!', she says, 'I thought it would not teach you to feel either duty, or affection, for your relations, who have treated you like their own daughter!' (*Udolpho*, p. 281). This is, of course, a misunderstanding, but it is one which recurs again and again, for Emily's sensibility does in fact render her incapable of the gross and rapid responses necessary to active social participation, and sinks her more and more dangerously in the world of her over-stimulated imagination.

The good side of sensibility, on which Radcliffe dwells more than Lewis, is represented by its visionary quality, which is again at its height in the character of Emily. Her many visions – for instance, those of Hannibal and of Troy – clearly show that the strength of the sensitive individual is in terms of her inner life, and that sensibility allows and encourages this to expand at the expense of communicative contact. But it is precisely because of this that Emily's perceptions of the *real* world go sadly amiss, as when, for instance, she continually imagines her fellow prisoner at Udolpho to be Valancourt. There is not the slightest reason why it should be Valancourt, except that this would fit into Emily's inner vision of life; and, of course, it turns out that it is indeed not Valancourt. The individual endowed with sensibility becomes increasingly unable to accept the messiness and untidiness of life and sees everywhere the operations of poetic justice, and in their portrayals of the continual defeat of this poetic justice Radcliffe and Lewis become cruel to the point of sadism. Lewis's torture of Antonia is unpleasant enough; but there is something just as jarring in the way Radcliffe allows her villains to taunt their unfortunate victims on the practical uselessness of their fine speeches and 'heroic' behaviour.[9]

It is also sensibility which lays the individual open to the inroads of 'superstition', and here we come to one of the crucial contradictions of Gothic writing. There is a fine irony in the text from *Julius Caesar* with which Radcliffe prefaces one of the chapters in *Udolpho*: 'I think it is the weakness of mine eyes,/That shapes this monstrous apparition./It comes upon me!' (*Udolpho*, p. 241). But the implicit question raised is never answered, for although Emily is indeed prey to 'imaginary terrors' she is also assailed by real difficulties, while it is Montoni who is allowed to hold the balanced and reasonable view of superstition: 'I am not superstitious', he says at one point, 'though I know how to despise the commonplace sentences, which are frequently uttered against superstition' (*Udolpho*, p. 291). We spend the whole book hoping that Emily will come to a similar position, but she never really does. When Radcliffe says, quite late in the book, that 'she now sunk, for a moment, under the weakness of superstition' (*Udolpho*, p. 530), it is difficult to know what the reader is meant to think, for this is what she has already been doing for 500 pages.

In Lewis's case, the failing of superstition is a mainspring of the action, for it is this tendency in Agnes's parents which has consigned her to convent life, and which thus precipitates her later sufferings; furthermore, Ambrosio's condition is blamed on the same fault in his background, for he was brought up by monks who 'terrified his young mind, by placing before him all the horrors with which superstition could furnish them' (*Monk*, p. 188). Here the contradiction in the text is even more remarkable, for Lewis is at the same time inveighing against superstition and depicting its manifestations as real. In a sense, both authors are playing a confidence trick on the reader, by using all the resources in their power to convince us of the reality of phantoms and then sneering at belief. A similar thing happens in *The Italian* in connection with the mysterious Nicola, who makes various appearances which can hardly be explained in other than supernatural terms. Vivaldi, finally confronting him, experiences a moment of severe doubt:

> The conduct of the mysterious being, who now stood before him, with many other particulars of his own adventures there, passed like a vision over his memory. His mind resembled the glass of a magician, on which the apparitions of long-buried events arise, and as they fleet away, point portentously to shapes half-hid in the duskiness of futurity. An unusual dread seized upon him; and a superstition, such as he had never before admitted in an equal degree, usurped his judgement. He looked up to the shadowy countenance of the stranger; and almost believed he beheld an inhabitant of the world of spirits.
>
> (*Italian*, p. 320)

Radcliffe's eventual explanation of Nicola's behaviour is massively unconvincing, adding weight to the idea that, behind the apparent differences between the 'explained' and 'unexplained' supernatural, all of these texts work by having it both ways: by persuading to belief while withholding full authorial confirmation of that belief. The problem cannot be resolved, precisely because realist coordinates are partly or completely absent. For both Radcliffe and Lewis, susceptibility to superstition is the price to be paid for perceptual sensitivity: the question of whether it is worth paying cannot really be raised, for it would call on distinctions between subjective and objective which have been undermined by the placing of characters in impossible and isolated situations, in which conventional norms of explanation have no validity.

For in Gothic fiction, the distortion of perception caused by excessive sensibility is situated in dialectical relation to the further distortion occasioned by social isolation. Characters already prone to misjudgement find themselves cut off – in castle, convent, dungeon – from anything that might help them to correct their mistakes. This dislocation from everyday norms is a prevalent general feature of tragedy – *Hamlet, Lear, Othello* all hinge on it – but what is curious in Radcliffe and Lewis is that, by evolving a comprehensive symbolic language in which to represent isolation, they threaten to remove all criteria for character judgement. We cannot ask whether Emily or Antonia would have behaved differently, or even more 'realistically', under different circumstances, because, as with the heroines of *The Recess*, it is never clear to what extent those circumstances are genuinely imposed on the characters by outside forces and to what extent they are projections of paranoia and vulnerability – as Emily's ghosts, for instance, prove to be. For Emily, undoubtedly, forges her own shackles: 'she looked upon Count Morano with horror', we read,

> but apart from him, a conviction, if such that may be called, which arises from no proof, and which she knew not how to account for, seized her mind – that she would never see Valancourt again. Though she knew, that neither Morano's solicitations, nor Montoni's commands had lawful power to enforce her obedience, she regarded both with a superstitious dread, that they would finally prevail.   (*Udolpho*, p. 209)

The vision of the Bleeding Nun which haunts Raymond so alarmingly in *The Monk* may seem more tangible than these insubstantial terrors, but in the end there is nothing the text itself can do to remove the suspicion that the Nun too may be a projection – of Raymond's guilt about elopement and his fears for Agnes's safety.

The end-point of these doubts, again as in *The Recess*, is madness, the complete dislocation of the mind under pressures which cannot even be accurately categorised as internal or external. Emily blames herself 'for suffering her romantic imagination to carry her so far beyond the bounds of probability, and determined to endeavour to check its rapid flights, lest they should sometimes extend into madness' (*Udolpho*, p. 342), and finds that there are moments 'when she could almost have believed herself the victim of frightful visions, glaring upon a disordered fancy' (*Udolpho*, p. 407); and at one point at least her maid Annette does indeed assume she is mad. Sensibility and distorted perception are perhaps always closely linked: Radcliffe and Lewis engineer fictional situations in which they are forced into identity, and character and reader become part of a vertiginous dance with death.

Under such stress, the Gothic victim turns naturally to the consolations of landscape. A major symbol for this is the turret-room in the convent of San Stefano, to which Ellena in *The Italian* retreats during her imprisonment, and in which she derives comfort from the scenes of sublime grandeur with which the convent is fortunately surrounded. Radcliffe cannot, and does not seriously try to, explain how it is that Ellena is allowed this retreat; and this is surely because the turret-room is largely an image for the interior of Ellena's own mind, the only resource left to her as a refuge from inhumanity. For Ellena, abandonment to natural sublimity is a counterforce against human injustice. For villains, the situation is naturally otherwise: Montoni, Madame Cheron, Ambrosio, Schedoni all have a marked lack of interest in and respect for their environment – although there is one remarkable moment in *The Italian* when Schedoni becomes wonderingly alive to a particular aspect of nature:

> 'The evening is closing fast,' continued Ellena, 'and I shall be overtaken by the storm.'
> Schedoni still mused, and then muttered – 'The storm, say you? Why ay, let it come.' (*Italian*, p. 222).

At first glance, it might seem that the villain is simply impervious to the effects of landscape, but in fact he has a marked, non-contemplative affinity with the wilder side of nature. In all three novels, the much-dreaded 'banditti' are described as the natural inhabitants of certain kinds of scenery:

> Sometimes, indeed, a gigantic larch threw its long shade over the precipice, and here and there a cliff reared on its brow a monumental cross, to tell the traveller the fate of him who had ventured thither before. This spot seemed the very haunt of banditti; and Emily, as she looked down upon it, almost expected to see them stealing out from some hollow cave to look for their prey. (*Udolpho*, p. 54)

Banditti are less human robbers than nature spirits of a particular kind, the spirits of the wild; and in *The Italian* Vivaldi points out a mountain which itself 'stands like a ruffian, huge, scarred, threatening, and horrid!' (*Italian*, p. 158). Montoni – the name itself is significant – and the mountains excite related feelings in Emily: they inspire awe and fear, yet they are also curiously reassuring, in that their potential for destruction renders pettier fears pointless and trivial. It may seem remarkable in *Udolpho* how often Emily, who is supposed to be terrified of Montoni, throws herself under his protection: but then Montoni is, in a sense, inevitable, and the inevitable is a powerful palliative in the face of less predictable dangers.

Radcliffe and Lewis are also highly specific in their perception of the social and psychological tendencies which produce the contradiction and strain which their characters experience. Partly what lies behind the novels is a concern with hypocrisy: with that fine dividing line between the kind of social and sexual hypocrisy which is encouraged by, and perhaps necessary to, regularised social intercourse, and that kind which is destructive and repressive. In *Udolpho*, it is noticeable that even in the idyllic early part of the book Emily and her father spend a lot of time concealing their emotions from one another. For her father's own good, Emily conceals from him her premonitions of his death; for his daughter's good, St Aubert conceals the fate of his sister, which is going to cause her such anguish later. And, of course, the relations between Emily and Valancourt are couched throughout in terms of the permissible hypocrisy which characterised relations between the sexes at the time. But it cannot be ignored that, for all the contemporary normalcy of these concealments, their fictional consequences are appalling; and this is hardly surprising in view of the degree of sexual segregation practised at the time. The kind of situation which Radcliffe dramatises is the result of the actual process of female education which Fielding describes so frighteningly in *Joseph Andrews:*

> thou must know, that as the passion generally called love exercises most of the talents of the female or fair world, so in this they now and then discover a small inclination to deceit; for which thou wilt not be angry with the beautiful creatures when thou hast considered that at the age of seven, or something earlier, miss is instructed by her mother that master is a very monstrous kind of animal, who will, if she suffers him to come too near her, infallibly eat her up and grind her to pieces: that, so far from kissing or toying with him of her own accord, she must not admit him to kiss or toy with her: and, lastly, that she must never have any affection towards him; for if she should, all her friends in petticoats would esteem her a traitress, point at her, and hunt her out of their society. These impressions, being first received, are farther and deeper inculcated by their school-mistresses and companions; so that by the age of ten they have contracted such a dread and abhorrence of the above-named monster, that whenever they see him they fly from him as the innocent hare doth from the greyhound. Hence, to the age of fourteen or fifteen, they entertain a mighty antipathy to master; they resolve, and frequently profess, that they will never have any commerce with him, and entertain fond hopes of passing their lives out of his reach, of the possibility of which they have so visible an example in their good maiden aunt. But when they arrive at this period, and have now passed their second climacteric, when their wisdom, grown riper, begins to see a little farther, and, from almost daily falling in master's way, to apprehend the great difficulty of keeping out of it; and when they observe him look often at them, and sometimes very eagerly and earnestly too ... they then begin to think of their danger; and, as they perceive they cannot easily avoid him, the wiser part bethink themselves of providing by

other means for their security. They endeavour, by all methods they can invent, to render themselves so amiable in his eyes, that he may have no inclination to hurt them . . . [10]

It is from this central contradiction between fear and longing that Fielding goes on to derive all the arts of sexual hypocrisy.

Emily is very much a victim of a situation which forbids the truth, and because of her inability to ask direct questions is reduced to direct lies; only the old servant Theresa tries to break through the patina of hypocrisy which is destroying the relationship, and she gets short shrift for her pains:

> 'Dear! dear! to see how gentlefolks can afford to throw away their happiness! Now, if you were poor people, there would be none of this. To talk of unworthiness, and not caring about one another, when I know there are not such a kind-hearted lady and gentleman in the whole province, nor any that love one another half so well, if the truth was spoken!' (*Udolpho*, p. 626)

Emily thereupon rises from her chair 'in extreme vexation', which is certainly the strongest moment of anger she ever experiences, and the truth is by no means spoken.

Lewis lovingly exposes the dangerous attractiveness of false modesty in his account of Ambrosio's interest in Antonia; cloyed with Matilda's all too available charms, the monk finds a more perverse pleasure in the contemplation of Antonia's innocence and reserve:

> Matilda gluts me with enjoyment even to loathing, forces me to her arms, apes the harlot, and glories in her prostitution. Disgusting! Did she know the inexpressible charm of modesty, how irresistibly it enthrals the heart of man, how firmly it chains him to the throne of beauty, she never would have thrown it off. (*Monk*, p. 192)

Momentarily, Lewis would have us believe that Ambrosio's feelings are comparatively pure; he then proceeds to insist that this apparent purity tends inexorably towards, firstly the fantasy, and at length the reality, of rape.

The fictional world to which these perceptions refer is, of course, primarily the world of Richardson, characterised by Watt as 'a universe where the calm surface of repressive convention and ingrown hypocrisy is momentarily – but only momentarily – threatened by the irruption of the secret violences which it provokes but conceals' (Watt, pp. 219–20). This moment of disruption is considerably prolonged by Radcliffe and Lewis, and is further emphasised by their characters' inefficient handling of the conventions themselves. In the conflict between Vivaldi and Schedoni in *The Italian*, a conflict conditioned anyway by indirectness of dialogue, Vivaldi is further hampered by the fact that he can tell nothing whatever from Schedoni's face, whereas Schedoni can read him like a map. There is a strong emphasis on physiognomy in all the books, but the actual descriptions, of for instance the Wandering Jew in *The Monk*, are less interesting than the vacillations of interpretation felt by the characters, some of whom are clearly aware that facial expression is all they have to go on in their attempts to assess other minds and intentions. Clarissa Harlowe, admittedly, finds the conventions less than fully adequate to her desperate situation; but these characters find them actually harmful.

Hindered on the one hand by the complexities of hypocrisy and on the other by the paradoxically superior mind-reading skills of stony-hearted villains, they are martyrs also to the inadequately repressed parts of their own psyche. Among the major enemies of Emily, Antonia, Ellena are their own passions; Lewis refers to them as 'despotic', and images of the kingdom of reason being 'over-powered' and 'dominated' by these unruly subjects abound.[11] The problem clearly has to do with the cogency or otherwise of the model of the psyche set up by the rationalists, which gives no room for the autonomous action of the passions.

> *Passions, like Elements, tho' born to fight,*
> *Yet, mix'd and soften'd, in his work unite:*
> *These 'tis enough to temper and employ;*
> *But what composes Man, can Man destroy?*
> *Suffice that Reason keeps to Nature's road,*
> *Subject, compound them, follow her and God.*[12]

If the rational person's attitude to passion is to dominate and subject it, as Pope here claims, revolt and rebellion are unsurprising, but the effects wrought are nonetheless terrifying. Many of the lesser tales in the novels – that of Laurentini in *Udolpho*, that of Beatrice in *The Monk* – are versions of this revolt of passion against virtue; Matilda claims to Ambrosio that the power of her passions is driving her towards madness; and the unspecified assault which Emily so fears derives partly from within, from the 'disordering' of her mind by repressed and uncomprehended desire. By conceiving of the passions as enemies, the Gothic victim admits a Trojan horse and also loses grip on the facts of his or her own psychology; when, in *The Italian*, we read that Ellena's joy at Vivaldi's arrival in the convent was 'not subdued, though it was frequently obscured' (*Italian*, p. 122) by various other considerations, we can only wonder at the confusion and lack of self-understanding which the naïve faculty psychology of the Augustans created.

It is in the context of these features of the novels that their symbolic structure needs to be assessed, for this structure hinges on a particular set of relations between psychological tendencies and the social conditions which encourage these tendencies. Radcliffe and Lewis clearly share anxieties about certain social institutions, in particular about the family and the Church. But these anxieties are only really about the extent to which such institutions confirm the 'deeper' problems of hypocrisy, lack of communication and the bondage of convention. In the case of the family, for instance, the tragic situations through which Ellena and Vivaldi pass in *The Italian* can be seen as the direct result of the aristocratic pride of the Marchese and his wife; but in fact, the Marchese becomes towards the end a figure of fun, and his wife repents movingly on her death-bed. Similarly, *The Monk* is obviously antagonistic to monastic life, but it is a curious feature of the book that the part the Inquisition plays is actually beneficent, while Radcliffe takes up a consistently ambiguous attitude towards religious institutions, evidenced principally in the parallel but opposite qualities of San Stefano and Santa della Pieta, one convent being seen as horrific, the other as a refuge and a place of safety.

Family and Church, the constant bugbears of Gothic fiction, offend Radcliffe and Lewis only at the point where they become claustrophobic instruments of isolation, and reinforce the errors of social communication which stem originally from longstanding convention. As readers, of course, we may choose to refer these very conventions back to previously existing social structures, and indeed many contemporary writers – Blake is a major example – did so; but Radcliffe and Lewis were more interested in the particular vicissitudes of the psyche, and they made an eclectic use of social phenomena and settings to reinforce this depiction, although it is worth keeping in mind the contemporary significance of their ecclesiastical symbols: there were, after all, no convents at the time in England, and the Inquisition was still operating in southern Europe through the eighteenth century.

Insofar as Church and family may, by over-zealous protection and isolation – imaged as imprisonment – contribute to rendering the individual less than completely fit for the exigencies of outside life, they contribute also to a lack of balance which is both the major character weakness of Gothic and also the major feature of the fictional world through which the characters move. Sensibility is one manifestation of this; but there is a more sinister oscillation between extremes of love and terror which runs through the books, as, of course, it runs through romanticism. Emily is constantly finding relief in 'melancholy pleasures', and obtaining moments of peace in which she may savour the full horror of her situation and wonder at mankind's capacity for violent extremes. Vivaldi is at one point quite overwhelmed by similar reflections:

> Can this be in human nature! – Can such horrible perversion of right be permitted! Can man, who calls himself endowed with reason, and immeasurably superior to every other created being, argue himself into the commission of such horrible folly, such inveterate cruelty, as exceeds all the acts of the most irrational and ferocious brute.
>
> (*Italian*, p. 198)

Vivaldi may wonder, but Radcliffe herself is sure that he can, and that beauty and death are inseparable; perhaps it was this that made Keats so admiring of her works. And when, in *The Monk*, Ambrosio goes to the crypt to find the catatonic Antonia, he finds an archetypal scene in the tomb: 'by the side of three putrid half-corrupted bodies lay the sleeping beauty' (*Monk*, p. 298). The only garment which Antonia has to protect her from the monk is a shroud. This kind of extremism, of course, derives very directly from the Elizabethan and Jacobean writers, and later from the graveyard poets; it is a quality quite foreign to other eighteenth-century literature, and foreign to the realist novel.

But Radcliffe and Lewis are not only not realist writers, in certain important senses they are, like Walpole, antirealist writers. The insistence on a poetic cogency of thematic oppositions at the expense of narrative probability; the self-conscious references to the very processes of fictionalisation; the refusal to distinguish decisively between character trait and environmental pressure: all these produce a literary mode which is 'bracketed' from reality from the very outset, and which, although it bears an important relation, as it must, to wider societal concerns, mediates these concerns through a symbolic structure which was already coming to have its own conventions and acceptances. Distancing in time and place was coming to serve a double function: on the one hand, it lowered the pressure on the writers to compromise with developmental realism of character or situation, while on the other it allowed a depiction of social and psychological tendencies, of states of mind, in extreme and grotesque form. The process reminds one irresistibly of Freud's notion of sublimation, whereby unwillingness or incapacity directly to confront experiential contradiction finds expression in an apparently different, but in fact related, system of meanings in which the pain of contradiction is cancelled by the pleasure of fantasy. Freud points out that the reader's responses to literature cannot be dissociated from a recognition of the very unreality of the fictional world:

> The unreality of the writer's imaginative world . . . has very important consequences for the technique of his art; for many things which, if they were real, could give no enjoyment, can do so in the play of fantasy, and many excitements which, in themselves, are actually distressing, can become a source of pleasure for the hearers and spectators at the performance of a writer's work. (*Works*, IX, 144)

The dramatic theory of catharsis has always been self-consciously related to some such idea, and it is the cathartic pretensions and ambiguities of the drama of Webster and Tourneur which reappear in Gothic works apparently as far apart as *Udolpho, The Monk* and Keat's *Lamia* (1819).

There is a connection between this heightening of the unreal and the concept of the sublime, as the very word 'sublimation' suggests. That sublimity is a major feature of Radcliffe's works is obvious: all her descriptive material, and her notion of the relations between individual and landscape, hinge on the concept of the sublime as a peak of emotional experience. But it is also a significant element in *The Monk*: Ambrosio's voice, we are told, contains 'all the terrors of the tempest' (*Monk*, p. 14), and Lewis devotes much space to the exposure of this false sublimity, finally, in a beautiful and extravagant irony, transporting the monk to meet his fate in the Sierra Morena, surrounded by precisely those sublime delights from which he has forever alienated himself by his duplicity. Ambrosio is a character with sublime potential, cheated of his heritage by his own weaknesses and, inseparably, by the distortions of conventual life.

Longinus's connection between sublimity and the unreal is followed through in *Udolpho* when Blanche de Villefort is shown standing before a set of windows,

> which were numerous and large, descended low, and afforded a very extensive, and what Blanche's fancy represented to be, a very lovely prospect; and she stood for some time, surveying the grey obscurity and depicturing imaginary woods and mountains, vallies and rivers, on this scene of night . . . (*Udolpho*, p. 471)

Blanche cannot 'see' anything at all; but this very obscurity stimulates her imagination to produce a world over against the inadequacy of reality. Ambrosio's fantasies are similarly represented as

75

running riot precisely because of the lack of stimulus offered by the limited environment of the convent. Claustrophobia and fantasy are inextricably linked, for sublimity is seen as the solace of the deprived senses. But the sublime, as we have seen in Longinus, is related not only to the imaginative construction of an alternative reality but also to the limits of communication. It can be hinted and suggested, but never described; when Emily and her father are in the mountains, we find that they had 'no words to express the sublime emotions they felt' (*Udolpho*, p. 43). These two attributes of the sublime are linked, for satisfactory expression demands a recognisable subject and object, and in the world of the imaginative sublime such a distinction is not valid. Gothic characters in the 1790s are creatures of indirect expression, occasioned by convention and often confirmed by actual confinement, and they value highly that 'poetic' indirectness and the natural phenomena which encourage it by overwhelming the word beneath an avalanche of feeling; and they are also characters whose sense of reality constantly tends towards distortion, sublimation and the production of an imaginary world, just as Radcliffe and Lewis themselves, dissatisfied with the restrictions implicit in realist writing, turned to the dubious pleasures of terror-stricken fantasy and carved new paths through the associated problems of expression.

To read *Udolpho*, *The Monk* and *The Italian* in series is to work on through the evolving and closely related set of attempts in the late eighteenth century to question the realist fabric and to find an alternative structure for prose fiction. Yet in the end, of course, it is true that Radcliffe and Lewis were very different writers. The question of explanation of the supernatural, especially in view of the fact that Radcliffe's works *do*, in fact, contain at least one unexplained phantom, is an inadequate ground of distinction, while exploration of theme only brings the two writers closer together. In order to grasp the real distinctions between them, we have to turn to a different area, to questions of tone and narrative stance, and to the models of author/reader relations which the texts imply. There is a simple question here about the attitude taken by the writer to the problems and characters which he or she discusses, but there is also a more complex and interesting question about the possible attitudinal positions offered to the reader by the text, and in respect of these not only is Lewis quite different from Radcliffe, but *The Italian* offers a significant development from the world of *Udolpho*.

In *Udolpho*, the principal tonal problems centre on Emily. The attitude which Radcliffe seems to want to encourage towards her heroine is a kind of indulgence: she is perfect in many of her attitudes and feelings, yet she is too perfect for a profane world, which causes an occasional odd irascibility in the writing. When, leaving La Vallée, Emily finds that one of her books has been removed and replaced with Valancourt's volume of Petrarch, Radcliffe notes that she 'hesitated in believing, what would have been sufficiently apparent to almost any other person' (*Udolpho*, p. 58); her moral perfection is, like her sensibility, sometimes inappropriate and even silly. Radcliffe wants us, however, to recognise that there is no reason why Emily *herself* should know that in order to survive reality she must 'downgrade' her behaviour; but she expects us, as readers, to know that the *world* will ceaselessly require her to do that. As readers, therefore, we experience both a superiority and an inferiority to Emily, as we would to a marvellous child; and our sense of her as a delightful but ingenuous daughter is reinforced generally by her absence of sexuality and locally by such matters as her inability to think of the obvious reason why her father should have preserved his memento of the Marchioness de Villeroi. It is perhaps because of these tendencies and attitudes that the author has come down to us through history as 'Mother' Radcliffe; and while reading we find that we are constantly expected to collaborate with her as wise but acceptably worldly parents. Although sensibility is criticised, she puts up virtually nothing in its place, for this would be to question or sacrifice those childlike virtues which demand our protective approbation.

Radcliffe's attitude comes out particularly strongly at those many points where she implicitly enjoins her reader to believe that Emily is clever and capable. She suggests that her handling of her emotions is deliberate and well calculated, even at moments of extreme stress; that she has a kind of native practicality, although her actions rarely demonstrate it; and even, late on in the book, that she had 'detected the fallacies at Udolpho' (*Udolpho*, p. 537), although any such detection on Emily's part was tardy and largely accidental. Thus she carefully undermines any adverse impressions we might form of Emily's behaviour, and supplies instead a favourable interpretation which distorts the actual occurrences while preserving her heroine's claims to virtue and intelligence.

With Montoni the situation is very different, for in certain important ways she fails to present him as a consistent character. The novel requires that he be depicted, at least potentially, as evil incarnate, but he constantly becomes assimilated to a less extreme model of the adult male, and even his dubious behaviour cannot prevent

Radcliffe from also showing him as a protective and stable figure. His wickedness comes over not as a positive force but as a kind of unfeelingness, laziness or irresponsibility; he cannot even be bothered to do his own courting of Madame Cheron, but retains a useful friend to do it for him. Yet alongside these faults, and despite his ferocious and threatening demeanour, he retains many good qualities – strength, loyalty, courage – and he is not even a particularly ruthless criminal; the reader feels that he could surely have obtained Cheron's estates much more easily if he had really tried, and in fact it even turns out that he did not commit some of the nastier crimes – for instance, the murder of Laurentini – with which the narrative at times appears to charge him.

Radcliffe's protective attitude to Emily, and her ambiguity about Montoni, which sometimes verges on covert admiration, fit together if we suggest that the social model in which *Udolpho* enjoins its readers to participate is largely familial. The kind of anxiety felt about Montoni is the kind felt about the proverbial 'black sheep': he may betray his family responsibilities, but at heart he is aware of them, and, like a rather tame wicked uncle, his fire and splutter are much more impressive than his actual capacity for violence. It is important in this context that St Aubert and his wife are removed so quickly and easily from the scene, because their continuing presence would interfere with the distribution of parental roles among the readers, and it is their places which the readers are required to fill as a counterbalance to the perverted family life of the castle itself.

Condemnation of Montoni is limited by the fact that, for better or worse, he has a role within the family of the novel; it is forces and influences outside the family which draw down Radcliffe's more whole-hearted disapproval. Underlings and servants are mostly malicious in *Udolpho*, and when they are not they are foolish and presumptuous. City life, as in the works of so many of Radcliffe's contemporaries, is portrayed as wholly destructive of real, familial virtue: it is from a sojourn in the city that all Valancourt's moral difficulties stem, and the whole book is framed within an essentially conservative rural idyll, centred on the transcendent and neo-aristo-cratic moral virtue of 'retirement'. Even the more unpleasant aristocrats, like Count Morano, are allowed to despise those, like Monsieur Quesnel, whose fortune and status are connected with the city and with commerce.[13] And this nostalgic emphasis on the family unit as inviolable and sacred – an emphasis often in direct contradiction with the themes of claustrophobia and confinement – is reflected in Radcliffe's style, which in *Udolpho* is based on a very direct relationship between narrator and reader and includes from time to time a descriptive immediacy which belies the supposed historical dimension of the novel.

By contrast, the social world of *The Monk* is a much wider and more general one. Unlike Radcliffe, Lewis places considerable emphasis on crowd scenes and on the public ramifications of private disaster and tragedy: Ambrosio's fate is not only his own but simultaneously an aspect of the wider decadence and hypocrisy of a mythical Madrid. The reader – whom I shall assume, perhaps contentiously, for Lewis to be masculine – is given no family role to fill; rather, he is required to see himself as a spectator at a dramatic entertainment which deliberately highlights and parades the more spectacular aspects of life. Lewis is deeply conscious of the position in which this practice puts the writer:

> An author, whether good or bad, or between both, is an animal whom everybody is privileged to attack; for though all are not able to write books, all conceive themselves able to judge them. . . . In short, to enter the lists of literature is wilfully to expose yourself to the arrows of neglect, ridicule, envy, and disappointment. Whether you write well or ill, be assured that you will not escape from blame.   (*Monk*, p. 157)

But he is, of course, not really worried by this: the public eminence of Ambrosio and the importance of his reputation should be seen as analogies of the fate of the writer, but Lewis was clearly more concerned with the pleasure of public idolisation than with its dubious moral causes and effects. There are risks in sensationalism, but they are risks which he was happy to run for the sake of admiration.

And in *The Monk* the reader's admiration is deflected from the characters, even from the virtuous Antonia, on to Lewis's own sleight of hand. Many of the lurid qualities and sensational oppositions in the text are calculated more to show us the range of the author's dramatic abilities than to provide any profound comment on life. Satan's 'explanation' of Ambrosio's worst crimes at the end of the book has not the slightest narrative justification; it is a piece of deliberate extremism, and the same is true of Lewis's juggling with Matilda's human-ness or otherwise. The book is full of psychological contrasts which have little to do with the verisimilitude of the portrayal of particular characters, but are meant to enhance the general sense of precariousness which Lewis wishes to encourage; he tries constantly to challenge his audience, to upset its security, to give the reader a moment of doubt about whether he may not himself be guilty of the complicated faults attributed to Ambrosio. Nothing in *The Monk* is what it seems, for any state can slide into the repression of its opposite. The more attractive and suitable a man or woman may seem as a potential partner, the more 'dangerous' he or she is; the sexual roles of Ambrosio and Matilda even become reversed as Matilda gains more and more ascendancy over the monk and threatens to change back into the man she had once pretended to be. The motif of this process is, of course, the double appearance of the demon; in his transformation from beauty to savagery is summarised the disturbing trickery Lewis joyfully practises on his audience.[14]

The high points of his style are short, almost surreal, dramatic scenes: Lorenzo's extraordinary dream about the rape in the cathedral, Ambrosio's overheated nightmares and his vision of the naked Antonia. In episodes like these, the reader is not expected to participate, for Lewis is too egocentric to want our participation; instead, we are supposed to be shocked, and unwillingly seduced, for Matilda's magic mirror, which reflects hidden and unwelcome sexual fantasies, is also the author's. The celebrated passage where he inveighs against the Bible seems to fall into the same category (*Monk*, pp. 205–6); when *The Monk* was published, this passage was particularly condemned as sacrilegious, but this misses the point for in the context of the narrative as a whole it has almost no meaning. It is purely a bravura performance, comparable with the magnificent dramatic speeches which Lewis gives to Ambrosio and Agnes, and which would be more at home as stage monologues.

Lewis wants his reader to be impressionable, admiring, spectatorial, and open to sudden doubt about whether the author's paradoxes do not in fact undermine his own moral pretensions and show him unwholesome and repressed aspects of his own psyche. Above all, he wants the reader to see essentially private faults exposed mercilessly on a more or less public stage, and he wants to mock his confused reactions. For Lewis, at all points, tries to be more cynical than his audience, and to dominate it by means of this cynicism. The reader – at least the modern reader – can cope easily with the author when he says – and shows – that 'nobody dies of mere grief', and that 'men have died, and worms have ate them, but not for love' (*Monk*, pp. 243, 314); it is harder to cope with the remarkable viciousness of that part of the denouement in which the unfortunate Antonia gets not only murdered but also replaced in her erstwhile lover's affections, at the wave of a magic wand, by a girl who has hardly taken any previous part in the story. It is not merely the content of *The Monk* which makes it a disturbing book, and which has caused it to be censored almost continuously since the time it was written; it is also the unnerving mixture of inadequacy and revulsion in the reader which Lewis deliberately sets out to produce, and the sense the reader gets that he is himself the main object of the author's savage animosity. It is worth noting in this context that Lewis knew of the work of de Sade, and apparently bought a copy of *Justine* in 1792. The extent of the influence is hard to judge, but certainly de Sade saw clearly the connections between Lewis and himself, and makes much of them in his own analysis of the terror-novel.[15] He refers to *The Monk* as 'superior in all respects to the exotic outbursts of Radcliffe's brilliant imagination'. Of the whole genre he says, very reasonably, that 'it was the inevitable outcome of the revolutionary upheavals experienced throughout the whole of Europe', and he argues that the importance of *The Monk* lies precisely in its role as a response to these social and religious changes. Certainly there appears to be a distinct streak of sadism in Lewis's relations both to his characters and to his readers, although this tendency within Gothic probably antedated the influence of de Sade, which was always fairly limited; Tomkins mentions the anonymous *Elfrida* (1787) for its analysis of 'morbid' situations and states of mind (Tompkins, p. 179), and, as we have seen, we can find very similar material in Smollett's *Ferdinand Count Fathom* considerably earlier. The most suggestive critical phrase is Railo's, when he speaks of the 'sexual excitement of a neurasthenic subject' (Railo, p. 281) as the crucial motif in this branch of Gothic; and the reaction of the reader to excitement of this kind is necessarily ambivalent.

In some ways, the world of *The Italian* is as familial, parochial and conservative as that of *Udolpho*: so strong is Radcliffe's sense of natural justice that even the dreaded Inquisition is here again portrayed as essentially virtuous in its workings. But there are significant differences between *Udolpho* and *The Italian*, some of which relate to Lewis's techniques, and all of which combine to render the later book considerably less reassuring and conventionally acceptable than the earlier, and to suggest that Radcliffe did not find the accommodation of bourgeois and aristocratic values which characterised *Udolpho* entirely easy.

Schedoni is covertly admired, as was Montoni, and is granted a kind of harsh approbation: like the earlier villain, he has extraordinary strength and a natural and aristocratic superiority to lesser criminals. But he has a dimension of introspection which Montoni entirely lacked, and indeed the whole book shows a much greater psychological sophistication than did *Udolpho*. There is, for instance, the remarkably suspenseful scene where Ellena, after going through enormous difficulties to secure a note which Vivaldi has managed to pass her despite her virtual imprisonment in the convent, and which we know to contain information which can lead to her escape, accidentally drops the lamp which gave her her only chance of reading it. The skill here is in judging the psychology of her readers, but Radcliffe is also better at depicting particular characters in half-shades rather than the monochrome of *Udolpho*: Vivaldi's conversation with the Abate, who holds it in his power to release Ellena but is too concerned with a peaceful life to interfere, could not have occurred in the fierce and simple world of *Udolpho*.

The debt to Lewis's less familial, more individualist stance shows itself particularly in obsessional matters: the nightmares, for instance, which the minor villain Spalatro suffers and which cause him to shudder before the undertaking of new crimes are reminiscent of the frenzied vacillations of Ambrosio, and the convent death cell to which Ellena is nearly confined is a close reproduction of Agnes's crypt in *The Monk*. The evil Marchesa too seems to display much of the perverse strength of Matilda, and to rest rather uneasily within the conventional sexual boundaries which otherwise characterise Radcliffe's world.

But the most important development in *The Italian* lies in Radcliffe's movement away from the familial model. Much more than either *Udolpho* or *The Monk*, *The Italian* is, as much later Gothic is to be, a book about conspiracy and about the complex social relations between conspirators, and it is in this context that Schedoni and the Marchesa come most startlingly alive. There was an anticipation of this in *Udolpho*; often, when Emily thought that Montoni was engaged on some horrible crime or other, Radcliffe tells us that in fact he had been occupied with political discussion with his cohorts. In fact, the picture the reader gets of the castle of Udolpho is very much of the ladies 'retired' in their rooms upstairs while Montoni and the other men discuss the affairs of the world over port and cigars. It is true that they are actually concerned with practical and violent interventions in the affairs of their country; but except for this factor, which Radcliffe never actually describes in detail, this is obviously a grotesquely exaggerated but thoroughly recognisable picture of eighteenth-century home life. In the later book, the conversations between Schedoni and the Marchesa, the Inquisition scenes, the final battle of wills between Schedoni and Nicola, are all grotesque extensions of what Radcliffe seems to have regarded as a distinctively masculine discourse, and the world of *The Italian* is built partly on a stronger pressure to deal with her fear of, and alienation from, this discourse and the feminine powerlessness which it entails.

The 'women's world' which Radcliffe and many other female novelists of the time depict is 'dependent on an obscure male world of action and business, which its occupants can seldom envisage, but of which they feel the reverberations' (Tompkins, p. 128). Tompkins goes on to analyse the general consequences of this perception in the fiction of the 1790s, pointing out that one disturbing aspect is that while the 'henpecked husband' and the 'presumptuous wooer' are frequently ridiculed the tyrant and the seducer are not, 'for to be a victim, as these women saw it, is to gain rather than lose in dignity' (Tompkins, p. 134). Essentially, the point goes back again to the issue of sexual hypocrisy. As has been well popularised in the work of Christopher Hill and others, a significant marriage crisis occurred in the eighteenth century, largely due to problems of inheritance, problems which figure very considerably in novelists from Richardson to Austen.[16] The crisis appears to have been caused by contradictions between patriarchal and individualistic family-structures, and to have been partly responsible for the worship of concealment of feeling. Because, as Hill puts it, financial and status considerations were at stake, it became a crime against the social code for any woman to admit her real feelings or to confess to passion, and the main purpose of the education of 'ladies of condition' becomes this suppression of feeling and passion. Under these circumstances, one could say that male and female discourse developed increasingly into separate languages, insulated from each other by the different interests of the sexes in relation to the maintenance of the social order. It was at the end of the eighteenth century that this disparity was forced out into the open, precisely because it was then that women started writing themselves; their main themes, says Tompkins, were, hardly surprisingly, 'pursuit and endurance' (Tompkins, p. 138). This is not to say, of course, that one can derive a wholesale analysis of the problems of sexual division from Radcliffe or from any of her contemporaries, but in *The Italian* the *problem* is certainly present, and there is a strong connection, which we will come across time and time again, between the Gothic novel in general and the evolution of perceptions about the subjection of women and the covert social purposes of marriage and marital fidelity.

From this starting-point, *The Italian* goes on to make much play with the potentially delusive power of words: Schedoni himself is described as a man with a hatred of truth but a profound love of disputation and argument, which could presumably also be said of the Inquisition. The reader is cast, as he or she will be again in so much later Gothic, as a kind of detective, placed within a closely knit social situation but not fully of it, trying to find truth amid the multiple hypocrisies and deceptions of conspirators, an extension of the reader's role with regard to historical fact in *The Recess*. It is in this context that the framing of the narrative as a received document is important, for it enables Radcliffe to distance herself from the story, and she often implies limits to her own knowledge of the events, which makes the reader's task all the more difficult. The reader is required not to collaborate or to marvel, but to discover a path through a maze of half-heard and half-understood conversations, much as Emily in *Udolpho* had had to try to infer the truth from whisperings overheard in distant rooms. Radcliffe no longer forestalls our interpretation, but suspends judgements and even deliberately withholds important evidence to ensure that the reader's attention can never be relaxed.

The development in sophistication which Gothic fiction displays in this brief span of years is remarkable; where *Udolpho* accepted many of the narrative conventions of earlier fiction, and *The Monk* strove to upset them directly by simple reversal of previously accepted boundaries of the communicable and the permissible, *The Italian* has already moved a long way towards the unsettling convolutions of fantasy and fiction which will bear fruit in the extraordinary complexities of Maturin's *Melmoth the Wanderer*. Already the best Gothic works are by no means escapist, nor are they 'light reading'; on the contrary, they have come to demand a type of discrimination largely unnecessary in the reading of earlier realist fiction and only dimly foreshadowed by Walpole, Reeve or Lee, for they are based on the ambiguity of fantasy and on the virtually insoluble problem of the text which lies. Where Fielding and Richardson allow the reader to distrust certain characters but are usually careful to provide indications by which we may make judgements, in *The Italian* Radcliffe begins to build on Lee's sugges- tion of a kind of fiction in which we may have to distrust the narrator herself, and therefore to construct imaginatively our own text from the hints, conversations and documents set out piecemeal before us.

Lewis's and Radcliffe's novels of vision and obsession necessarily tend towards certain new kinds of role for the reader because relations between reader, narrator and character differ according to the extent to which public or private aspects of character are at stake. When a narrator describes a character's face, we normally accept the description without question; when he or she describes a character's mental processes and emotional responses, we balance these against what we are told of external reality and make judgements on this basis; but when the narrator points out to us that the character's grasp on reality is at best shaky and at worst quite deluded, we are forced into a different order of response, and our interpretative role becomes both greater and more ambiguous. In *Udolpho* we certainly experience this dislocation, but largely within the circumscribed limits of the castle itself, and Radcliffe later formally dispels our doubts. In *The Monk*, the dislocation is clearly greater, but it seems to matter less because the whole novel is, like *Otranto*, more obviously grotesque, and we can merely shrug at those doubts. But *The Italian* slides dizzily between distortion and the real, making us attribute different values and statuses to different elements in the story, and demanding that we separate out the various subtexts which Radcliffe has welded together. From familial collaborator and half-willing victim, the reader has turned suddenly into creative participant. In this developed form, the Gothic is revealed as not an escape from the real but a deconstruction and dismemberment of it, which we as readers can only put together by referring its materials to our own assumptions about the relations between world and mind and by entering actively into the self-conscious play of the text, a process for which *The Recess, Udolpho* and *The Monk*, by disturbing our assumptions of the real in different but connected ways, have already partly prepared us.

Notes and references

1. **Charlotte Smith** was the author of, among other works, *Emmeline, the Orphan of the Castle* (1788); *Ethelinde, or, The Recluse of the Lake* (1789); *Celestina* (1791); *The Old Manor House* (1793).
2. See *Sir Walter Scott on Novelists and Fiction*, ed. Ioan Williams (London, 1968), p. 103.
3. 'The Bravo of Venice' (anon. rev.), *The Critical Review* (Series III), V (July, 1805), 253.
4. Summers, at pp. 234 ff., mentions among many other works **Charlotte Dacre**, *Zofloya, or, The Moor* (1806); **E. T. A. Hoffmann**, *Die Elixiere des Teufels* (1816); several works of **G. W. M. Reynolds**, including *Wagner, the Wehr-wolf* (on which see below, pp. 160–3); and **T. P. Prest**, *The Black Monk, or, The Secret of the Grey Turret* (1844).
5. **Coleridge**, *Biographia Literaria*, ed. J. Shawcross (2 vols, London, 1907), II, 183.
6. **Ann Radcliffe**, *The Mysteries of Udolpho*, ed. Bonamy Dobrée (London, 1970), p. 221.
7. **Matthew Lewis**, *The Monk* (London, 1973), p. 111.

8. **Radcliffe**, *The Italian, or, The Confessional of the Black Penitents*, ed. Frederick Garber (London, 1971), p. 284.
9. See *Italian*, pp. 84, 187.
10. **Fielding**, *Joseph Andrews*, ed. A. R. Humphreys (London, 1968), pp. 239–40.
11. See, e.g. *Monk*, pp. 16, 97.
12. **Pope**, *Poems*, III, i, 68–9.
13. See *Udolpho*, p. 215; also p. 521.
14. Lewis is also, of course, consolidating a symbolic tradition of the 'beautiful demon' which passes from Beckford's Eblis and Blake's Orc through into common romantic currency.
15. See *Oeuvres Complètes du Marquis de Sade* (16 vols, Paris, 1966), X, 15.
16. See, e.g. **Christopher Hill**, 'Clarissa Harlowe and her times', in *Puritanism and Revolution* (London, 1968), pp. 351–76, and the references Hill cites.

CHAPTER 4

Gothic and romanticism

Blake, Coleridge, Shelley, Byron, Keats, John Polidori, Mary Shelley

In looking at the Gothic fiction of the 1790s, it is important to keep in mind that this was not a strange outcropping of one particular literary genre, but a form into which a huge variety of cultural influences, from Shakespeare to 'Ossian', from medievalism to Celtic nationalism, flowed. And one concomitant of this is that most of the major writers of the period 1770 to 1820 – which is to say, most of the major *poets* of that period – were strongly affected by Gothic in one form or another. And this was not merely a passive reception of influence: Blake, Coleridge, Shelley, Byron and Keats all played a part in shaping the Gothic, in articulating a set of images of terror which were to exercise a potent influence over later literary history.[1] In this chapter I want to outline some aspects of the engagement of the romantic poets with the Gothic and then to examine in a little more detail the three principal symbolic figures which run through their Gothic work: the wanderer, the vampire, and the seeker after forbidden knowledge. Finally, I want to look at two prose works which, in 1818 and 1819, arose from this stock of symbols: John Polidori's story 'The Vampyre', and Mary Shelley's *Frankenstein*. One of the features of Gothic fiction which distinguishes it historically from many other forms of 'sensational' writing is the power which it exerted over this group of undeniably major writers; this is both part of its validation as a focus of critical interest, and also a major source of its continuing historical vitality. It needs to be said at the outset that it has become conventional to suppose that Gothic was a mode of writing which each of the romantics 'outgrew', an immature expression of their concerns; this, as we shall see, is not quite the case. The engagement of Blake and Coleridge continued, albeit in changing forms, throughout their lives; and with the other three writers it is hard to see any evidence of curtailment of interest in the short years which they had at their disposal.

All five of these poets use Gothic forms and styles as models for their poetry; particularly, of course, early in their work, in terms of direct, 'training' imitations, but also later. These models are as various as the eighteenth-century notion of Gothic allows. In the case of Blake, there are the early imitations of Spenser and other 'reclaimed' writers; his interest in the ballad form, from the anti-quarian crudities of 'Fair Elenor' through to the thematically complex but formally translucent works in the Pickering Manuscript; the Ossianic structure of the prose pieces in the *Poetical Sketches*; and his continuing interest in the graveyard poets, evidenced not only in his illustrations to Young and Blair, but in his constant preoccupation with morbid vocabulary, as strong in *Vala, or, The Four Zoas* (1795–1804) and *The Keys to the Gates* (*c.* 1818) as in his 'apprentice work'. Coleridge returns constantly to graveyard topics, to pain, disappointment and melancholy, and again imitates Ossianic poetic prose and the form of the ballad, from 'Anna and Harland' in 1790 to 'Alice du Clos' in 1828. In 'The Destiny of Nations' (1796), the voices of Gray and Young form a background to his meditations on history and politics, in lines like –

> As through the dark vaults of some mouldered Tower
> (Which, fearful to approach, the evening hind
> Circles at distance in his homeward way)
> The winds breathe hollow, deemed the plaining groan
> Of prisoned spirits . . . [2]

In the case of Shelley the early involvement is even stronger, with a work like *Rosalind and Helen*, begun in 1817, taking shape as a mosaic of ballad, legendry and graveyard motifs:

> This silent spot tradition old
> Had peopled with the spectral dead.
> For the roots of the speaker's hair felt cold
> And stiff, as with tremulous lips he told
> That a hellish shape at midnight led
> The ghost of a youth with hoary hair,
> And sate on the seat beside him there,
> Till a naked child came wandering by,
> When the fiend would change to a lady fair!
> (*Works*, II, 11)

And there are passages in *The Triumph of Life*, the work on which Shelley was engaged at the time of his death in 1822, which develop no less surely from graveyard poetry than do the primitive exercises in *Original Poetry by Victor and Cazire* (1810). Byron's poetry comprehends a full range of the Gothic registers: the ballad ('Oscar of Alva'), imitation of 'Ossian' ('The Death of Calmar and Orla'), Chaucerian archaism (as in *Childe Harold's Pilgrimage*), and a constant concern with the nature of feudalism and monasticism (as in *Lara*, and in 'The Song of the Black Friar' from *Don Juan*). The case of Keats, perhaps, is the most marginal, not in that there was no Gothic influence, but in that Keats was largely interested in the 'white' Gothic of Spenser, Hurd and vanished chivalry; but even with Keats we find passages in, for instance, *Isabella, or, The Pot of Basil* (1818) which show clearly how deeply rooted Gothic assumptions had become:

> Who hath not loiter'd in a green church-yard,
>   And let his spirit, like a demon-mole,
> Work through the clayey soil and gravel hard,
>   To see skull, coffin'd bones, and funeral stole;
> Pitying each form that hungry Death hath marr'd,
>   And filling it once more with human soul?[3]

The actual contributions which the poets made to the development of these registers of discourse were diverse. Blake, from the start, was attracted by the potential political dimensions of Gothic: his ballads 'Gwin, King of Norway' and 'The Grey Monk' originate in the conception of the ballad as a democratic, antiauthoritarian form, the voice of the people, and the pictures of horror which he draws so continually and so effectively are invariably to do with the horror of domination and political violence – as, for instance, in *The French Revolution* (1791), where he shows us the inmates of the Bastille:

> In the tower nam'd Order, an old man, whose white beard cover'd the stone
>   floor like weeds
> On margin of the sea, shrivel'd up by heat of day and cold of night; his den
>   was short
> And narrow as a grave dug for a child, with spiders webs wove, and with
>   slime
> Of ancient horrors cover'd, for snakes and scorpions are his companions...
>   (Erdman, p. 284)

Terror in Blake is always to do with distortion, whether it be the distortion which an all-dominant faculty of reason imposes on the passions, or the distortion of a social and sexual code which destroys the human body and pollutes the mind with repression,

> *Till she who burns with youth, and knows no fixed lot; is bound*
> *In spells of law to one she loaths: and must she drag the chain*
> *Of life, in weary lust! must chilling murderous thoughts, obscure*
> *The clear heaven of her eternal spring? to bear the wintry rage*
> *Of a harsh terror driv'n to madness, bound to hold a rod*
> *Over her shrinking shoulders all the day; & all the night*
> *To turn the wheel of false desire: and longings that wake her womb*
> *To the abhorred birth of cherubs in the human form*
> *That live a pestilence & die a meteor & are no more.*
>
> (Erdman, p. 48)

What Blake makes very plain is that those kinds of fear arising from lack of communication which Radcliffe and Lewis depict are basic to a society which enshrines division, between sexes, between classes, between individuals; and that these kinds of fear are not merely, as it were, superstructural, but are embedded in the deepest levels of the psyche – those levels which Thel explores:

> *The eternal gates terrific porter lifted the northern bar:*
> *Thel enter'd in & saw the secrets of the land unknown;*
> *She saw the couches of the dead, & where the fibrous roots*
> *Of every heart on earth infixes deep its restless twists:*
> *A land of sorrows & of tears where never smile was seen.*
>
> (Erdman, p. 6)

This 'land of sorrows & of tears' is surely the unconscious, pining for expression but held down by Urizen's torturing rationalism and by his opposition to physicality. Blake is the great poet of the shattered human body:

> *The shapes screaming flutter'd vain*
> *Some combin'd into muscles & glands*
> *Some organs for craving and lust*
> *Most remain'd on the tormented void:*
> *Urizens army of horrors.*
>
> (Erdman, p. 87)

His symbolic world is an interplay between distorted giant forms, the 'Giants' of *The Marriage of Heaven and Hell* (1790–3), who 'formed this world into its sensual existence and now seem to live in it in chains' (Erdman, p. 39), and its dominant forces are the 'Spectrous' Urizen and the 'Terror' which is Orc, who both depend for their being on mutual fear and strife.[4]

But if the body in Blake is 'broken' by repression, it is tortured even more fiercely by the ravages of industrialisation:

And Los's Furnaces howl loud; living: self-moving: lamenting
With fury & despair, & they stretch from South to North
Thro all the Four Points: Lo! the Labourers at the Furnaces
Rintrah & Palamobron, Theotormon & Bromion, loud labring
With the innumerable multitudes of Golgonooza, round the Anvils
Of Death. But how they came forth from the Furnaces & how long
Vast & severe the anguish eer they knew their Father; were
Long to tell & of the iron rollers, golden axle-trees & yokes
Of brass, iron chains & braces & the gold, silver & brass
Mingled or separate: for swords; arrows; cannons; mortars
The terrible ball: the wedge: the loud sounding hammer of destruction
The sounding flail to thresh: the winnow: to winnow kingdoms
(Erdman, p. 226)

Blake builds, with the help of Gothic tools, a universe of man/ machine chimeras, of dehumanised men and women and of machines with a curious and malevolent mode of life. In this universe all is threat and violence, and the comfortably traditionalist features of the Gothic are pressed into the service of an all-embracing vision of the horror of the fallen world.

Coleridge's use of terror is, in many ways, more conventional than Blake's; poems like 'Dura Navis', 'Song of the Pixies' and the minor contributions to *Lyrical Ballads* bespeak this general interest in Gothic and the supernatural, which is also evident in the dramas. But in two ways, he is close to Blake. In a poem like 'Religious Musings' (1794–6), the problems of commerce, war and sexual exploitation are again made the subject of a prevailingly Gothic image-language:

O thou poor Wretch
Who nursed in darkness and made wild by want,
Roamest for prey, yea thy unnatural hand
Dost lift to deeds of blood! O pale-eyed form,
The victim of seduction, doomed to know
Polluted nights and days of blasphemy . . .
(*Poems*, p. 119)

As with Blake, there is here no motive of mere sensationalism, but a use instead of Gothic exaggeration as a means of conveying the underlying horror of the everyday world. And Blake's 'Giant Forms' also return in Coleridge in a slightly changed guise: in the 'Verses' of 1796 addressed to Horne Tooke, he refers to those –

Mists in which Superstition's pigmy band
Seem'd Giant Forms, the Genii of the Land!
(*Poems*, p. 151)

Among other things, these are the giant shapes of 'Ossian', but

Coleridge, like Blake, perceives these brute elder gods as repressive; their shadows intervene between man and his self-realisation, a line of argument to which Shelley returned in more detail.

Where Blake's concept of Gothic springs direct from British anti-quarianism, Coleridge is already very conscious of the Gothic in its more recent forms, of Radcliffe, many of whose trappings appear in 'The Old Man of the Alps', of Lewis, in 'The Mad Monk', and of Schiller, to whom Coleridge addressed these well-known lines:

> *Ah! Bard tremendous in sublimity!*
> *Could I behold thee in thy loftier mood*
> *Wandering at eve with finely-frenzied eye*
> *Beneath some vast old tempest-swinging wood!*
> *Awhile with mute awe gazing I would brood:*
> *Then weep aloud in a wild ecstacy!*
> *(Poems, p. 73)*

And whereas Blake finds in Gothic a mode of representing the fears of a society, Coleridge is in the end more concerned with finding correlatives for his personal psychological predicament. The tone of alienation which pervades his work is struck in the 'Lines' written at Shurton Bars:

> *And there in black soul-jaundic'd fit*
> *A sad gloom-pamper'd Man to sit,*
> *And listen to the roar:*
> *When mountain surges bellowing deep*
> *With an uncouth monster-leap*
> *Plung'd foaming on the shore.*
> *(Poems, p. 98)*

Coleridge's ghosts are conjured by his own feelings of guilt; 'The Pains of Sleep' (1803) is very close to *Night Thoughts*, not only in the structure of feeling which it manifests, but also in the exaggerated, lurid terms in which Coleridge tries to objectify his nightmares:

> *But yester-night I prayed aloud*
> *In anguish and in agony,*
> *Up-starting from the fiendish crowd*
> *Of shapes and thoughts that tortured me:*
> *A lurid light, a trampling throng,*
> *Sense of intolerable wrong,*
> *And whom I scorned, those only strong!*
> *(Poems, p. 389)*

This sense of persecution, which continues into work as late as 'Limbo' (1817) and beyond, is distinctively modern in its awareness of its own psychological origins; Coleridge was well aware that the ghosts which tortured him were of his own imagining, but he was equally aware that this made them no whit less potent.

Shelley appears to have been the most immersed of the poets in contemporary Gothic writing. The influences of Lewis, Godwin and Charlotte Dacre show clearly in the two short Gothic romances, *Zastrozzi* and *St Irvyne*, which he wrote in his youth, and he was also heavily influenced – for instance in *The Revolt of Islam* (1817) and *The Cenci* (1819) – by Schiller and the German Gothics. Mary Shelley writes, rather caustically, that 'he was a lover of the wonderful and wild in literature; but had not fostered these tastes at their genuine sources – the romances of chivalry of the middle ages; but in the perusal of such German works as were current in those days';[5] but this is only part of the point. Shelley found in the Germans a sanction for the portrayal of extreme, 'wild', violent situations, particularly again in *The Cenci*; but what he also found was a political content which aroused his admiration. A crucial text here was *Die Räuber*, in which Gothic, melodramatic apparatus is used to teach the directly political lesson that individual violence is the product of social injustice. *Queen Mab* (1813), *The Cenci*, *The Revolt of Islam* all hinge on this argument; the outlaw becomes justifiable when he is seen to be responding to an unjustifiable society. But the conjunction of Gothic vocabulary and political thinking can be seen at its strongest in a passage from *The Triumph of Life*:

> *The earth was gray with phantoms, and the air*
> *Was peopled with dim forms, as when there hovers*
>
> *A flock of vampire-bats before the glare*
> *Of the tropic sun, bringing, ere evening,*
> *Strange night upon some Indian isle; – thus were*
>
> *Phantoms diffused around; and some did fling*
> *Shadows of shadows, yet unlike themselves,*
> *Behind them; some like eaglets on the wing*
>
> *Were lost in the white day; others like elves*
> *Danced in a thousand unimagined shapes*
> *Upon the sunny streams and grassy shelves;*
>
> *And others sate chattering like restless apes*
> *In vulgar bands,*
> *Some made a cradle of the ermined capes*
>
> *Of kingly mantles; some across the tiar*
> *Of pontiffs sate like vultures; others played*

> *Under the crown which girt with empire*
>
> *A baby's or an idiot's brow, and made*
> *Their nests in it. The old anatomies*
> *Sate hatching their bare broods under the shade*
>
> *Of demon wings, and laughed from their dead eyes*
> *To re-assume the delegated power,*
> *Arrayed in which those worms did monarchise,*
>
> *Who made this earth their charnel....*
>
> *(Works, IV, 183–4)*

Part of the argument here is simply that phantoms, skeletons, 'the old anatomies' serve to mock the things of this earth, as the grave-yard poets had insisted; but Shelley goes farther than this in showing these phantoms as specifically attracted to those in power. Monarchs and pontiffs only possess delegated power, in two different senses: first in that their power will be stripped away by death, but second, and more importantly, in that the particular *kind* of power which they exercise is itself a power of death and repression. Kings and priests rule through terror, and in this sense their power is identical with the power of the spectre. The connection between this and conventional notions of the Gothic is made in, for instance, *Queen Mab*:

> *Low through the lone cathedral's roofless aisles*
> *The melancholy winds a death-dirge sung:*
> *It were a sight of awfulness to see*
> *The works of faith and slavery, so vast,*
> *So sumptuous, yet so perishing withal!*
> *Even as the corpse that rests beneath its wall.*
> *A thousand mourners deck the pomp of death*
> *Today, the breathing marble glows above*
> *To decorate its memory, and tongues*
> *Are busy of its life: to-morrow, worms*
> *In silence and in darkness seize their prey.*
>
> *(Works, I, 130)*

The Gothic for Shelley is a point of access to history; cathedral and castle ruins both remind us of the days of 'faith and slavery', and assure us of the transience of these forms of domination. In *The Revolt of Islam* there are passages very similar to some in Lewis, but serving the very different purpose of reminding us of the horror of famine and war:

As thus she spake, she grasped me with the strength
Of madness, and by many a ruined hearth
She led, and over many a corpse: – at length
We came to a lone hut, where on the earth
Which made its floor, she in her ghastly mirth
Gathering from all those homes now desolate,
Had piled three heaps of loaves, making a dearth
Among the dead – round which she set in state
A ring of cold, stiff babes; silent and stark they sate.

(*Works*, I, 342)

Alongside this political interest runs Shelley's general fascination with the coexistence of beauty and horror, as in the well-known poem on da Vinci's Medusa, with the 'tempestuous loveliness of terror' (*Works*, III, 299). This is a development from the 'dreadful pleasure' of Radcliffe and the theorists of the sublime, and the hero-figures of most of Shelley's narrative poems are imbued with these contradictory qualities:

He was so awful, yet
So beautiful in mystery and terror,
Calming me as the loveliness of heaven
Soothes the unquiet sea: – and yet not so,
For he seemed stormy, and would often seem
A quenchless sun masked in portentous clouds;
For such his thoughts, and even his actions were;
But he was not of them, nor they of him,
But as they hid his splendour from the earth.
Some said he was a man of blood and peril,
And steeped in bitter infamy to the lips.

(*Works*, IV, 132)

The apotheosis of this beautiful, terrifying, outlaw hero occurs, of course, in Byron, who builds in this and other respects on Radcliffe and Lewis, whom he much admired, although this did not prevent him from mocking them. 'The horrid crags, by toppling convent crowned' in *Childe Harold* (1812–13),[6] and the description of Newstead Abbey –

Yes! in thy gloomy cells and shades profound,
The monk abjur'd a world, he ne'er could view;
Or blood-stain'd Guilt repenting, solace found,
Or Innocence, from stern Oppression, flew.

(*Poetry*, I, 118)

– are straightforward references to the Gothic conventions; the description of the apparition near the end of *Don Juan* is supposed to occasion a more complex and ironic reaction:

> It was no mouse – but lo! a monk, arrayed
> In cowl and beads, and dusky garb, appeared,
> Now in the moonlight, and now lapsed in shade,
> With steps that trod as heavy, yet unheard;
> His garments only a slight murmur made;
> He moved as shadowy as the Sisters weird,
> But slowly; and as he passed Juan by,
> Glanced, without pausing, on him a bright eye.
>
> (*Poetry*, VI, 578)

Byron's attitude towards Gothic, in fact, is itself complexly poised. In some ways he uses it for purposes similar to Shelley's, for instance to indict political and religious repression, as in the 'Prayer of Nature' (1806):

> Let bigots rear a gloomy fane,
> Let Superstition hail the pile,
> Let priests, to spread their sable reign,
> With tales of mystic rites beguile.
>
> Shall man confine his Maker's sway
> To Gothic domes of mouldering stone?
> Thy temple is the face of day;
> Earth, Ocean, Heaven thy boundless throne.
>
> (*Poetry*, I, 225)

But Byron is less certain about the past than Shelley. There is a sense of aristocratic nostalgia which sits uneasily with the political radicalism throughout Byron's work; the uneasiness comes out strongly in a meditation in Canto III of *Childe Harold*:

> Beneath these battlements, within those walls,
> Power dwelt amidst her passions; in proud state
> Each robber chief upheld his arméd halls,
> Doing his evil will, nor less elate
> Than mightier heroes of a longer date.
> What want these outlaws conquerors should have
> But History's purchased page to call them great?
> A wider space – an ornamented grave?
> Their hopes were not less warm, their souls were full as brave.
>
> (*Poetry*, II, 244–5)

Perhaps, Byron is saying, it is true that the heroes and conquerors of history were mere robbers and slaughterers; but equally possibly, perhaps even those robbers possessed a glory now absent from the world. Or, again, perhaps our whole relation to the past is a trick of time:

> There is given
> Unto the things of earth, which Time hath bent,

A Spirit's feeling, and where he hath leant
His hand, but broke his scythe, there is a power
And magic in the ruined battlement,
For which the Palace of the present hour
Must yield its pomp, and wait till Ages are its dower.
                                    (*Poetry,* II, 425)

Byron, in fact, is more concerned than Shelley with musing on the meaning of the past; where Shelley sees in history a long object-lesson in the transience of empire, Byron suspects that the aesthetic aspects of the Gothic ruin play an important part in conditioning our political responses. His description of a Gothic mansion in Canto XIII of *Don Juan* is not merely a description, but also an attempt at explanation:

> *Huge halls, long galleries, spacious chambers, joined*
>   *By no quite lawful marriage of the arts,*
> *Might shock a connoisseur; but when combined,*
>   *Formed a whole which, irregular in parts,*
> *Yet left a grand impression on the mind,*
>   *At least of those whose eyes are in their hearts:*
> *We gaze upon a giant for his stature,*
> *Nor judge at first if all be true to nature.*
>   (*Poetry,* VI, 500–1)

This is strongly reminiscent of Walpole, but without Walpole's literal-mindedness; Byron sees the past as peopled by giants, but he knows that the imagination is responsible. As he implies in *Lara* (1814), the Gothic is to do with a kind of expressionism; what we see in the past is in part the exaggerated shadow of the reality:

> *He wandering mused, and as the moonbeam shone*
> *Through the dim lattice, o'er the floor of stone,*
> *And the high fretted roof, and saints, that there*
> *O'er Gothic windows knelt in pictured prayer,*
> *Reflected in fantastic figures grew,*
> *Like life, but not like mortal life, to view:*
> *His bristling locks of sable, brow of gloom,*
> *And the wide waving of his shaken plume,*
> *Glanced like a spectre's attributes – and gave*
> *His aspect all that terror gives the grave.*
>   (*Poetry,* III, 331)

In lines like these, many things come together. Blake's notion of 'Giant Forms'; Coleridge's nightmare phantoms; Shelley's portrayal of the grandeur of Ozymandias: in relation to all of these, Gothic can be seen as a way of imagining the unimaginable, whether it be the distant depths of history or the even more distant soundings

97

of the unconscious. The Gothic is a distorting lens, a magnifying lens; but the shapes which we see through it have nonetheless a reality which cannot be apprehended in any other way. In the late eighteenth and early nineteenth centuries, the Gothic seems to have been in part a limited but genuine substitute for the sciences of history and of psychology, a way of gaining access to, and understanding of, those barbaric areas where knowledge had not quite penetrated. The Gothic castle is a picture seen out of the corner of the eye, distorted yet real; and if it vanishes when you swing to look at it full on, this is only because of the historical limitations of perception.

The case of Keats, as we have said, is rather different. His poetry, particularly his early poetry, has much to do with Gothic in the sense of chivalry, of a vanished purity and beauty. In 'Specimen of an Induction to a Poem' (1816) he asks,

> *how shall I*
> *Revive the dying tones of minstrelsy,*
> *Which linger yet about lone gothic arches,*
> *In dark green ivy, and among wild larches?*
> (Garrod, p. 12)

But he is also capable of seeing the dark side of the old legends, as in *Endymion* (1817):

> *Groanings swell'd*
> *Poisonous about my ears, and louder grew,*
> *The nearer I approach'd a flame's gaunt blue,*
> *That glar'd before me through a thorny brake.*
> *This fire, like the eye of gordian snake,*
> *Bewitch'd me towards; and I soon was near*
> *A sight too fearful for the feel of fear:*
> *In thicket hid I curs'd the haggard scene –*
> *The banquet of my arms, my arbour queen,*
> *Seated upon an uptorn forest root;*
> *And all around her shapes, wizard and brute,*
> *Laughing, and wailing, groveling, serpenting,*
> *Showing tooth, tusk, and venom-bag, and sting!*
> *O such deformities!*
> (Garrod, pp. 141–2)

But there is something uncongenial in such descriptions, something evidenced in the generalised nature of the scene, in the imprecision of 'haggard', in the overprotesting note of 'O such deformities!', which suggests that Keats is not at home in such realms. Even in *Isabella*, one of his most obviously Gothic poems, he apologises for his graveyard pictures:

> *Ah! wherefore all this wormy circumstance?*
> *Why linger at the yawning tomb so long?*
> *O for the gentleness of old Romance,*
> *The simple plaining of a minstrel's song!*
>   (Garrod, p. 231)

What Keats adds to the Gothic is in a different area, in his apprehension of the terrifying transience of beauty, and in *The Fall of Hyperion* (1819), in his fear of the proximity of beauty and decay:

> *But yet I had a terror of her robes,*
> *And chiefly of the veils, that from her brow*
> *Hung pale, and curtain'd her in mysteries*
> *That made my heart too small to hold its blood.*
> *This saw that Goddess, and with sacred hand*
> *Parted the veils. Then saw I a wan face,*
> *Not pin'd by human sorrows, but bright blanch'd*
> *By an immortal sickness which kills not . . .*
>   (Garrod, p. 516)

The Eve of St Agnes (1819), again, is a poem with a conventionally Gothic plot, but there is a dreaminess and a lack of event in it which conveys a very distinctive impression. Keats is at his best, not when describing the events themselves, but when, at the end of the poem, he relegates the whole action to the world of dream:

> *And they are gone: ay, ages long ago*
> *These lovers fled away into the storm.*
> *That night the Baron dreamt of many a woe,*
> *And all his warrior-guests, with shade and form*
> *Of witch, and demon, and large coffin-worm,*
> *Were long be-nightmar'd. Angela the old*
> *Died palsy-twitch'd, with meagre face deform;*
> *The Beadsman, after thousand aves told,*
> *For aye unsought for slept among his ashes cold.*
>   (Garrod, p. 256)

Real terror in Keats arises from the conjunction between this world of dream and the world of reality, as in 'La Belle Dame sans Merci', and in *Endymion*:

> *Straight he seiz'd her wrist;*
> *It melted from his grasp: her hand he kiss'd,*
> *And, horror! kiss'd his own – he was alone.*
>   (Garrod, p. 173)

Terror is not nightmare, but the freezing touch of reality. The past remains, on the whole, a vision of beauty, but this very fact renders the present the more appalling. But although this is so, Keats was not untouched by the more conventional Gothic, and some of his descriptions in *The Eve of St Agnes* achieve a dazzling beauty:

> *And in the midst, 'mong thousand heraldries,*
> *And twilight saints, and dim emblazonings,*
> *A shielded scutcheon blush'd with blood of queens and kings.*
> (Garrod, p. 246)

Blake, Coleridge, Shelley, Byron and Keats all found in the Gothic elements which they used for distinctive purposes; and in doing so, they simultaneously widened the scope of Gothic and made explicit certain connections which had previously been only implicit. What they also did was, in various works, embody the central symbols of terror of an age; and largely because of these imaginative embodiments, those symbols were to resonate right through the nineteenth century. The first of these symbols is the Wanderer, who figures in work by Coleridge, Shelley and Byron, as well as in Maturin's *Melmoth the Wanderer* and a host of other poems and novels of the period – including, of course, *The Monk*. The ancient legends of the Wanderer come from a variety of sources: from various parts of the Bible, from the Koran, from early historians like Roger of Wendover and Matthew of Paris. Railo traces these sources, and notes the Wanderer's occasional presence in Italian, Spanish, German and English literature of the sixteenth and seventeenth centuries (Railo, pp. 191–217). In Germany in the 1770s and 1780s a resurgence of interest in the symbolic connotations of the figure occurs in the form of, for instance, various fragments by Goethe, of C. F. D. Schubart's 'Der ewige Jude' (1783) and of Schiller's *Der Geisterseher*; novels based on the theme appeared in 1785 and 1791.

The essence of the body of legendry concerns the idea of a man who, for an ultimate crime against God, often blasphemy or unbelief, is doomed to a perpetual life on earth. This perpetual life is never pleasant, but the interpretation of its significance varies a great deal. In some cases, it is characterised by a perpetual weariness and tedium, the quintessence of *Weltschmerz* and superhuman melancholy; in others, the life of the Wanderer is read as a kind of Promethean or Titanic defiance. The Wanderer is hero and/or victim. He is usually possessed of supernatural powers, often the gift of reading the future; and it was often said that his task on earth was to find another person who, out of despair, would exchange destinies with him, a task in which he never succeeds. As a symbol, the Wanderer is almost infinitely flexible; the connotations range from the defeated aspirations of humanity towards perfection, to a dreadful warning of the consequences of defiance.

This symbol fascinated the romantics. We can see a glimpse of it

in Blake's *Jerusalem* (1804–20), when Albion enters upon the state
of Eternal Death, saying:

> *I have girded round my cloke, and on my feet*
> *Bound these black shoes of death, & on my hands, deaths iron gloves:*
> *God hath forsaken me, & my friends are become a burden*
> *A weariness to me, & the human footsteps is a terror to me.*
>
> (Erdman, p. 179)

Albion's condition at this point is of alienation from the divine.
This alienation marks him out as the perpetual outcast, the man
who bears on his own shoulders the wrath of God. For Coleridge,
haunted as he was by feelings of alienation and guilt, the symbol
had a peculiar potency: we can see it, for instance, in a description
from 'The Wanderings of Cain' (1798):

> the mighty limbs of Cain were wasted as by fire; his hair was as the
> matted curls on the bison's forehead, and so glared his fierce and sullen
> eye beneath: and the black abundant locks on either side, a rank and
> tangled mass, were stained and scorched, as though the grasp of a
> burning iron hand had striven to rend them; and his countenance told
> in a strange and terrible language of agonies that had been, and
> were, and were still to continue to be. (*Poems*, p. 289)

And, of course, the Ancient Mariner is in the same position, abandoned by God because of an unforgiveable crime and doomed to
wander the world as a living demonstration of divine vengeance.
Shelley, again, in *Queen Mab*, in 'Ghasta, or the Avenging Demon!!!'
and in various other early pieces, makes use of the symbol, principally as a device for embodying a vision of history; since the Wanderer has walked the world for many centuries, he is also imbued
with the wisdom of ages, and is a fit commentator on worldly
transience. Byron's Childe Harold, although not superhuman, fulfils
a similar role:

> *But my Soul wanders; I demand it back*
> *To meditate amongst decay, and stand*
> *A ruin amidst ruins; there to track*
> *Fall'n states and buried greatness . . .*
> (*Poetry*, II, 347)

There are many possible reasons for the romantic articulation of
this symbolic figure. One thing which is clear is that the Wanderer,
whatever his original crime, has long since expiated his sin; or, as
in the case of the Ancient Mariner, the sin is not seen as fully
deserving the punishment. The God who is punishing him is a
jealous God, jealous of human aspiration. Certainly the Wanderer

101

committed the primal crime, but often in ignorance. He is, therefore, the victim of a terrible persecution, one which he cannot
alleviate; he is the exemplary sacrifice to repression. He is the
symbol of a severance of communication, of wholeness; and at
the same time he is the living evidence of the terror at the heart
of the world. And yet he is himself beyond fear; he has defied God,
and, by a familiar mythic process, has now himself acquired the
taboo he transgressed, he is himself a source of terror.[7] He has
dared to touch that which cannot be touched – God, the remote
past, the hidden desire – and is now himself untouchable. He
represents a primal anomaly, that of 'the mortal immortal' (to quote
the title of a story by Mary Shelley)[8] and the threat which he carries
with him is of the wholesale disturbance of the natural order, that
order so beloved of the writers of the early eighteenth century.

The vampire is also an anomaly, and one which crops up repeatedly in the works of the romantics. In Shelley's 'Invocation to Misery'
(1818), the figure of Misery bears a strong resemblance to the
vampire:

> *Kiss me; – oh! thy lips are cold:*
> *Round my neck thine arms enfold –*
> *They are soft, but chill and dead;*
> *And thy tears upon my head*
> *Burn like points of frozen lead.*
>
> *Hasten to the bridal bed –*
> *Underneath the grave 'tis spread:*
> *In darkness may our love be hid,*
> *Oblivion be our coverlid –*
> *We may rest, and none forbid.*
> (*Works*, III, 205)

What we have here is the perverse union of passion and death
which is the essence of the vampire. Again, the symbol has many
references: like the Wanderer, the vampire transgresses the law of
mortality, and also like the Wanderer he is a curious inversion of the
Christian myth of sacrifice. Interestingly, several of the vampires
in romantic writing are women, the outstanding examples being
Geraldine in Coleridge's 'Christabel' (1797), and Keats's 'La Belle
Dame sans Merci', who sucks the blood not only from the hero of
the poem but also from the entire surrounding world, leaving it
pallid, meaningless, stripped of aura:

> *I saw pale kings, and princes too,*
> *Pale warriors, death-pale were they all;*

They cried – 'La Bella Dame sans Merci
Hath thee in thrall!'

I saw their starved lips in the gloom,
With horrid warning gaped wide,
And I awoke and found me here,
On the cold hill's side.
(Garrod, p. 243)

To an even greater extent than the Wanderer, the vampire appears as a symbol of taboo. The one mentioned in Byron's *The Giaour* (1813) is untouchable even by other phantoms and ghouls:

Wet with thine own best blood shall drip
Thy gnashing tooth and haggard lip;
Then stalking to thy sullen grave,
Go – and with Gouls and Afrits rave;
Till these in horror shrink away
From spectre more accursed than they!
(*Poetry*, III, 123)

And Shelley, in *Prometheus Unbound* (1819), makes the point that this untouchable quality is only one-way: the vampire himself is dangerous precisely as a source of infection:

None, with firm sneer, trod out in his own heart
The sparks of love and hope till there remained
Those bitter ashes, a soul self-consumed,
And the wretch crept a vampire among men,
Infecting all with his own hideous ill . . .
(*Works*, II, 240)

The vampire is a very widespread symbol, examples occurring in almost every European and Asian mythology; but there are distinctive features of his romantic manifestation, and many of them are summarised in John Polidori's short story, 'The Vampyre'.[9]

In the first place, the story barely deals at all with the concrete matter of bloodsucking; it is, like 'Christabel' and 'La Belle Dame sans Merci', almost entirely about sex. The protagonist, Lord Ruthven, is indeed said to have a vampire's curious habits, but the damage he wreaks is largely effected by more conventional forms of seduction and dishonour. Also, this wreckage he causes in the social fabric is not exactly his fault: Polidori hints strongly that those who are ruined by his attentions are really the victims of their internal weakness – either they are themselves criminals, gamblers, sharpers, or they are merely 'frail'. Ruthven transgresses the social norms, but he does so with the collaboration of his victims; he

103

merely acts as a catalyst for repressed tendencies to emerge into the light of day. It is specifically said that he is extremely attractive; and it is also, much more interestingly, hinted that he may be a dream-object. When young Aubrey first meets him,

> He watched him; and the very impossibility of forming an idea of the character of a man entirely absorbed in himself, who gave few other signs of his observation of external objects, than the tacit assent to their existence, implied by the avoidance of their contact, allowing his imagination to picture everything that flattered its propensity to extravagant ideas, he soon formed this object into the hero of a romance, and determined to observe the offspring of his fancy, rather than the person before him.

The connections between the vampire and dream are very strong; both are night phenomena, which fade in the light of day, both are considered in mythological systems to be physically weakening, both promise – and perhaps deliver – an unthinkable pleasure which cannot sustain the touch of reality. Also the vampire, like the dream, can provide a representation of sexual liberation *in extremis*, indulgence to the point of death. The question of power is central: to the vampire's victim, the vampire seems all-powerful, compelling, hypnotic, yet this can also be seen as a transfer of responsibility; as within the walls of Udolpho, no blame attaches to submission to the inevitable.

The figure of Lord Ruthven became a model for the English vampire. The most important of his particular attributes is that he is, like the vampires of central European legend, an aristocrat, and it would be foolish to overlook the obvious connection between this feature and his sexual potential. What Ruthven exercises over his victims is a kind of *droit de seigneur*, that kind of absolute sexual privilege which is a concomitant of absolute power, and which is at the same time a predictable object of middle-class fantasies. Ruthven is indeed modelled in some ways on Byron, but this is less important; Ruthven is the representation not of a mythologised individual but of a mythologised class. He is dead yet not dead, as the power of the aristocracy in the early nineteenth century was dead and not dead; he requires blood because blood is the business of an aristocracy, the blood of warfare and the blood of the family.

The vampire in British culture, in Polidori, in Bram Stoker and elsewhere, is a fundamentally antibourgeois figure. He is elegant, well dressed, a master of seduction, a cynic, a person exempt from prevailing socio-moral codes. He thus takes his place alongside other forms of Gothic villain, as a participant in a myth produced by the middle class to explain its own antecedents and its own fears. Significantly, the vampire in Polidori is capable of 'winning'; by the time we come to Stoker's version almost a century later, he is defeated by the assorted forces of science, rationalism and ethical conformism. He is a rebel, not by virtue of turning from society, but by having pre-dated it; he is the unassimilable aspect of the past – which, of course, has to do with the Wanderer too.

Alongside the Wanderer and the vampire in the romantic bestiary we have to place the seeker after forbidden knowledge. Psychologically, that seems almost like a pun, since the ultimate forbidden knowledge is presumably sexual, and that is far from irrelevant when one considers that the knowledge Frankenstein attains to is precisely the knowledge of human reproduction, albeit by unconventional means. Coleridge, however, in 'Quae Nocent Docent' (1789), sets the tone for the overt romantic search:

> But o'er the midnight Lamp I'd love to pore,
> I'd seek with care fair Learning's depths to sound,
>   And gather scientific Lore:
> Or to mature the embryo thoughts inclin'd,
> That half-conceiv'd lay struggling in my mind,
> The cloisters' solitary gloom I'd round.
>
> *(Poems,* p. 9)

The forbidden knowledge which the romantic ostensibly seeks is similar to that of the alchemists: the knowledge of eternal life, the philosophers' stone, those kinds of knowledge which will make men gods – although, again, Coleridge's language of 'mature', 'embryo', 'half-conceiv'd' alerts one to the fact that there is another level to this search. Like the graveyard poets, Shelley seeks these kinds of knowledge through the study of death:

> I have made my bed
> In charnels and on coffins, where black death
> Keeps record of the trophies won from thee,
> Hoping to still these obstinate questionings
> Of thee and thine, by forcing some lone ghost
> Thy messenger, to render up the tale
> Of what we are.
>
> *(Works,* I, 177)

The survival of death is clearly a root motif in all three symbols; and so is a certain conception of desire. The Wanderer, the vampire, the seeker, all have desires which are socially insatiable; that is to say, their satiation would involve social disaster, as well as transgression of boundaries between the natural, the human and the divine. They are individualist disruptives – all of them aristocrats of one kind or another – who are not content with the restrictions placed on them by a settled and ordered society. They burst out of the eighteenth century suddenly and furiously; none of them, indeed, were new symbols at the time, but their resurgence and the attention lavished on them nonetheless cannot be explained ahistorically.

The figure of the seeker after forbidden knowledge turned, in 1818, into the most significant and popular of modern terror-symbols with the writing of *Frankenstein*. The durability and influence of Mary Shelley's book has been enormous; perhaps no work in the Gothic tradition has entered more fully into the cultural imagination. And yet, of course, the question of its relation to this tradition is tendentious. We know that it was planned as a horror story; and we also know that during the years 1814–18 Mary Shelley had read work by Beckford, Radcliffe, Lewis, Godwin (her father) and Charles Brockden Brown, as well as several of the German terror-novelists. But there are also many other connections, most notably to the myths of Prometheus and Faust, which enter into *Frankenstein* in a transmuted form. Prometheus, the archetypal seeker after forbidden wisdom, incurred in his search a terrible and eternal punishment: the punishment not of perpetual wandering but of perpetual torture. Shelley and Byron both wrote of Prometheus, and these lines of Byron's aptly summarise the romantic perception of his plight:

> *Titan! to thee the strife was given*
>   *Between the suffering and the will,*
>   *Which torture where they cannot kill;*
> *And the inexorable Heaven,*
> *And the deaf tyranny of Fate,*
> *The ruling principle of Hate,*
> *Which for its pleasure doth create*
> *The things it may annihilate,*
> *Refused thee even the boon to die . . .*
>   *(Poetry, IV, 49–50)*

The relation, however, between *Frankenstein* and the Prometheus and Faust legendary is oblique, and careful distinctions are needed here, principally because the characteristics of the Promethean hero are divided by Mary Shelley between the scientist Frankenstein and the 'monster' which he creates. It is Frankenstein who defies God by creating life, but it is the monster who bears at least part of the punishment.

Frankenstein has a simple plot, which is greatly complicated by sophisticated narrative devices. Frankenstein aspires to the creation of a living being and, by dint of hard work and obsessive concentration, achieves his end. The being he creates, however, proves less tractable than he had hoped, and becomes progressively alienated from his creator, eventually committing a series of hideous crimes. They finally confront each other, and the monster demands that Frankenstein create a mate for him. Frankenstein, however, refuses, and the book concludes with the two of them locked in a perpetual mutual pursuit and conflict. But within this framework there are many problems, principally to do with Mary Shelley's stance towards the relationship between Frankenstein and his creation. It appears that she intended to demonstrate the wrongness of Frankenstein's efforts, at the same time as showing the monster as a fundamentally morally neutral creature who is made evil by circumstances; but these twin goals sit very uneasily together, and there are many moments when it is difficult for the reader to know whose behaviour is the most unjustifiable.

To appreciate these problems, it is necessary first to consider the actual process of creation which Frankenstein undertakes. Near the beginning of the book, he tells us the nature of his intellectual interests:

> I confess that neither the structure of languages, nor the codes of governments, nor the politics of various states, possessed attractions for me. It was the secrets of heaven and earth that I desired to learn; and whether it was the outward substance of things, or the inner spirit of nature and the mysterious soul of man that occupied me, still my inquiries were directed to the metaphysical, or, in its highest sense, the physical secrets of the world.[10]

Frankenstein's task is thus conceived as a purely scientific one; he has no interest in matters social or moral, but considers himself as a 'pure enquirer after truth'. It is in keeping with this that the methods which he uses are not Faustian alchemy, but the processes of actual science. Thus far, Mary Shelley appears to be directing her book against the illusion of pure scientific enquiry; this is one of the major arguments of the text, and one which has certainly helped to keep the myth alive.

Her disapproval of this conception of the possibilities of science is underlined in several ways. She emphasises that Frankenstein's researches take him unhealthily through engagement with death and sickness, in that he has to find the parts of the monster's future body in charnel-houses and morgues. She also emphasises that, while engaged in his creation, he forgets all other ties of human affection, forgets his family, and passes into a state of dreamlike, obsessive absorption in the task on hand. This, she is saying, is an unnatural birth, and can have only unnatural consequences.

Yet despite this setting, the mood of the book abruptly changes once the monster is brought to life. The description of his physical appearance is important:

> How can I describe my emotions at this catastrophe, or how delineate the wretch whom with such infinite pains and care I had endeavoured to form? His limbs were in proportion, and I had selected his features as beautiful. Beautiful! – Great God! His yellow skin scarcely covered the work of muscles and arteries beneath; his hair was of a lustrous black, and flowing; his teeth of a pearly whiteness; but these luxuriances only formed a more horrid contrast with his watery eyes, that seemed almost of the same colour as the dun white sockets in which they were set, his shrivelled complexion and straight black lips.
>
> (*Frankenstein*, p. 51)

It is clear that Frankenstein has formed a fixed judgement about his creation already, has in fact classified him as a monster, purely on the grounds of his physical appearance. Instead of feeling a quasi-paternal affection for him, he rejects him out of hand. Yet the monster is not, cannot be, inherently evil, as Mary Shelley repeatedly tells us. One could expect from this that she would continue to blame Frankenstein for his 'unnaturalness', and yet she appears not to, but rather to want to retain some considerable portion of the reader's sympathy for the wretched scientist. Later on, the monster relates his version of the early events of his life, showing himself to have been a total innocent:

> It was dark when I awoke; I felt cold also, and half-frightened, as it were instinctively, finding myself so desolate. Before I had quitted your apartment, on a sensation of cold, I had covered myself with some clothes; but these were insufficient to secure me from the dews of night. I was a poor, helpless, miserable wretch; I knew, and could distinguish, nothing; but feeling pain invade me on all sides, I sat down and wept.
>
> Soon a gentle light stole over the heavens, and gave me a sensation of pleasure. I started up, and beheld a radiant form rise from among the trees. I gazed with a kind of wonder. It moved slowly, but it enlightened my path; and I again went out in search of berries. I was still cold, when under one of the trees I found a huge cloak, with which I covered myself, and sat down upon the ground. No distinct ideas occupied my mind; all was confused. I felt light, and hunger, and thirst, and darkness; innumerable sounds rung in my ears, and on all sides various scents saluted me: the only object that I could distinguish was the bright moon, and I fixed my eyes on that with pleasure.
>
> (*Frankenstein*, pp. 104–5)

Mary Shelley is here concerned to present the monster in the light of Rousseauistic and Godwinian theories, as born innocent, a *tabula rasa*, a being who will have his psyche formed by his contacts with circumstance.

But the corollary of this, one would again expect, would be for her to point out that the monster's early experiences of rejection must have played a large part in turning him into the evil being which he becomes. Yet she does not do this. The crucial episode here is the confrontation between the two protagonists, when Frankenstein, having pursued the monster, encounters him in the Alps. When he sees him, Frankenstein says,

> I trembled with rage and horror, resolving to wait his approach, and then close with him in mortal combat . . . rage and hatred had at first deprived me of utterance, and I recovered only to overwhelm him with words expressive of furious detestation and contempt.

This indeed Frankenstein proceeds to do, calling him 'devil' and 'vile insect', to which the monster responds with surprising forbearance:

> 'I expected this reception,' said the daemon. 'All men hate the wretched; how, then, must I be hated, who am miserable beyond all living things! Yet you, my creator, detest and spurn me, thy creature, to whom thou art bound by ties only dissoluble by the annihilation of one of us.'   (*Frankenstein*, p. 100)

This is surely a very reasonable point; but it certainly does not seem so to Mary Shelley. She wants, on the one hand, not to blame the monster for being as he is, while on the other not to blame Frankenstein for hating him with a furious, bitter and almost incoherent hatred, but this is impossible. Constantly in the book Mary Shelley tries to produce in the reader an effect of alienation from the monster, which misfires because it really seems that the original reason for Frankenstein's rejection of him was mere aesthetic disappointment. Crucially, we wonder why Frankenstein will not provide him with a mate. He appears to fear the production of a race of monsters, but the monster's request is nonetheless not unreasonable. Mary Shelley's final act of authorial contempt towards the monster whom *she*, after all, has also 'created', is a bitter one; she gives him no name, and the consequences of that are only too apparent.

The problem appears to be that *Frankenstein* works at several different levels, and they do not coincide; this, on the one hand, vitiates the coherence of the text, but it has also kept it in being as a viable myth for a number of different purposes. First of all, behind the book is the shadow of an optimistic theory. Mary Shelley nominally subscribed to Godwin's belief in the eventual perfectibility of man, and any doctrine of the *tabula rasa* must suppose that, if circumstances were only right, perfection of the individual is a possibility. On the other hand, the book embodies many local doubts about scientific progress; it emphasises, in a very modern way, the need for care and responsibility in matters scientific. If Frankenstein had taken the trouble to know a little about politics, psychology, education, he might have been able to *rear* his creation as well as simply bringing him to life.

In these ways, at least, the book embodies a rational conflict; but there are other levels as well. Principally, there is an intense fear of the ugly, the unpredictable, the disruptive, which prevents the author from dealing fairly with the monster. Frankenstein may have committed a heinous sin, or a social crime, but in the end he is 'one of us': the monster may not be wholly blameworthy, even for his later acts of violence, but nonetheless he is *different*, and must be chastised as such. And further below the surface, still darker things stir. At one point, Frankenstein's brother William is murdered; while mourning him, Frankenstein perceives –

> in the gloom a figure which stole from behind a clump of trees near me; I stood fixed, gazing intently: I could not be mistaken. A flash of lightning illuminated the object, and discovered its shape plainly to me; its gigantic stature, and the deformity of its aspect, more hideous than belongs to humanity, instantly informed me that it was the wretch, the filthy daemon, to whom I had given life. What did he there? Could he be (I shuddered at the conception) the murderer of my brother? No sooner did that idea cross my imagination, than I became convinced of its truth; my teeth chattered, and I was forced to lean against a tree for support. The figure passed me quickly, and I lost it in the gloom. Nothing in human shape could have destroyed that fair child. *He* was the murderer! I could not doubt it.
>
> (*Frankenstein*, pp. 73–4)

The language is the language of schizophrenia. The monster is the creature, the embodiment of Frankenstein's desire, just as Hyde is the desire-creature of Doctor Jekyll; thus the extraordinary strength and virulence of Frankenstein's transfer of guilt. If the monster is a creature of circumstance, and if his creator has the responsibility for such circumstance, then Frankenstein must share in the guilt for his brother's death.

But not only can Frankenstein not do this; Mary Shelley cannot either. The monster undoubtedly could have been 'acculturated';

instead, he is exiled. *Frankenstein,* at root, is a book about the rejection of the strange, at both social and psychological levels. And yet, of course, the matter is not as simple as this. Karl Mannheim says of the romantics that they tried to rescue 'repressed irrational forces, espoused their cause in the conflict, but failed to see that the mere fact of paying conscious attention to them meant an inevitable rationalisation',[11] and this seems applicable, in varying degrees, to much of the Gothic. In *Frankenstein,* the contradictions occasioned by this rationalisation are particularly strongly marked, precisely because Mary Shelley took her moral and political purposes more seriously than did Radcliffe or Lewis; where they were content to allow narrative itself a limited degree of autonomy, she requires all the time to subject her narrative to intellectual scrutiny.

This is in no way to regard *Frankenstein* as an inferior work; on the contrary, in *Frankenstein* contradictions emerge which are suppressed in many other Gothic and Gothic-influenced texts. A great deal of Gothic is about injustice, whether it be divinely inspired, or meted out by man to his fellow men and women. The Wanderer and Frankenstein's monster are powerful symbols of that injustice; and so, in one way, is the vampire, who after all merely acts in the way which is laid down for him, and is himself under a kind of doom. The question of why these symbols of injustice and malevolent fate should be conjured up at a particular historical period is a delicate one, and one which we shall return to later, but we can advance one or two possibilities now.

It is conventional, and reasonable, to say that the society which generated and read Gothic fiction was one which was becoming aware of injustice in a variety of different areas, and which doubted – principally in the persons of the great romantics – the ability of eighteenth-century social explanations to cope with the facts of experience. We can see it in the dawning consciousness of inequality in the relations between the sexes; in the romantic emphasis on the partiality and non-neutrality of reason as a guiding light for social behaviour; in the increasing awareness that there are parts of the psyche which do not appear to act according to rational criteria; in the constantly reiterated thought that, after all and despite so-called natural law, it is still often the sins of the fathers which are visited on their descendants. This last may well be the strongest argument in connection with *Frankenstein.* It seems sensible to assume that there must be historical reasons for this: and two possibly relevant facts stand out.

The first is that Gothic writing emerges at a particular and definable stage in the development of class relations: we may define this as the stage when the bourgeoisie, having to all intents and purposes gained social power, began to try to understand the conditions and history of their own ascent. This, surely, is the reason for the emphasis in the literature on recapturing history, on forming history into patterns which are capable of explaining present situations; it is as clear a motivation in Gibbon as in Shelley. The second, related point, is an economic one and is suggested by Lucien Goldmann in his description of 'classical liberal society' as a society in which 'there is no conscious regulation of production and consumption at any level. In such a society, of course, production is nevertheless regulated. . . . But this regulation operates in an *implicit* way, outside the consciousness of individuals, imposing itself on them as the mechanical action of an outside force.'[12]

The coming of industry, the move towards the city, the regularisation of patterns of labour in the late eighteenth century, set up a world in which older, 'natural' ways of governing the individual life – the seasons, the weather, simple laws of exchange – become increasingly irrelevant. Instead, individuals are propelled along paths of activity which make sense only as parts of a greater, less easily comprehended whole. The individual comes to see him- or herself at the mercy of forces which in fundamental ways elude understanding. Under such circumstances, it is hardly surprising to find the emergence of a literature whose key motifs are paranoia, manipulation and injustice, and whose central project is understanding the inexplicable, the taboo, the irrational. And one further point needs to be suggested from this, before we go on to examine more of the literature itself; and that is that if Gothic is thus a form of response to the emergence of a middle-class-dominated capitalist economy, and if such an economy prevails in important respects through the nineteenth century and on into the twentieth, it may be possible to explain the persistence of the central Gothic symbols in the same terms. These symbols, we may say, were forged as a response to a period of social trauma; and perhaps that trauma is one which British culture is still trying, in increasingly sophisticated ways, to understand.

Notes and references

1. It seems to me correct to exclude Wordsworth from this argument; but see Rodway, pp. 51, 56, 59, 71.
2. *The Poems of Samuel Taylor Coleridge*, ed. Ernest H. Coleridge (London, 1912), p. 141.

3. *The Poetical Works of John Keats*, ed. H. W. Garrod (Oxford, 1958), p, 229. All subsequent Keats references are to 'Garrod'.

4. See, e.g. Erdman, pp. 143, 334–5.

5. **Mary Shelley,** 'Notes to *Queen Mab*', in Shelley, *Works*, I. 167.

6. *The Works of Lord Byron: Poetry*, ed. Ernest H. Coleridge (7 vols, New York, 1966), II, 34.

7. See Freud's psychoanalytic interpretation of anthropological evidence in *Totem and Taboo*, in *Works*, XIII, 1–161; see also *Works*, XI, 200 ff.

8. See **Mary Shelley,** *Tales and Stories*, introd. Joanna Russ (Boston, Mass., 1975), pp. 148–64.

9. In *Gothic Stories of Horror and Romance, 1765–1840*, Vol. I, *Great British Tales of Terror*, ed. Peter Haining (London, 1972), pp. 251–69.

10. **Mary Shelley,** *Frankenstein*, introd. R. E. Dowse and D. J. Palmer (London, 1963), p. 28.

11. **Karl Mannheim,** *Essays on Sociology and Social Psychology*, ed. Paul Kecskemeti (London, 1953), p. 89.

12. **Lucien Goldmann,** *Towards a Sociology of the Novel*, trans. Alan Sheridan (London, 1975), p. 136.

CHAPTER 5

The dialectic of persecution

William Godwin, C. R. Maturin, James Hogg

We have said that many of the basic coordinates and conventions of Gothic can be found in the works of Ann Radcliffe and Matthew Lewis, works written during the commercial 'boom period' of Gothic in the 1790s. We have also suggested that a large part of the originality of their fiction, and also a large proportion of its narrative and other difficulties, arise from the problem that the tradition with which they deal has less to do with the earlier development of the novel than with a longer and more diffuse poetic and dramatic tradition; and thus it is in some ways natural that Gothic flows readily back into the work of most of the major romantic poets. However, it is now necessary to turn back to the Gothic novel itself, and to examine a further group of important works.

The number of Gothic novels written in this period from the 1790s to the 1820s was colossal. Popular writers in the genre appear to have become increasingly able to turn out a formulaic product in a matter of weeks, and the eventual decline in Gothic's popularity was clearly at least partly to do with a flooding of the market, and also with the way in which the hold of the early Gothic masters tended to stultify originality. It would be impossible here to attempt a survey of the field; and those critics, like Summers, who have attempted it have quickly found themselves bogged down in a morass. A single example, hopefully, will suffice to summarise many lesser works, and as good a one as any is *The Midnight Bell*, by Francis Lathom. This was one of the works cited in *Northanger Abbey* as among Catherine Morland's Gothic diet, and it has had the highly dubious distinction of being referred to by Varma as 'a Gothic masterpiece'. Lathom, he ludicrously claims, was 'skilled in dialogue and dramatic incident, in which this novel abounds' (Varma, p. 5); but what Lathom actually appears to have been skilled in was producing a series – a long series – of works which satisfactorily trod the line between reliance on his distinguished predecessors and provision of the occasional unexpected thrill. Lathom, who became known chiefly as a Gothic playwright, was writing novels early on in the period: *The Castle of Ollada* appeared in 1794, an auspicious year, and *The Midnight Bell* in 1798. All of his early fiction is thoroughly Radcliffean in most of the important ways: settings, the class stereotyping of character, the emphasis on sensibility are all out of the world of *Udolpho*. Where *The Midnight Bell* differs from this tradition, it is picking up on other recognisable influences. In particular, Lathom had clearly been reading German terror-writing; we can find evidence for this in the speed and crudity of the bloodshed and death which figure largely in the book, and, in a more sophisticated way, in the way Lathom utilises the increasingly available stock of German stereotypes. His banditti, like those of Schiller, Godwin and many later writers, are 'avowed enemies to tyranny',[1] forgivable outcasts who offer a tempting sanctuary from the pressures of social normalcy. His prisons, on the other hand, are precisely the outward and visible sign of tyranny, little Bastilles, one of which is destroyed by lightning to the anticipated joy of the audience. This kind of undeveloped but pervasive political content is, of course, akin to what we have already found in the poets; for Lathom as for many others, it was again the outcome of a reading of Schiller and a vaguely voyeuristic attitude to German political and cultural life. *Midnight Bell* reads as a good sketch for a novel; it is narratively compelling, but it starves us of any real involvement with, or investigation of, character and situation. This is, in a sense, not to judge Lathom harshly; he knew perfectly well that the gaps he was leaving would be automatically filled in by the reading *cognoscenti*, much as a modern science fiction writer can reasonably assume, on the strength of his predecessors, that he need not spend time going into the practical details of the possibility of space travel. A minor point about Lathom which colours his fictional world is his apparent familiarity with de Sade; but he appears to have seen de Sade as giving a kind of 'permission' for certain kinds of crude psychological depiction, rather than as significantly altering his perception of the motivations of his puppet characters.

The minor fiction of the period is characterised by a number of oft-repeated themes, present in Lathom and in many others. The pact with the devil; the liability of convents to become infested with demoniac rites; the mortifying outcome of the search for forbidden knowledge; the shocking effect of the corruption and death of beauty; the debilitating results of the longing for revenge: all of these provide structural elements for a wide range of novels and magazine stories. The important point, though, is that these particular themes are not – *in themselves* – peculiar to the Gothic; as is immediately recognisable, they can be found in Jacobean drama, and most of them owe a great deal to English – or occasionally German – folklore. To find the really distinctive features which allow this range of themes to be transformed into works of imaginative power and historical originality, it is necessary to set the themes in the context of, first, the general psychological concern which colours their resurgence in this period, and second, the *formal* characteristics of the more interesting Gothic works. We said earlier that Gothic fiction played a large part in the historical development of the 'novel of plot' in general, and there are Gothic works which should interest us much more for their strugglings with formal innovation, with the problems of inculcating suspense and narrative doubt, than for their largely legendary and traditional content.

If one looks at Gothic in these terms – that is, if one attempts to describe the parameters of Gothic in terms of its specific formal differences from other novelistic acceptances of the time, and in terms of the particular *kind* of preoccupation with terror which it embodies – three works stand out, and have done in the history of criticism: William Godwin's *Caleb Williams* (1794); Charles Robert Maturin's *Melmoth the Wanderer* (1820); and James Hogg's *Confessions of a Justified Sinner* (1824). At first glance, this seems a very disparate group of texts, and of writers. *Caleb Williams* and Hogg's *Confessions* are usually – and, I believe, reasonably – included in discussions of the Gothic, although this is often only because of the extreme difficulty of relating them to anything else; I hope to show that the mainsprings of these two works are indeed Gothic, and that a large part of their interest derives from their different attempts to embody Gothic preoccupations in guises which do not pay lip-service to the dominant environmental trappings of the genre. All three of the writers have an eccentric relation to Gothic fiction: Godwin took to writing fiction as part of a larger, predominantly political and philosophical, intellectual project; Hogg, of course, was principally a poet, and the *Confessions* has often been found singularly inexplicable in terms of his other excursions into fiction; Maturin, indeed, played the part of a 'Gothic novelist' to a more considerable extent, but he was also a dramatist, a writer of historical and Irish novels, and a clergyman with a pronounced doctrinal interest which motivates much of his fiction.

And yet these three novels, between them, identify many of the principal concerns of Gothic. We suggested earlier that Radcliffe's strengths as a novelist were her interest in character psychology, her use of a poetic and symbolic mode to intensify her tales and her constant blurring of the boundaries of reality and fantasy; we do not find any of these characteristics in a genre-writer like Lathom, but we do in Godwin, Maturin, Hogg. And what we also find in these writers – or rather, in these three *books* – is a bending of each of these qualities to the service of a common object. For the object of *Caleb Williams*, of *Melmoth* and of the *Confessions* is the same; it is actually to *investigate* the extremes of terror. Jacobean drama – and much of the lesser 'Gothic' fiction – was not quite concerned with this; it was concerned, often for other purposes, with *portraying* extreme terror, but not with setting up experimental structures in which the audience is led, gradually and sometimes hesitantly, into new territories where terror can have full rein, independent of the constraints of the real world. These three books are nightmare books, in the particular sense that moral purpose – often initially present – is in each case eroded by the pressures of psychological obsession. The difficulty of ascribing clear ethical intent to any of them, despite their authors' apparent wishes, is evidenced by the way in which critics have had to try to deal with them: if Godwin's purpose, for instance, is, as one might deduce from biographical information that it ought to have been, to depict the evil of tyranny, he fails, because his interest in the psychological interplay of his two principals undermines the putative political argument.

And in the case of *Caleb Williams*, *Melmoth*, *Confessions*, we can be even more explicit about the kind of terror with which they are concerned; it is a terror which has to do with persecution. It may seem an irrelevant biographical point to make, but it is worth pointing out that their three authors were all men with, in one way or another, good reason to regard themselves as persecuted: Godwin for his political principles, Hogg for his odd position *vis-à–vis* the literary and cultural establishment, Maturin because the writing of Gothic fiction was not supposed ideally compatible with the duties of an Anglican clergyman, and also because there is evidence that he was of a paranoiac cast of mind. The worlds which they encourage us to enter are surprisingly modern worlds compared with those of

Radcliffe or Lewis, in that they look forward to the more recent nightmare worlds of Dostoevsky and particularly Kafka, where again the nightmare is one in which on the one hand there is suspension of ethical imperatives while on the other poetic justice never really comes. And this feature is, as we shall see, connected in each case with formal considerations: all three books are, in their context, radical formal departures from previous fiction, and this is at least partly because all three tend towards the use of complex verification techniques to assure us of the validity of the highly improbable stories which they recount. It is as if each author were assured of the psychological truth of what he says, but in order to convince his readers of its truth 'in the world' he has to invent his own means of internally guaranteeing that the story is true. This we can see, however, in more detail by turning to the books themselves.

William Godwin is best known as the author of *An Enquiry Concerning the Principles of Political Justice* (1793), the seminal work of philosophic anarchism, but he also wrote six novels, of which perhaps only *Caleb Williams* and *St Leon* (1799) are still read. *St Leon* was one of the first of many novels to deal with Rosicrucianism, which was to become a staple element in the Gothic fiction of the early nineteenth century. His influence on later writers was considerable: Maturin, Shelley and Charles Brockden Brown all show important traces of Godwin's themes and preoccupations. In more specific terms, and still within the boundaries of Gothic, Conan Doyle can be seen as following in Godwin's footsteps as far as the planning of fiction was concerned; but his strongest influence was exerted on Bulwer Lytton and, through Lytton, on Dickens. Lytton's *A Strange Story* owes a great deal to *St Leon*, and it is interesting in this context that it was Lytton who eventually wrote the story of Eugene Aram, the 'philosophical murderer', which Godwin had at one time planned to write.

It would be fair, however, to characterise *St Leon* as 'metaphysical Gothic', concerned as it is with the problems of everlasting life, while *Caleb Williams* is undoubtedly 'political Gothic', and played a formative role as such in the work of the Shelleys. This is not to say that it falls within the German tradition of idealisation of the feudal past, for *Caleb Williams* is rather aggressively set in the present; but it is overtly concerned with the problems of social interaction within a class-divided society, and with the injustice which that society is capable of meting out to the innocent. In this respect, it belongs with the leftist novels of Thomas Holcroft and Robert Bage;[2] and yet, as the plot develops, the situation of the supremely unfortunate

Caleb comes to remind us of the plight of Frankenstein's monster more than of their afflicted but very human heroes.

Caleb, alone in the world, is taken on as secretary to a wealthy but reclusive squire with the pleasingly cosmopolitan name Ferdinando Falkland. He decides that Falkland is not all he seems and, from a motive of sheer curiosity, sets himself to discover his secret. Disastrously for him, he does; an old retainer reveals that Falkland was once put on trial for the murder of an intolerably boorish neighbour named Tyrell, who had grossly insulted him, but was acquitted. By dint of ceaseless vigilance and some remarkable strokes of luck, Caleb establishes that Falkland did in fact commit the murder, but Falkland turns the tables on him by pointing out that Caleb's knowledge of this secret means that he, Falkland, must keep him under his thumb for the rest of his life. Caleb starts to realise the extreme peril of his situation and begins a long series of attempts, which take up the latter two-thirds of the book, to evade Falkland. Every step he takes plunges him further into the toils of misery and persecution, since Falkland's power of retaliation is seemingly infinite. Caleb is propelled from humiliation to prison to temporary exile, and everywhere Falkland and his minions contrive to ruin his reputation and blast his hopes. In the end, desperate, Caleb manages to persuade the authorities of the truth of his story, only to suffer a terrible last-minute agony of guilt at ruining Falkland who, for all his past crimes, nonetheless still curiously appears to Caleb as a model of nobility.

The story is extremely meticulously, even mechanically, planned; indeed, Godwin is celebrated for having thought of the pursuit situation first, and then invented a set of events to provoke it. The last portion in particular modulates from the effect of a received manuscript into almost direct speech in an alarming fashion, making one feel very strongly the imminent closing in of the book's maleficent forces. Walter Allen suggests that part of *Caleb Williams's* concentrated power stems from Godwin's intellectualism; it is written, he says, in 'the coldest, most intellectual, most abstract prose possible'.[3] Yet this is only true in certain respects. The *plan* of the book certainly appears to work according to the dictates of reason rather than of imagination, and it has also been noted that *Caleb Williams* has a claim to being the first novel in the language without any kind of love-interest; but Allen himself puts the other side of the case when he says that whatever Godwin's intentions may have been, he was not in the least a 'realistic' novelist (*CW*, p. xi). The kind of abstractness which the book has is not, in fact, by any means the abstractness of a cold intellectual system, but rather that of a world which operates according to its own immutable and barbaric laws, a world in which characters oscillate between the most violent extremes of passion. On one occasion when Caleb seems near to discovering the secret of his guilt, Falkland's behaviour is described in a way far from reasonable:

> He left his employment, strode about the room in anger, his visage gradually assumed an expression as of supernatural barbarity, he quitted the apartment abruptly, and flung the door with a violence that seemed to shake the house. (*CW*, p. 123)

This is reminiscent of the poor manners of the average Gothic villain, and indeed the phrase 'supernatural barbarity' well summarises the treatment which Caleb fears, and in part receives, at Falkland's hands. 'What was it', he expostulates at one point,

> that fate had yet in reserve for me! The insatiable vengeance of a Falkland, of a man whose hands were, to my apprehension, red with blood, and his thoughts familiar with cruelty and murder. How great were the resources of his mind, resources henceforth to be confederated for my destruction! (*CW*, p. 145)

But then, it is difficult to know quite how far Caleb's fears are justifiable, for Godwin begins, as do many other Gothic writers, by pointing out to us that both of his principal characters are afflicted by an interest in romance, that cast of mind so fatal to Radcliffe's heroines. Caleb, in his youth, 'panted for the unravelling of an adventure with an anxiety, perhaps almost equal to that of the man whose future happiness or misery depended on its issue' (*CW*, p. 2). This susceptibility makes him a somewhat unreliable witness; while in the case of Falkland, the whole of his crime is attributed to his over-serious and archaic sense of honour, which Godwin also takes care to connect with a love of chivalry and romance.

To be sure, there are points in the book where Godwin's rationalism comes over strongly, particularly in his extended disquisition on the evils of prison. He also shows us a band of 'philosophic banditti' and enters into great detail about their arguments in favour of a life of crime, and about Caleb's position on this. And this, of course, connects with Godwin's pronounced and general interest in criminal psychology; it is difficult to think of a book in which a prison escape is described in such enormous detail. But on the whole, the world of *Caleb Williams* is a curiously distorted one; although Caleb himself passes through many different scenes in the course of his flight, these pass like shadows, while Falkland – who in fact is rarely physically present – possesses an overwhelming reality for Caleb which he is barely able to forget for an instant.

Godwin is very skilled at building up suspense; one way in which he does it is by constantly – and consistently – reminding us that the book is Caleb's *present account of the past:* thus, while we are watching him flee across England we are also hearing his present voice, fraught with the burden of his wasted years: 'I have not deserved this treatment. My own conscience witnesses in behalf of that innocence, my pretensions to which are regarded in the world as incredible' (*CW,* p. 1). In the first part of the book, Caleb often holds out promises of horrors to come, horrors which all too strongly suggest 'supernatural barbarity', as 'the death-dealing mischief advances with an accelerated motion, appearing to defy human wisdom and strength to obstruct its operation' (*CW,* p. 39). For Falkland, through the eyes of Caleb – and that is, of course, our only vantage-point – is scarcely human; that is not to say that he is evil or Satanic, but rather that, like so many Gothic figures, he is a creature who embodies total *will.* For Falkland, there is only the smallest of gaps between decision and operation: his conviction of the necessity of hounding and silencing Caleb is sufficient to enable him to disregard the laws of probability. This leaves Caleb at a loss for words: the 'catastrophe' he is about to relate, he says at one point, 'will be found pregnant with horror, beyond what the blackest misanthropy could readily have suggested' (*CW,* p. 85).

What Godwin has done in *Caleb Williams* is to attempt to set up a situation from which there is no escape, in which persecution by our enemies in unavoidable. But it is, of course, very hard if not impossible to do this within a realist framework, basically because such an extreme situation requires no intrusion of luck, chance, the unexpected. The operations of fate must be inexorable. Caleb summarises the totally *enclosing* nature of his fate thus:

> The voice of an irresistible necessity had commanded me to 'sleep no more'. I was tormented with a secret, of which I must never disburthen myself; and this consciousness was, at my age, a source of perpetual melancholy. I had made myself a prisoner, in the most intolerable sense of that term, for years – perhaps for the rest of my life. Though my prudence and discretion should be invariable, I must remember that I should have an overseer, vigilant from conscious guilt, full of resentment at the unjustifiable means by which I had extorted from him a confession, and whose lightest caprice might at any time decide upon everything that was dear to me. The vigilance even of a public and systematical despotism is poor, compared with a vigilance which is thus

goaded by the most anxious passions of the soul. Against this species of persecution I knew not how to invent a refuge.

(*CW*, p. 151)

If Falkland's methods are so much more effective and terrifying than those of the state, then it is clear that the one cannot be taken as a metaphor for the other. Although the kind of power which Godwin is depicting has a connection with political power (and is, at crucial points of the story, sustained by the authorities) it is not in itself political power. It is better described as the power of subjection, and as such it operates partly through Caleb's mind. 'Though my prudence and discretion should be invariable', he says; and in admitting that degree of hopelessness, he marks his own unintentional collaboration with the forces of persecution.

It is impossible to establish objectivity within a first-person narrative. Caleb certainly is persecuted, but we find ourselves looking through the cracks in his account of the persecuting universe. In the first place, it is not true that his is the position of 'conscious innocence'; his curiosity – one might call it spying – causes Falkland's actions. Also, there are occasions when Caleb entirely mistakes Falkland's intentions towards him and conjures them into an overmalevolent form. And finally, Caleb's feelings clearly partake of rejected love: through all his vicissitudes he bears with him a still, small acceptance of Falkland's tremendous worth, which, of course, renders his feelings all the more bitter. The crucial question, however, is whether we should decide on evidence of this kind that Caleb himself is an exaggerator, given to misinterpreting and overdramatising his situation, or whether the informing consciousness behind the whole novel is transgressing realist conventions and producing a world of deliberately heightened dimensions. There is plenty of evidence for the former: 'here I am', says Caleb late in the book,

> an outcast, destined to perish with hunger and cold. All men desert me. All men hate me. I am driven with mortal threats from the sources of comfort and existence. Accursed world! that hates without a cause, that overwhelms innocence with calamities which ought to be spared even to guilt! Accursed world! dead to every manly sympathy; with eyes of horn, and hearts of steel! (*CW*, p. 277)

And later,

> There is no end then ... to my persecutors! My unwearied and long-continued labours lead to no termination! Termination! No; the lapse

of time, that cures all other things, make my case more desperate!
(*CW*, p. 297)

But then, the world through which Caleb moves, so simple and reassuring at the beginning, becomes progressively more and more the world of Gothic romance. The prisons are those peculiarly intolerable prisons of the Inquisition, where the greatest efforts have been made to ensure maximum discomfort of the soul: 'he that has observed the secrets of a prison, well knows that there is more torture in the lingering existence of a criminal, in the silent intolerable minutes that he spends, than in the tangible misery of whips and racks!' (*CW*, p. 198). And the old lady who forms an animosity towards Caleb while he is with the banditti expresses herself very strongly on the subject when Caleb on one occasion exhorts her to leave him: 'Leave you! No: I will thrust my fingers through your ribs, and drink your blood! . . . I will sit upon you, and press you to hell! I will roast you with brimstone, and dash your entrails into your eyes!' (*CW*, p. 254). We are thus confronted with a situation characteristic of Gothic, in which a suspicion of paranoia on the part of the protagonist is accompanied by a development in the expressionist characteristics of the world through which he moves. As with Radcliffe's heroines, it is pointless to ask of Caleb how he *might* behave; the world in which he increasingly finds himself is not properly amenable to the laws of probability, according to which escape could hardly be so difficult. What is certain is that there is, for the *reader*, no escape from the nightmare which is *Caleb Williams;* and what is remarkable in Godwin is that he manages to achieve this sense of claustrophobia and paralysing doubt precisely by leading us only gradually from an initial situation which reminds us more of Fielding than of the Gothics.

If we are to look for a way in which *Caleb Williams* relates to Godwin's other interests, it is not through any kind of rationalism but more in terms of Freud's statement, in *Totem and Taboo*, that a paranoiac delusion is a caricature of a philosophic system,[4] but it is important to remember that to use the concept of paranoia in this Freudian sense is not to refer to a small and special class of aberrants, but rather to a very basic mental orientation. Caleb's sufferings are in no way purgative; they improve neither his character nor his morals – nor his health. In one sense, *Caleb Williams* can be seen as the apotheosis of the eighteenth-century novel of justice versus the law, as in Fielding, Smollett and others; but what makes it very different is the intentness with which Godwin pursues his protagonist, the inevitability which sweeps him from degradation to degradation, the utter lack of irony which is Godwin's paradoxical strength. *Caleb Williams* is a kind of caricature, a Punch and Judy show of tyranny; but it is also a powerful statement about the way in which social persecution produces and nourishes its own victims.

To move from Godwin to Maturin is to exchange devilry's lay avatars for the demoniac in person, and to move away from a present world seen through a distorting lens into a dizzying maze of interlocking legends and religous motifs. The strand which appears to link his Irish novels, his Gothic plays, his sermons and *Melmoth* itself is an anticlericalism, surprising in a priest, which makes Lewis look playful. *Melmoth* is to a large extent recognisable in its immediate ancestry: Schiller, Radcliffe, Lewis and twenty intervening years during which so many old and evil folk-tales had been recaptured and set once again in motion. Maturin even lifts names from *The Italian* and from Lewis's *Alfonso,* and throws off casual references to vampires and the Black Mass with an aplomb which was not lost even on *Blackwood's:* Maturin is gifted, they said, 'with a genius as fervently powerful as it is distinctly original', and 'walks almost without a rival, whether dead or living, in many of the darkest, but, at the same time, the most majestic, circles of romance'.[5] *Melmoth* was a vastly influential book, although it was overtaken eventually by the decline in those reading habits which sustain works of such length and complexity; Balzac, Baudelaire, Poe and Robert Louis Stevenson all bear the marks of *Melmoth,* and Scott was willing to testify to Maturin's power,[6] but now it seems to look too capacious, too encyclopaedic a record of the obsessions of an age, to be given the attention it deserves. There is a comment Maturin himself makes in the course of it, that 'there are some *criminals of the imagination,* whom, if we could plunge into the "oubliettes" of its magnificent but lightly-based fabric, its lord would reign more happy'.[7] He is referring to particular psychological obsessions, ghosts which it is difficult to lay, but the phrase sounds well as a description of *Melmoth* itself and of its protagonist, who comes nearer than any other romantic hero/villain to summing up in his awesome person the multifarious qualities which go to make up the archetype of the cursed outcast.

Varma says that Maturin 'has a much deeper, clearer, and more organised vision of the place of evil and horror in the world than his predecessors' (Varma, p. 166), and this is crucial: *Melmoth,* despite its size and its extraordinary narrative structure, is a highly organised work, and to understand it requires the uncovering of that heavily encrusted principle of organisation which sustains its rococo decoration. To recount 'the story' is not easy; however, one can at least pick out the general lines. Young Melmoth, attending at the decease of an aged relative in Ireland, inherits a manuscript. With the unwisdom conventional in the genre, he proceeds to read it (in inauspicious weather conditions) and finds that it relates the tale of one Stanton and his encounters with a mysterious figure who, first, promises Stanton that he will encounter much misfortune, culminating in a spell in a madhouse, and then, when this prophecy is fulfilled, appears to him in his adversity offering to give him his freedom in exchange for . . . a certain gift. This figure is identified as a relative of young Melmoth's who ought by rights to have been dead long before. While he is wondering at this manuscript, a shipwreck brings to his door a Spaniard called Monçada, who tells him his own story, which is even more horrific, and which involves the Wanderer in a similar capacity.

At this point, the book has barely started; the stories come thick and fast, most of them now related by Monçada to young Melmoth. They are set across 150 years, and range through Europe to the Indian Ocean. Most of them are highly coloured and grim with death and horror, although one or two minor tales are tedious in the extreme. It is all grist to Maturin's mill; almost at the end of the book, Monçada shows signs of starting all over again, with a second series, as it were. In all the tales the Wanderer figures; in all of them he is a figure of superhuman powers who appears at moments of the most profound despair, making his devilish offer. Maturin remains gentlemanly to the end in not revealing the Wanderer's terms, although it is perfectly clear from the first encounter that he is a seeker of souls, and it is reasonably assumed that we will be familiar with the story of the Wandering Jew. Finally the Wanderer himself appears to his relative, announcing that his quest has failed and that he has come home to await the end; the end consisting in his being dragged away by demons, initially into the sea, but, we presume, thence into the flames which he has failed to avoid.

Thus summarised, the book sounds confused and derivative; but Maturin shares with his predecessors the ability to bring ancient sources to life in a remarkable way. One of the unexpected things about *Melmoth* is that it is extremely witty. The Spanish sections owe a great deal to Cervantes, and Melmoth himself, when he appears at any length, is a kind of cosmic satirist. One of his victims is a nature-child called Immalee, and she at one point entreats him not, at a time of extreme danger, to manifest 'sophistry or levity', or 'that wild and withering eloquence that flashes from your lips, not to enlighten but to blast' (*Melmoth*, p. 514).

We can best see the flavour of Maturin's supremely self-conscious wit in the transactions between Melmoth and a Spanish merchant called Don Aliaga. Aliaga, on a journey home, encounters the mysterious stranger at a tavern, who tells him the lengthy and conventionally Gothic 'Tale of Guzman's Family'. When the tale finishes, we discover that in fact Aliaga, a practical man, has been asleep for some time and is not in the least interested in the tale. The stranger, in no way piqued by this, proceeds to offer another tale, to which Aliaga hastily responds, 'my curiosity has been completely satisfied by the narrative I have already listened to' (*Melmoth*, p. 437), and makes to leave. The stranger, not to be shaken off, promises that they will meet again, overtakes him on the road and subjects him to another, much less interesting story called 'The Lover's Tale' which is set in England, a country about which Aliaga knows nothing at all. When this tale ends, Aliaga finds himself in a state of resentful wonderment:

> 'It is inconceivable to me', said Don Aliaga to himself, as he pursued his journey the next day – 'it is inconceivable to me how this person forces himself on my company, harasses me with tales that have no more application to me than the legend of the Cid, and may be as apocryphal as the ballad of Roncesvalles . . .' (*Melmoth*, p. 502)

But the world of *Melmoth* is one in which one does not reject stories so lightly: the Wanderer – for it is of course he – proceeds, with surprising terseness, to tell Aliaga the story towards which all this has been tending, that of the misfortunes which are, back at home, besetting *him*. Aliagia, however, showing remarkable resistance, takes not the slightest notice and is duly punished.

It is partly through the lips of Melmoth the satirist that Maturin passes his commentary on religion, and this causes problems. To Melmoth, all religions are equally delusory; the only reality behind religion is divine vengeance. Maturin's position is clearly against Catholicism in particular and all its works, but time and time again particular characters go beyond what is necessary to defend this position. At one point, a dying and very evil monk offers a neat summary of his views on the falsity of religious belief:

> All saints, from Mahomet down to Francis Zavier, were only a compound of insanity, pride, and self-imposition; – the latter would have been of less consequence, but that men always revenge their impositions on themselves, by imposing to the utmost on others. (*Melmoth*, p. 115)

This speech is undercut by Maturin's implications about the nature of the speaker, but the response from Monçada, who is by no means an evil character, is to comment that 'there is no more horrible state of mind than that in which we are forced by conviction to listen on, wishing every word to be false, and knowing every word to be true'. Certainly the overall impression derived from the book is that Maturin vastly exceeds his brief against the Catholic Church, and brings most of the edifice of religion down on his head.

Like *Caleb Williams, Melmoth* is a book in which sheer intensity and savagery of feeling – antityrannical feeling – overwhelms fine doctrinal discrimination. Maturin's power of discrimination is elsewhere: he is at his most masterful in his depiction of the complexity, and often the paradoxicality, of extreme emotional states – generally, of course, states of extreme terror and despair. Examples are legion. Monçada is tortured at one point by monks who, in order to break his resistance to taking the vows, enter into a communal pretence that he is mad, and affect to be frightened of him:

> The terror that I inspired I at last began to feel. I began to believe myself – I know not what, whatever they thought me. This is a dreadful state of mind, but one impossible to avoid. In some circumstances, where the whole world is against us, we begin to take its part against ourselves, to avoid the withering sensation of being alone on our own side. (*Melmoth*, p. 158)

He attempts to escape with a companion, and is thwarted at the last moment when their light expires: 'we lay', he says,

> not daring to speak to each other, for who could speak but of despair, and which of us dared to aggravate the despair of the other. This kind of fear which we know already felt by others, and which we dread to aggravate by uttering, *even to those who know it*, is perhaps the most horrible sensation ever experienced. The very thirst of my body seemed to vanish in this fiery thirst of the soul for communication, where all communication was unutterable, impossible, hopeless. (*Melmoth*, p. 195)

Again, Monçada receives the confession of a dying monk that his life has been wasted on hypocrisy: in the monk's words, Monçada says,

> I could not help recognising that *simplicity of profound corruption*, – that frightful paralysis of the soul, which leaves it incapable of receiving any impression or making one, – that says to the accuser, Approach, remonstrate, upbraid – I defy you. My conscience is dead, and can neither hear, utter, or echo a reproach. (*Melmoth*, pp. 111–12)

In each of these cases, Maturin takes a psychological commonplace

– the terror of being regarded as mad, the longing for communication in moments of stress, the simplicity and honesty of the deathbed confession – and turns the screw one notch further. It is also usually Maturin's practice at these points to generalise, to seek to involve us in the situation of his characters by depicting their torments and reversals as those of humanity at large. He is at his best, perhaps, on the fear of insanity. There is a passage when Stanton is in the madhouse which is worth quoting at some length. The Wanderer arrives to tempt him, and says:

> Stanton, do you imagine your reason can possibly hold out amid such scenes? – Supposing your reason was unimpaired, your health not destroyed . . . A time will come, and soon, when, from mere habit, you will echo the scream of every delirious wretch that harbours near you; then you will pause, clasp your hands on your throbbing head, and listen with horrible anxiety whether the scream proceeded from *you* or *them*. The time will come, when, from the want of occupation, the listless and horrible vacancy of your hours, you will feel as anxious to hear those shrieks, as you were at first terrified to hear them, – when you will watch for the ravings of your next neighbour, as you would for a scene on the stage. All humanity will be extinguished in you. The ravings of these wretches will become at once your sport and your torture. You will watch for the sounds, to mock them with the grimaces and bellowings of a fiend. The mind has a power of accommodating itself to its situation, that you will experience in its most frightful and deplorable efficacy. Then comes the dreadful doubt of one's own sanity, the terrible announcer that *that* doubt will soon become fear, and *that* fear certainty. Perhaps (still more dreadful) the *fear* will at last become a *hope* . . .   (*Melmoth*, p. 56)

And Melmoth goes on to develop the possibilities at much greater length. This is typical of the speeches of temptation which form the culmination of each story; and the terrors depicted in them show a luxuriant variety which fully justifies Maturin's claims as a practitioner of psychopathological taxonomy. 'The heartless and unimaginative are those alone who entitle themselves to the comforts of life, and who can alone enjoy them', says Melmoth; 'beyond that, all is the dream of insanity, or the agony of disappointment' (*Melmoth*, p. 476).

Melmoth the Wanderer, like *Caleb Williams*, is a paranoiac text, in which malevolence becomes its own justification. The world is not purged by the death of Melmoth, as it is by the death of Lewis's Ambrosio or of Radcliffe's Schedoni, because Melmoth is not a *principal* of evil but an agent of the perennial evil of others. His absence will in no way affect the existence of the 'enormous engine' of persecution which Monçada describes (*Melmoth*, p. 91), and which beats at its strongest in those secret places of the soul, those 'monasteries' characterised by the midnight search and the carefully placed interrogation lamp. If you die a heretic, says Melmoth in a phrase strikingly similar to lines in Poe, 'all your relations in their gala robes would shout their hallelujahs to your dying screams of torture' (*Melmoth*, p. 344).

Melmoth has his own moments of sadism, and they are breathtakingly depicted. About to consummate his demon-marriage to Immalee, he exults in the evil which will result:

> Perish to all the world, perhaps beyond the period of its existence, but live to me in darkness and in corruption! Preserve all the exquisite modulation of your forms! all the indestructible brilliancy of your colouring! – but preserve it for me alone! – me, the single, pulseless, eyeless, heartless embracer of an unfertile bride, – the brooder over the dark and unproductive nest of eternal sterility, – the mountain whose lava of internal fire has stifled, and indurated, and inclosed for ever, all that was the joy of earth, the felicity of life, and the hope of futurity! (*Melmoth*, p. 354)

But these are mere words; Melmoth is powerless to harm Immalee unless she acquiesces. Meanwhile, the horror of the world goes on: the consigning of the innocent to the madhouse, the hideous lynching of the parricide, the behaviour of the 'amateur in suffering', the gentleman who makes a point of being present at every execution to savour the screams of the dying (*Melmoth*, p. 147), these incidents owe nothing to Melmoth; he merely exults in them, and offers a way of escape which is consignment to worse torture hereafter.

We said that the world of *Caleb Williams* becomes progressively nightmarish, and the same is true of *Melmoth*. Maturin describes various dreams during the course of the book, and by the time we reach the scene of Immalee's marriage to the Wanderer the world has become a thing of shadow. The scene is worth quoting in full (Immalee's name, on her return to civilisation from the Indian isle where she was brought up, has been changed to Isidora):

> At that moment the moon, that had so faintly lit the chapel, sunk behind a cloud, and every thing was enveloped in darkness so profound, that Isidora did not recognise the figure of Melmoth till her hand was clasped in his, and his voice whispered, 'He is here – ready to unite us.' The long-protracted terrors of this bridal left her not a breath to utter a word withal, and she leaned on his arm that she felt, not in confidence, but for support. The place, the hour, the objects, all were hid in darkness. She heard a faint rustling as of the approach of another person, – she tried to catch certain words, but she knew not what they were, – she attempted also to speak, but she knew not what

she said. All was mist and darkness with her, – she knew not what was muttered, – she felt not that the hand of Melmoth grasped hers, – but she felt that the hand that united them, and clasped their palms within his own, was as *cold as that of death*. *(Melmoth*, p. 394)

From this point on, the plight of Isidora becomes less and less clear, as if she is being wafted away from the world. At one point we find her pregnant with Melmoth's child on the day assigned for her wedding to another man. And this tendency towards dream is confirmed right at the end of the book when the Wanderer, having returned to Ireland, spends his last moments on earth dreaming of the terrors to come. There is, indeed, a crucial comment which Isidora, at this time in the dungeons of the Inquisition for her association with the Wanderer, makes on her death-bed. She claims to have been visited by him the previous night, and her confessor suggests that this must have been a dream. 'My father, I have had many dreams', answers Isidora, 'many – many wanderings, but this was no dream' (*Melmoth*, p. 532). At this moment, 'dream' and 'wandering' become the same word, and the being of the Wanderer fades into the chimerical world of the unconscious, from when perhaps he came. In *Eros and Civilisation*, Herbert Marcuse, summarising Freud's theory of the return of the repressed, says that 'the memory of prehistoric impulses and deeds continues to haunt civilisation: the repressed material returns, and the individual is still punished for impulses long since mastered and deeds long since undone'.[8] This, surely, is the microcosmic form of the world which Maturin displays in macrocosm: a world in which suffering is in no way proportionate to guilt, in which no amount of civilised behaviour can prevent the breaking-out of those forces which still haunt the mind of the individual and the mind of the culture.

Caleb Williams and *Melmoth* both display forms of tyranny: the tyranny of social classing and the conventional injustice of authority, and the tyranny of dogmatism and inhumane religion. Alongside these wide-ranging themes, the material from which Hogg's *Confessions of a Justified Sinner* is forged is liable to seem a little parochial, since the particular tyranny which most exercises Hogg is the evil produced by antinomianism, the extreme Calvinist doctrine that those who are Elect, 'saved by God', will remain so regardless of their works on earth. But this is only the starting-point of the *Confessions;* for on this basis Hogg produces a detailed and terrifying account of schizophrenia, tracing it through its stages of development with considerable psychological skill. One aspect of the book relates closely to folklore; the inset tale of the notorious 'Auchtermuchty preachment' reminds one of Scott, and also of Stevenson's later Scottish tales, and Hogg is at his descriptive best on local superstitions and customs. On the other side, Hogg appears to have owed a debt to more obviously Gothic writers, like Hoffmann, whose *Die Elixiere des Teufels* was translated just before the writing of the *Confessions*, and Maturin, whom he resembles in his interlocking of different accounts to build up narrative ambiguity.

Walter Allen claims that the *Confessions* contains the most convincing representation of the power of evil in the literature,[9] and there is a sense of *proximity* in the narrative, a sense of the closeness of the events to the reader, which goes to support this judgement. The book consists of two major parts: the so-called 'Editor's Narrative', and the 'Confessions' proper. The editor's narrative recounts the story of the Colwan family. The old Laird marries, late in life, a younger woman who is a strict Calvinist, much under the influence of a 'fire and brimstone' preacher named Wringhim. The couple are rapidly estranged, but she bears the Laird two sons. The elder, George, is acknowledged and brought up as heir to the estates. The younger, however, the Laird does not acknowledge: his wife brings him up with the assistance of Wringhim, who bestows on him his own name. The younger Wringhim begins to 'haunt' his brother, claiming to regard him as one of the 'Reprobate', and using every means to taunt and provoke him. Shortly after George finally retaliates, albeit mildly, he is found dead under mysterious circumstances. Wringhim, who is associating with a mysterious friend who appears to have shape-changing powers, succeeds to the estates of Dalcastle, whereupon his behaviour becomes even more reprehensible. The authorities are persuaded of the possibility that he murdered his brother, but a search for him fails; he has disappeared.

Then follow the Confessions proper, which are the account of the same, and other, events written by Wringhim himself. He tells how he was brought up by the elder Wringhim to regard himself as one of the Elect, and how he meets his mysterious friend, who asks to be known as Gil-Martin. By dint of various sophistries, Gil-Martin persuades Wringhim that his work on earth is to purge it of the Reprobate, and provokes him into murdering a recalcitrant preacher. He then aids and abets him in his harassment of his brother, and eventually in his murder. All the time, Wringhim persuades himself that his friend is a benefactor, and that he is helping him to perform the work of the Lord. When he has succeeded to the lairdship, however, he begins to suffer from memory lapses and other curious symptoms, and his life becomes progressively nightmarish. He also begins to be beset by demons; Gil-Martin claims that only through his protection can they be held at bay. Wringhim is forced to flee Dalcastle on being accused of murder, rape and other crimes, and roams the country in the utmost misery, pursued by the demons and, since his presence anywhere leads to supernatural disturbance, unable ever to stay in one place. He eventually succumbs to the temptation of suicide, which Gil-Martin claims, again, will be forgiven him because he is of the Elect.

The relationship between the two accounts is not simple. Clearly Wringhim's story is unreliable, and it remains doubtful to what extent Gil-Martin really 'appears' or is a figment of his imagination. The editor's account appears more objective, but even this seems not to be Hogg's voice. Hogg is trying to draw a line between an acceptable and an unacceptable form of Calvinism; but over against Wringhim's antinomianism, he places an 'editor' who is very little impressed by religion at all. Early in the editor's narrative, the old Laird rebukes Wringhim senior – 'in short, Sir, you are a mildew, – a canker-worm in the bosom of the Reformed Church, generating a disease of which she will never be purged, but by the shedding of blood'[10] – but the Laird himself seems to regard religion as merely a matter of form. Hogg's opinion, however, comes out when he says that the tenets of the young Lady Dalcastle 'were not the tenets of the great reformers, but theirs mightily overstrained and deformed' (*Confessions*, p. 2); and this emphasis on the *eventual* tendencies of Calvinist doctrines, when taken to extremes, runs through the book. When Wringhim first meets Gil-Martin, they conduct theological discussions: 'in every thing that I suggested', says Wringhim, 'he acquiesced, and, as I thought that day, often carried them to extremes, so that I had a secret dread he was advancing blasphemies' (*Confessions*, p. 118). But he fails to act upon this doubt; and since he remains convinced of the angelic purposes of Gil-Martin, his perception of the world is correspondingly distorted.

Hogg's witty portrayal of Wringhim's self-righteousness comes out in the latter's account of an incident when he is harassing George by getting in his way during a tennis match. The 'editor' has already told the story in a way which suggests that Wringhim was acting out of pure malice, but Wringhim claims that he was 'fired with indignation' at seeing his brother engaging in 'ungodly' sports – fired to the point of blows:

> Yes, I went boldly up and struck him with my foot, and ·meant to have given him a more severe blow than it was my fortune to inflict. It had, however, the effect of rousing up his corrupt nature to quarrelling

and strife, instead of taking the chastisement of the Lord in humility and meekness. He ran furiously against me in the choler that is always inspired by the wicked one; but I overthrew him, by reason of impeding the natural and rapid progress of his unholy feet, running to destruction.   (*Confessions*, pp. 148–9)

Needless to say, this is a reversal of the earlier account, according to which, George, trying to reach a ball, fell over Wringhim, Wringhim aimed a vicious kick at him, and George hit him lightly with his racket.

In effect, the book is the story of a dual persecution; in the first narrative the persecution of George by Wringhim, in the second Wringhim's persecution by Gil-Martin. George is bewildered by Wringhim's ability – which he owes. of course, to Gil-Martin – to pursue him with supernatural accuracy; he becomes 'utterly confounded; not only at the import of this persecution, but how in the world it came to pass that this unaccountable being knew all his motions, and every intention of his heart, as it were intuitively' (*Confessions*, p. 36). Indeed, 'the attendance of that brother was now become like the attendance of a demon on some devoted being that had sold himself to destruction' (*Confessions*, p. 37), and Wringhim comes to seem a demon to George in much the same way as Wringhim himself becomes demon-haunted.

His fate, however, is much the worse; George is merely murdered, but Wringhim suffers the graphically described tortures of the damned on earth. From being a friend, Gil-Martin becomes an inescapable and implacable pursuer. Wringhim is left with no choices: on one occasion, when he is thrown out of a house during the night because of the unaccountable noises which always accompany him, he says:

> I was momentarily surrounded by a number of hideous fiends, who gnashed on me with their teeth, and clenched their crimson paws in my face; and at the same instant I was seized by the collar of my coat behind, by my dreaded and devoted [*sic*] friend, who pushed me on, and, with his gilded rapier waving and brandishing around me, defended me against all their united attacks. Horrible as my assailants were in appearance, (and they had all monstrous shapes), I felt that I would rather have fallen into their hands, than be thus led away captive by my defender at his will and pleasure. . . .
>
> (*Confessions*, p. 233)

Gil-Martin has already grimly underlined the fact that Wringhim, having encouraged him, can now never escape:

> I am wedded to you so closely, that I feel as if I were the same person.

> Our essences are one, our bodies and spirits being united, so, that I
> am drawn towards you by magnetism, and wherever you are, there
> must my presence be with you.   (*Confessions*, p. 229)

And this, of course, raises the central ambivalence of the *Confessions*, as to the objective existence of Gil-Martin. This is a question
which Hogg does not answer. Others see Gil-Martin, in various
guises; but equally, Wringhim is clearly progressively subject to a
religious mania with close affinities to recognisable forms of schizophrenia. From the outset, he shows megalomaniac tendencies – 'I
was born an outcast in the world, in which I was destined to act so
conspicuous a part' (*Confessions*, p. 97) – and throughout his narrative he sees his life as a testimony to the glory of God:

> I come now to the most important period of my existence, – the period
> that has modelled my character, and influenced every action of my
> life, – without which, this detail of my actions would have been as a
> tale that hath been told – a monotonous 'farrago' – an uninteresting
> harangue – in short, a thing of nothing. Whereas, lo! it must now be
> a relation of great and terrible actions, done in the might, and by
> the commission of heaven. Amen.   (*Confessions*, p. 114)

Wringhim's religion teaches him to despise the 'things of this world':
'in particular, I brought myself to despise, if not to abhor, the beauty
of women' (*Confessions*, p. 113). Later, he begins to find it impossible
to hold himself together as an individual, and begins to suspect the
true meaning of his inseparability from Gil-Martin, his 'companion':

> When I lay in bed, I deemed there were two of us in it; when I sat up,
> I always beheld another person, and always in the same position from
> the place where I sat or stood, which was about three paces off me
> towards my left side. It mattered not how many or how few were
> present: this my second self was sure to be present in his place . . . The
> most perverse part of it was, that I rarely conceived *myself* to be any
> of the two persons. I thought for the most part that my companion
> was one of them, and my brother the other; and I found, that to be
> obliged to speak and answer in the character of another man, was a
> most awkward business at the long run.   (*Confessions*, p. 154)

It is shortly after this splitting of the personality that his memory
lapses begin, and he finds himself 'in the habit of executing transactions of the utmost moment, without being sensible that I did
them' (*Confessions*, p. 182). He loses whole months, and eventually
reaches a pitch of terror:

> Thus was I sojourning in the midst of a chaos of confusion. I looked
> back on my bypast life with pain, as one looks back on a perilous
> journey, in which he has attained his end, without gaining any
> advantage either to himself, or others; and I looked forward, as on a

darksome waste, full of repulsive and terrific shapes, pitfalls, and precipices, to which there was no definite bourne, and from which I turned with disgust.   (*Confessions*, p. 183)

Hogg's resolution of the various interpretations which might be placed on the book is left in the hands of the 'editor', but his is clearly not meant to be the last word. Instead, he expresses a careless scepticism which is clearly ironic:

in this day, and with the present generation, it will not go down, that a man should be daily tempted by the devil, in the semblance of a fellow-creature; and at length lured to self-destruction, in the hopes that this same fiend and tormentor was to suffer and fall along with him. . . . In short, we must either conceive him not only the greatest fool, but the greatest wretch, on whom was ever stamped the form of humanity; or, that he was a religious maniac, who wrote and wrote about a deluded creature, till he arrived at that height of madness, that he believed himself the very object whom he had been all along describing. And in order to escape from an ideal tormentor, committed that act for which, according to the tenets he embraced, there was no remission, and which consigned his memory and his name to everlasting detestation.   (*Confessions*, pp. 254–5)

In three crucial respects, *Caleb Williams*, *Melmoth* and the *Confessions* are similar, and these similarities are in areas which have to do with the concerns of the Gothic as exemplified by Radcliffe and Lewis. In the first place, the three novels are psychological investigations. Varma claims that 'by portraying mental states and emotions of characters,' the Gothic novelists 'enlarged the scope of the novel, and by sounding the whole gamut of fear, pointed towards the psychological novel of over a century later' (Varma, p. 215). This is characteristically overstated, but it is true that these books are deeply concerned with the nature of fear: so concerned, indeed, that they dispense with many other matters. The *Confessions*, like *Caleb Williams*, is devoid of a love-plot. *Melmoth* and the *Confessions* dispense with that central novelistic convention, identification with a single major protagonist, the *Confessions* by both breaking up the narrative form and ensuring the reader's alienation from the chief figure, Wringhim, and *Melmoth* by placing the protagonist both in the wings of much of the narrative and also on so superhuman a plane that the possibility of identification is made to appear virtually sacrilegious. None of the novels has a redemptive ending: Melmoth and Wringhim end in flames, while Caleb we presume to be proceeding to mortal agonies as bad as anything he has experienced in the course of the book. Smollett's Introduction to *Ferdinand Count Fathom,* from which we have already quoted, contained the following passage:

> The impulses of fear which is the most violent and interesting of all the passions, remain longer than any other upon the memory; and for one that is allured to virtue, by the contemplation of that peace and happiness which it bestows, an hundred are deterred from the practice of vice, by that infamy and punishment to which it is liable, from the laws and regulations of mankind. (*Fathom*, p. 3)

This sounded fairly specious, we can be sure, when Smollett wrote it; but the relation of even this residual moral tone to any of these three novels is tenuous in the extreme. In the case of *Caleb Williams,* Caleb has not manifested any particular vice to which we can ascribe his punishment, except the surely venial one of curiosity; while Falkland, who *might* be considered a vicious character (although this is far from clear) presumably clears his soul by his death-bed repentance. In *Melmoth,* evil consequences appear to flow without differentiation from vice *and* virtue; besides, even if we deemed ourselves instructed by any of the inset tales, we can gather little of moral use from Melmoth's own, supremely important fate, since his situation bears so little relation to that of the reader. And in the *Confessions,* although Wringhim is punished, and harshly, it is difficult to feel by the end of the book that he has been fully to blame for his misfortunes, since Hogg has taken such pains to demonstrate that he is, in any reasonable definition of the term, insane. Godwin's novel was written some thirty years before the other two, yet it is bound to them by a particular kind of modernity, that kind of modernity which takes very seriously the problems of social and psychological conditioning, and which therefore questions the supremacy of the realm of the 'moral'. We feel in all three novels that the scope for decisive interplay between characters is very limited, that there are larger, more objective, more inexorable factors which propel the characters along destined lines. And yet this feature is ambivalent: although it bears a relation to more modern intellectual developments, it also bears a relation back to myth and legend, but what it does in both these guises is step well outside the individualism of mainstream eighteenth-century fiction. We are, of course, concerned with what Caleb, Melmoth, Wringhim, do next at any given time; but we are, I believe, very doubtful as to whether this will make very much eventual difference to the working-out of their fates. The characters are caught, stuck like flies in amber, while the authors carefully dissect them, laying bare their obsessions and motivations.

The second point is rather different, and it concerns the formal nature of the texts themselves. Questions present themselves in all three cases. Why did Godwin adopt his unusual method of writing 'from the end'? Why does *Melmoth* emerge as a montage of oddly linked narratives? Why – and reviewers rather bitterly asked this at the time – did Hogg tell us his story twice? It would be dangerous to claim that there is a single answer to these three questions, but there are nonetheless connections, ones which also have a relevance to the narrative complexities of *Frankenstein*. In the broadest sense, all three writers were aware that they were not writing 'realist' novels; perhaps another way of putting that would be to say that they knew it was going to be difficult to persuade their readers that the world was 'really' like this. The mildest example of this is Godwin, who decided that extremely careful planning might serve as a suitable device for 'verifying' his text, for making readers feel an involvement which is different from that which we feel in a work of fantasy. The case is parallel to that of various later writers who seek to obviate the improbability of horror and detective stories by assuming a quietly reasonable tone designed to make us forget our disbelief.[11] We have only, I think, to put Godwin alongside a writer like Fielding to see the way in which the world he portrays is 'unreal': it has insufficient richness and variety, it is overintent, it is too *concentrated* – and it is also too laden with the apparatus of heroic flight and pursuit. Hogg is in an even more difficult position. How is a reader to be made to 'take seriously' a story in which the devil in person attaches himself for a considerable period of time to one fairly insignificant character? Hogg's answer, more radical though similar in kind to Mary Shelley's, is to verify his subtexts against each other. The doubts which we may feel about Wringhim's account are supposed to be allayed by the worldly-wise tone of the 'editor', and the appearance of Hogg himself near the end serves further to insert the text into a 'real' context. The most severe problem, of course, was Maturin's, and consequently his attempt at a solution is the most complex. The form of *Melmoth* appears to be this: a narrative is begun which appears to be highly improbable. Before it ends, another narrative begins which offers 'separate' corroboration of the first. And before that ends . . . No single character in *Melmoth* claims to be in absolute possession of the truth; no single subtext claims authority independently of the others. Maturin simply piles on the evidence, selecting his fields as widely as possible, so that the audience is brought gradually nearer and nearer to a kind of circumscribed credence necessary for continued interest.

The third point is related to this. I have referred throughout the chapter to the motif of persecution, and it is beginning to be clear that the depiction of persecution – social, religious, psychological – is a primary motif of the Gothic. But what is significant in these three books is that they are all told by narrators – Melmoth's intended victims, Caleb Williams, Wringhim (although he, of course, only tells half a story) – who are *themselves persecuted.* In this sense, it seems fair to refer to the three texts as paranoiac texts, for it is very difficult to know where the reader is situated in an encounter with a story of persecution told by the persecuted. The three persecuting figures are Falkland, Melmoth and Gil-Martin. According to their victims, they all possess virtually supernatural powers of pursuit. If you went into a police station with any of these stories, you would not be believed, and this is partly the point. Godwin, Maturin and Hogg all force us into reacting ambivalently. Yes, we say, Caleb is certainly unfortunate – but is Falkland really as malevolent and as powerful as that? What are the limits, if any, on the powers of Melmoth? Is Gil-Martin the devil?

Or, of course – and this is a somewhat rhetorical question – do the persecuting figures represent something more complicated? Are they powers conjured up, or at least encouraged, by their victims themselves? In other words, the problem with texts like these is that they open up the possibility that the narrator is himself paranoid, and this again seems to be a Gothic tendency. The Gothic is laced with conspiracies, many of which – like those of *Udolpho* – turn out to be rather less vicious than they appear at the time. But in these three books, nothing 'turns out' at all. We are left with our doubts, and it is this continual suspension which keeps us engaged.

These three elements – the shift towards the psychological, the increasing complexity of verification, the emphasis on the ambivalence of persecution – are all ones which we have come across before in Radcliffe and Lewis, and they establish certain parameters of the Gothic. However, what is also noticeable in Godwin, Maturin and Hogg is that one crucial element, that of historical interest, seems to have disappeared. In the next group of Gothic writers, however, it returns decisively although in an altered form, and we need now to return to the question of what these psychological and formal parameters of the Gothic have to do with the Gothic recapture of history.

Notes and references

1. **Francis Lathom,** *The Midnight Bell* (London, 1968), p. 145.
2. The most important comparisons are with **Robert Bage,** *Hermsprong, or, Man as he is not* (1796); **Thomas Holcroft,** *Anna St. Ives* (1792) and *The Adventures of Hugh Trevor* (1794–7).
3. **William Godwin,** *The Adventures of Caleb Williams, or, Things as They Are,* ed. Herbert von Thal, introd. Walter Allen (London, 1966), p. xv (Introduction). All subsequent references are to *CW.*
4. See *Works,* XIII, 73.
5. '*Melmoth the Wanderer,* etc.' (anon. rev.), *Blackwood's Edinburgh Magazine,* VIII (Nov. 1820), 161.
6. See *On Novelists and Fiction,* pp. 204–13, 273–97; also *The Correspondence of Sir Walter Scott and Charles Robert Maturin,* ed. F. E. Ratchford and W. H. McCarthy, Jr (Austin, Texas, 1937), pp. 7–8, 56–7, 101, etc.
7. **C. R. Maturin,** *Melmoth the Wanderer: A Tale,* ed. Douglas Grant (London, 1968), p. 250.
8. **Herbert Marcuse,** *Eros and Civilisation* (London, 1969), p. 62.
9. See **Walter Allen,** *The English Novel: A Short Critical History* (London, 1954), pp. 124–5.
10. **James Hogg,** *The Private Memoirs and Confessions of a Justified Sinner,* ed. John Carey (London, 1970), p. 15.
11. See below, pp. 315–29.

CHAPTER 6

Gothic, history and the middle classes

Scott, Bulwer Lytton, G. P. R. James, William Harrison Ainsworth,
G. W. M. Reynolds

The historical novel in the early nineteenth century was dominated by one great figure: Scott. Whereas before him historical fiction had proceeded on a parallel course with Gothic, or intertwined with it, Scott's novels mark a radical break in the process of mythologisation which characterises his predecessors. On the other hand, the new dimension of realism which Scott introduced into historical fiction did not produce the general change in approach which has some-times been assumed; when we look at the generation of popular writers of the 1830s and 1840s, we find instead certain elements of Scott's technique mixed again with older Gothic habits.

Scott was himself, of course, by no means free from Gothic influence. As a collector of folk-legends and ballads, he was in direct line of descent from the antiquarians of the eighteenth century. He contributed to Lewis's collection of ballads, *Tales of Wonder* (1801), and also wrote two heavily Gothic plays, *House of Aspen* (1799) and *Doom of Devorgoil* (1817). He wrote three tales of terror which are still regarded as models of the genre, 'The Tale of the Mysterious Mirror', 'The Tapestried Chamber' (both 1828) and the disturbing 'Wandering Willie's Tale' in *Redgauntlet* (1824). He also planned a longer Gothic work on the subject of Thomas the Rhymer; it was never completed, but the surviving fragment closely resembles the examples of the terrifying produced much earlier by Anna Laetitia Barbauld and Nathan Drake.[1]

There is, in fact, a curious paradox in Scott's relation to historical fiction: on the one hand, his industry and zeal, his sheer bulk of knowledge, his portrayal of whole panoramas of the past rather than merely of the aristocracy gave the historical novel a basis in the real which it had never before had, while on the other an intense and continuing interest in legendry and the supernatural provides a constant accompaniment to his version of the past. The two things are far from mutually exclusive: the point is that instead of mythologising *about* the past Scott tries to endow with new vitality the actual myths *of* the past, the beliefs by which our ancestors lived. If this makes occasionally for a certain confusion, this is hardly surprising, for as soon as one begins to probe those myths one realises the difficulty of assessing the belief structures of past ages. People in the seventeenth century may be said glibly to have believed in ghosts, but that is only the beginning of the problem: how did they believe in them, and as what?

His *Letters on Demonology and Witchcraft* (1830), which address themselves to this question, are also a compendium of themes and images utilised by the Gothic writers. The ostensible purpose of the book is to demonstrate the vicious contradictions underlying the witch-persecutions of the seventeenth century; Scott had, quite rightly, no doubts that accusations of witchcraft were important largely as devices for settling personal quarrels and for victimisation of the socially unwanted; a better and more cruel way of getting rid of the old and unproductive has perhaps never been devised. But in the course of prosecuting this argument, Scott also accedes to that demand for the supernatural which had been awakened by Percy, Macpherson and the antiquarians. In the *Letters* are collected together the strange account of supernatural events in the apocryphal Book of Tobit; the early vampire tale of Asmund and Assueit from Saxo Grammaticus; the extraordinary story of the living idol of the goddess Freya which, Scott points out, 'resembled in form the giant created by Frankenstein'; the story of 'the apparition of the Brocken mountain' which is identical to the gigantic apparition in Hogg's *Confessions*; and even a reference to lycanthropy.[2] Several passages, particularly the material on Indian religions, remind one strongly of parts of *Melmoth the Wanderer*; and to complete the list of Gothic obsessions, Scott inserts a partial history of the Inquisition, which was becoming a favourite topic among less scrupulous 'historians'.

But the tales and the *Letters* were minor work; it is obviously to the novels that one has to look to see the impact of Scott's relation to the Gothic. Birkhead claims that *The Bride of Lammermoor* (1819) is 'the only one of Scott's novels which might fitly be called a "tale of terror" ' (Birkhead, p. 153), and it is worth examining this claim for a moment. The plot of *Lammermoor*, certainly, is melodramatic. Edgar, the young Master of Ravenswood, representative of an ancient and noble Scottish family, succeeds to a heritage vastly impoverished by political troubles and the legalistic activities of the more influential upstart Whig lawyer, Sir William Ashton. Ashton has taken over the old castle of Ravenswood and its grounds while the Master himself lives in a desolate tower called Wolf's Crag on the, so to speak, edge of financial collapse. Ravenswood regards Ashton as a sworn enemy, but his urge for revenge is blunted when he falls in love with his daughter Lucy. Lucy pledges herself to the Master, but her mother, a much more powerful and vindictive figure than Sir William, foils any fruition of their relationship. The Master goes abroad, while Lucy falls increasingly into a totally passive state in which her mother manages to dispose of her in marriage to another, more acceptable, suitor. The Master returns on the day of the wedding to find Lucy in the act of breaking her promise to him, and accuses her of faithlessness. On the wedding night, cries are heard, and the guests, rushing to the bridal chamber, discover the bridegroom severely wounded. When they find the unfortunate Lucy, she is

> seated, or rather couched like a hare upon its form – her head-gear dishevelled; her night-clothes torn and dabbled with blood, – her eyes glazed, and her features convulsed into a wild paroxysm of insanity. When she saw herself discovered, she gibbered, made mouths, and pointed at them with her bloody fingers, with the frantic gestures of an exulting demoniac.[3]

She dies without recovering her sanity, while the Master is lost in a quicksand on his way to a duel with her brother.

It is a bleak and savage plot, set in bleak and savage country. The story bears some similarity to Maturin's *The Milesian Chief* (1812), and there are several other Gothic echoes. Alice, the old wise-woman who warns of trouble to come, is a by now conventional Gothic character, and so in some respects is Lucy herself:

> Left to the impulse of her own taste and feelings, Lucy Ashton was peculiarly accessible to those of a romantic cast. Her secret delight was in the old legendary tales of ardent devotion and unalterable affection, chequered as they so often are with strange adventures and supernatural horrors. This was her favoured fairy realm, and here she erected her aerial palaces.
> (*WN*, XIV, 45)

Ravenswood himself says that 'there is a fate on me' (*WN*, XIV,

291), and his doom is represented by an apparition, historically associated with the House of Ravenswood, who appears to him, in a scene reminiscent of a short story by Beckford, beside an ancient fountain.[4]

Yet this does not make *Bride of Lammermoor* a Gothic novel. One reason, undoubtedly, is Scott's handling of the relations between individuals and society. Ravenswood is a typical Scott hero, in that he is hardly master of his own fate but is buffeted by wider changes in political life which render him from time to time more or less powerful and independent. But this wider realm, which in a sense dictates the interaction of the characters, is not the symbolic vision of a persecuting society which looms so large in Radcliffe, but a thoroughly recognisable Scotland, locked in political and religious conflict. Lucy, certainly, is a persecuted heroine: but her mother's reasons for persecuting and dominating her are perfectly 'reasonable' in terms of the political intrigue which Scott is following through.

Scott, in effect, brings his readers too close to the motivations of his characters to allow any of the distinctive Gothic distortion of perspective. Apparently paradoxically, but with the same effect, the only scene in which a supernatural manifestation actually occurs, the apparition by the fountain, is distanced: whereas Scott has been recounting a direct narrative, he suddenly pauses as Ravenswood, meditating on the truth of old Alice's predictions, nears the fated fountain, and interpolates:

> We are bound to tell the tale as we have received it; and, considering the distance of the time, and propensity of those through whose mouths it has passed to the marvellous, this could not be called a Scottish story, unless it manifested a tinge of Scottish superstition. As Ravenswood approached the solitary fountain, he is said to have met with the following singular adventure . . .   (*WN*, XIV, 348)

The effect is to sever this portion of the story off as inappropriate to the kind of realism for which the book is striving.

In the last analysis, the question of the relation of Scott's novels to the Gothic is one which has to involve the term 'realism'. Realism is, as we have already seen, a very difficult concept to handle; it is difficult to conceive of the possibility of a literary text which is not in some way realist, although one is thus merely thrown back on to the question of different definitions of the real. What can perhaps be said about Scott, however, is in terms of the persuasive project of his fiction; and here the most distinctive feature is that he does not *over-persuade*. The impression received of realism from a book like *Bride of Lammermoor* is not likely to be due to knowledge on the part of the reader that 'history really was like that', but to the feeling that Scott is not trying to derive any particular advantage from distortion. If it could be said non-pejoratively, one would want to say that Scott's novels are singularly pointless; they do not strive to produce glamour, and they do not depend for their fascination on the overloading of costume detail typical of the earlier historical novel.

Another suspicion to be derived from a reading of Scott is that Gothic may be a very difficult, or even the wrong, term to use of single episodes, events, characters in fiction; that Gothic may most fitly be used as a term descriptive of *whole* works, because to bracket the supernatural, to assign it a role in an otherwise reasonable narrative, is to deprive it of a large part of its power. Scott appears, like Defoe earlier, to make a non-Gothic use of the supernatural;[5] the distinctive doubts and suspensions of belief which run through Radcliffe and Maturin are absent, and instead one feels the pressure of the undoubted sanity of the narrator acting to rob the phantom of its terrors.

But for the generation of popular writers who succeeded Scott and who claimed his influence, this was not true. I want to look here at four writers who were all, in rather different ways, best-sellers during the 1830s and 1840s, and who all owe a considerable debt to the Gothic: Bulwer Lytton, G. P. R. James, William Harrison Ainsworth and the remarkable G. W. M. Reynolds. They can be bracketed together on a number of different counts: perhaps the most important is that they were all writers with an alert sense of public taste. They were all closely involved in the practical business of earning a living by letters, and they were all extraordinarily prolific writers who took seriously the need to give their audiences what they appeared to want. In the case of Lytton, this involved trying his hand at almost every available kind of fiction; in the case of the others, finding a formula which sold and repeating it with modifications for as long as necessary; but with all of them, it involved among other things returning to Radcliffe and Lewis and revitalising those aspects of their writing which seemed most appropriate to the tastes of a different age.

The questions raised by this revitalisation are, in one sense at least, political ones. Gothic in the last years of the eighteenth century was, as we have seen, partly an attitude towards history; more specifically, it clearly had to do with the ways in which a social class sought to understand and interpret class relations in the past.

Gothic in the 1830s and 1840s had similar connections, but naturally the passing of several decades effected considerable changes in the nature of the problem. In Lytton, James, Ainsworth and Reynolds, we have a group of literary figures with a high degree of political involvement of one kind and another, and also with a fine range of affiliations. Lytton began a political career as a Radical Member of Parliament, ending up as a rather unusual kind of Tory with considerable political connections. James was a high Tory throughout; he also stood for Parliament, although with less success than Lytton. Ainsworth, like Lytton, and despite essentially conservative politics, was involved in the Newgate Novels controversy of the 1830s,[6] at the same time as voicing a polemical if rather outdated Jacobitism. Reynolds, at the far end of the scale, was involved in a whole range of radical political causes, was editor of several very important radical magazines, and was for a short time the effectual leader of the Chartists. It is incidentally interesting to note how their political interests have affected their reception into literary history: where Lytton, James and Ainsworth are each given space in standard histories of the novel, and have each also attracted biographical attention, Reynolds, who was in his day not only more popular than any of them but also more popular than Dickens and Thackeray, is critically ignored, as indeed he was even at the time of his death. The novels of all four of them – James, admittedly, less than the others – are politically charged, although often with a mixture of motifs and attitudes which now seems puzzling. And amid the archaisms and historical ambivalences of their fiction, we find in addition, in Lytton, Ainsworth and Reynolds, an important new development, the appearance of a sub-genre which we might term 'proletarian Gothic'.

Summers and Avrom Fleishman agree in seeing a considerable change in popular fiction occurring around 1827–30, and in saying that a new style was formed by Lytton, Ainsworth and James.[7] Margaret Dalziel in her book on the popular fiction of the period uses as evidence publication in the Parlour and Railway Libraries, which between them published fourteen of Ainsworth's novels, nineteen of Lytton's and a staggering forty-seven of James's.[8] Reynolds's sphere of popularity was somewhat different: his work was generally published in instalments, and during the 1840s it undoubtedly achieved a wider circulation than any other fiction of the period. To understand the nature of the change, and also the origins of this kind of popularity, it is necessary to say a few words about the preceding period.

The French Revolution had been accompanied, as is well known, by a considerable politicisation of the novel. Writers like Godwin, Holcroft, Bage, Mary Hays, and Mary Wollstonecraft all contributed to this development, and the influence of German literature also played a part. But this period of politicisation was brief. The ending of the long-drawn-out war with France produced a curious kind of cultural Indian summer, and the dominant mode of fiction during the period between 1815 and 1827 was so-called 'silver-fork' fiction, which was characterised principally by its exclusive dealings with the world of the aristocracy. Sadleir points out that this was hardly surprising, because the forms from which 'silver-fork' fiction had developed had themselves been preoccupied with the aristocracy.[9] The novel of sensibility; social satire; even reform fiction itself had shared this preoccupation, and of course so had the Gothic, in which, as Sadleir says,

> However humble the birth of the heroine, however obscure the origins of the hero, it was inevitable, by the end of any gothistic tale of the Radcliffian brood, that the lover should throw off the veil of mystery, enter into his hereditary glories and take his mistress with him. The leading villains also – on the principle that only persons of quality merit prominence even in crime – were generally titled; and if their titles were more often foreign than English, the convention was one of healthy nationalism, and was cheerfully reciprocated in French and German romances of the same school.　　(*Bulwer*, p. 122)

But the crucial feature of 'silver-fork' fiction was that, unlike the Gothic, satirical or reform novels of preceding decades, it was totally uncritical (until the publication in 1828 of Lytton's *Pelham*), and Lytton himself suggests why this was:

> The novels of fashionable life illustrate feelings very deeply rooted, and productive of no common revolution. In proportion as the aristocracy had become social, and fashion allowed the members of the more mediocre classes a hope to outstep the boundaries of fortune, and be quasi-aristocrats themselves, people eagerly sought for representations of the manners which they aspired to imitate, and the circles to which it was not impossible to belong.[10]

In short, the 'silver-fork' novel was a handbook for the post-war 'parvenu'. Essential to it was a revision of the assumed relations between aristocracy and bourgeoisie, and it is in this context that we need to see the fiction of the 1830s.

The emergence of Lytton's work against this background is strongly reminiscent of the relationship of the older Gothics to the sentimental novel, in the sense that he takes up the 'silver-fork' themes and attitudes but adds to them a distinctive note of romance which subtly transmutes their impact, particularly in *Pelham*. In youth, Lytton had been influenced by reading in his grandfather's library of old romances and works of chivalry, and whereas *Pelham* is apparently the story of a somewhat raffish aristocrat in the 'silver-fork' tradition, it is distinctive both in the ironic attitude which Lytton brings to bear on his characters and also in the Gothic scenes – Pelham's night walk through London, the murder of Tyrell – which recur within an ostensibly 'social' novel. Throughout Lytton's tremendously various fictional output, scenes of terror occur which challenge the reader's assumptions about the reality of the world which he is being shown; as Sadleir points out, the best evidence for the way in which this was regarded by his contemporaries is the fact that he was the dedicatee of the *Romancist and Novelists' Library* (1839–40), a series largely devoted to terror-fiction and including reprints of Walpole, Reeve, Radcliffe, Lewis, Maturin, Mary Shelley and Brown among others.[11]

Lytton's major stylistic influence in this area was undoubtedly Radcliffe. His work is characterised by a surging grandiloquence, a deliberate heightening of effect in terms both of the imagery of nature – in, for instance, *Falkland* (1827) – and of his descriptions of emotion. His characters, like Radcliffe's, move through a world of appalling dangers and exaggerated responses, even when that world is nominally mid-nineteenth-century London, and many of them share the Radcliffean tendency to see themselves as tragic heroes or victims despite the prosaic nature of their surroundings. But more important in terms of themes and interests is Godwin, in two respects: in Lytton's earlier works, there is a considerable debt to Godwin's interest in criminal psychology, particularly derived from *Caleb Williams*, while later on, when he acquired a more mystical tint, much of the material on Rosicrucianism derives from *St Leon* and also, probably, from Maturin. What brings the influences of Radcliffe and Godwin together is Lytton's strong interest in the psychology of the fearful, and in this respect there is also a detectable minor influence, particularly in the early *Mortimer* (1824), from John Moore's *Zeluco* (1786), a work very close to Lytton's in its blend of ironical detachment and horror.

In terms of style, Lytton can fairly be said to have run across the same problem as Radcliffe in respect of genres. Like her, he is not content to portray prosaic emotions. Even when the circumstances are not entirely appropriate, his characters choose to see the world through a lens of tragic symbolism; *Lucretia* (1846), for instance, is

147

a story ostensibly modelled on the life and crimes of Wainewright the poisoner, but sordidness and violence are transmuted as by an alchemist into the materials of metaphysical tragedy, a process which prompted the *Spectator* to condemn the work as being, like those of some of the Elizabethan poets, tainted with a 'mortal unhealthiness of mind'.[12] The *Spectator's* fear was that Lytton was endowing the criminal with a kind of world-historical status, very much on the lines of Schiller with his bandit-kings.

His unwillingness to remain within those realist confines which characterise the 'social novel' is also evident in terms of theme, particularly in the later books. *A Strange Story* (1862) takes up the idea of unnaturally prolonged life, following on from the tales of the Wandering Jew; and in 'The Haunted and the Haunters' (1857) Lytton wrote a full-blown tale of the apparently supernatural, at the same time employing contemporary pseudo-scientific explanations – which tend merely to deepen the mystery – to excuse himself. The most impressive feature of 'The Haunted and the Haunters' is Lytton's description of the apparitions: at one point, an enormous dark form is conjured up:

> my impression was that of an immense and overwhelming Power opposed to my volition; that sense of utter inadequacy to cope with a force beyond man's, which one may feel *physically* in a storm at sea, in a conflagration, or when confronting some terrible wild beast, or rather, perhaps, the shark of the ocean, I felt *morally*. Opposed to my will was another will, as far superior to its strength as storm, fire, and shark in material force to the force of man.[13]

Lytton does not make the mistake of trying to describe the form itself; he chooses rather to heighten its impact by leaving it vague and amorphous while closely specifying the developing feelings which it arouses.

But although one can pick out particular Gothic themes and stylistic elements in Lytton's work, these are only in a sense super-structural. What underlies them is a continuing dissatisfaction with the muddle and pettiness of the everyday: in an apparently social novel like *Pelham*, his tone looks forward to the world-dismissing aphorisms of Oscar Wilde, in his more metaphysical work back to the self-aggrandisement of characters in Radcliffe and Maturin. In the earlier work, we see characters striving against worldly restriction; in the later ones the world itself has become an arena for conflict between supernatural forces. Most of his novels can be seen as a series of exercises in a seemingly rather anachronistic 'grand style'; at its worst, this collapses into rhetoric and bombast, at its best, in for instance *Godolphin* (1833), it manages to take events and situations from the everyday world and suggests depths of metaphorical connection which create a sense of cloudy but potent allegory. Keith Hollingsworth says that in Lytton's time, 'very few recognised that the imaginative and symbolic methods which were known (if not always appreciated) in poetry could also enrich the novel' (Hollingsworth, p. 226); and although it is probably because of his poeticised prose that his novels have hardly survived the passing of time, clearly his contemporary popularity signified an appreciation of new forms of romance.

In these ways, then, Lytton can be seen as continuing Gothic traditions, but in two other ways he distinctively modifies these traditions in accordance with social changes. The first way has to do with the three novels *Paul Clifford* (1830), *Eugene Aram* (1832) and *Lucretia*, and with their attitudes towards the criminal. As early as *Pelham*, Lytton had introduced into his fiction a picture of the contemporary underworld; in these three novels, the first two of which were heavily involved in the Newgate Novel controversy, he develops this interest in a series of attempts to reconstruct the criminal mind and its relation to social pressures. His purposes are directly political:

> A child who is cradled in ignominy; whose schoolmaster is the felon; whose academy is the House of Correction; who breathes an atmosphere in which virtue is poisoned, to which religion·does not pierce – becomes less a responsible and reasoning human being than a wild beast which we suffer to range in the wilderness – till it prowls near our homes, and we kill it in self-defence.[14]

This passage from the 1848 Preface to *Paul Clifford* is clearly Godwinian, except for its mention of religion: Lytton's concern is with the nature of conditioning, the way in which society, through its hypocrisy, produces its own criminals. His method of bringing this point home to his audience is, in all three novels, Gothic: his feeling appears to be that, so blind are his contemporaries to the evils of prisons and the law, only exaggeration, the presence of gibbets, skeletons, thunderstorms, will open their eyes. These are novels of the social outsider, and written, to much contemporary critical alarm, very much from the outsider's point of view: Lytton tries to make us experience the terrors which characterise a life of poverty and repression, not so much to produce sympathy for his criminals as to demonstrate the actual barbarity of the apparently civilised. The result resembles a blend of Godwin and Maturin: the fictional dungeons and hovels conjured up resemble those of *Melmoth* in their lurid intensity, but the verdicts which his characters pass on the significance of their lives are Godwinian in their clarity, and in a curious kind of 'impassioned reasonableness' which characterises Lytton's view of their impossible social situation.

In order to see Lytton's other major contribution to the Gothic we need to look at the later work, and particularly at *Zanoni* (1842). There are many threads in this long and symbolically complex representation of the harmony of nature and art; but the principal one concerns Zanoni himself, a man who through diligent study of hermetic doctrines has given himself longevity and wisdom, and Glyndon, who aspires to be his pupil. Glyndon, however, tries to move too fast, and in doing so encounters 'The Dweller of the Threshold', a dread being which gains power over him and wrecks his life until he accepts that his role in the world can best be performed, not by attempting to quit the mundane sphere, but by exercising his artistic imagination and powers within the given environment.

Clearly, *Zanoni* is akin to the Faust legends, but there are significant differences. The knowledge which Zanoni and his own master, Mejnour, have acquired is not evil but neutral: Mejnour uses his largely for the achievement of personal purity and intellectual perfection, Zanoni tends rather to more humanitarian purposes. But the attainment of this knowledge is not directly compared with aspiration towards the divine, but rather symbolises the possibility of entering into a 'society of the immortals', who can exert influence over the destiny of the world. The political allegory is not far from the surface, although Lytton's attitude is ambivalent. He is attracted to the idea of a society of Illuminati who, through profound meditation and training, can choose, if they wish, to provide a kind of spiritual world-government, but by the end of the book Zanoni has renounced his immortality and sacrificed himself for the good of the world.

But, of course, he could not have done that without having trodden the path of wisdom in the first place; similarly, Glyndon abandons the attempt to reach the stars, but presumably the artistic and other work which he will go on to do on earth will be influenced by such knowledge as he has acquired. As with so many Gothic works, *Zanoni* assents to the proposition that there are people intrinsically endowed with extraordinary power, who therefore have an extraordinary responsibility to learn to use it aright.

The 'Dweller of the Threshold' is a powerful symbol of guilt. Like the apparition in 'The Haunted and the Haunters', it is described largely subjectively; it is the form in which the unconscious manifests its disturbance to Glyndon over the breaking of taboo. Glyndon seeks to transgress natural boundaries, but he does so prematurely and encounters the world of spirits before he has the strength to cope with it. As a result, this partial awareness of spirit reacts back on him, reducing every aspect of the material world to dust and ashes.

The final part of the book is remarkable. It is played out against the background of the Terror subsequent to the French Revolution, and Lytton uses this as a metaphor for fear in general. By his death, Zanoni is credited with the responsibility for bringing about the downfall of Robespierre and thus ending the Terror, just as his death involves the disappearance of the Dweller; it has, after all, been his aspirations, however well intended, which have opened the channel down which the Dweller has been able to come.

As an account of the problems of 'aristocracy', in the most general sense, the book is not an unfair representation of Lytton's own problematic position.[15] A member of an old family, himself seeking ennoblement yet retaining from his youth certain radical ideas, Lytton is first and foremost a writer who sets himself in opposition to the bourgeoisie. The fact of his popularity, on this reading, becomes ironic evidence of the extent to which the middle classes were willing to bear obscurantism, grandiosity and didacticism, provided it savoured of aristocratic origins. Lytton's favourite historical figure was Bolingbroke, whom he saw as a symbol of 'nobility in degradation', and much of the high-handedness of his style derives from his attempts to create fictional stages worthy of displaying the actions of a latter-day nobleman.

This is, however, by no means to call *Zanoni* a conservative book. If, by the end, we are convinced of the necessity of remaining within the mundane, this is only because we have been thus persuaded by those who are competent to tell us, the suffering aristocrats of the spirit who risk all to bring back fateful information from the realms of the stars; although the world may go on, Lytton suggests that the ways in which it is held together are not through the material ties so beloved of the bourgeoisie, but through an intricate web of universal correspondences known only to the initiate. The final act of the spiritual/political leader must be self-sacrifice; not at all because the middle-class world view is correct, but because the knowledge that they are wrong would be too much for them to bear.

Lytton's fiction is therefore in a crucial way in opposition to

Scott's. Where Scott reinterprets history in terms of the interest of an increasingly democratic age in the effects of society on a wide range of classes and types of individual, Lytton's focus is on the individual – be he criminal, rake or Rosicrucian – who is in one way or another excluded from society. That such an individual's attempt to manipulate it to his own ends seldom succeeds is a mark of the tragic element in Lytton's thinking, the tragedy of nobility trying to find a social and ethical position in a world apparently given over to a materialist law which renders the values of aristocracy – honour, elegance, reserve – increasingly irrelevant. The 'Dweller of the Threshold' is a terror only to the impatient and blundering Glyndon; his function with regard to the world of the initiates is protective, as the last defence against the destruction of hierarchy.

Yet this, again, is by no means to say that Lytton was a defender of the *existing* aristocracy, which he criticises bitterly, partly for having abandoned the privileges and responsibilities which should characterise it: Lytton's message is not conservatism but rejuvenation, in which respect he is very different from G. P. R. James, a writer who was much more seriously influenced by Scott. It was in fact Scott who originally noticed James's *Richelieu* (1829) and apparently saw it as a work after his own heart.[16] James was an even more prolific and popular writer than Lytton, although he achieved this by a repetitive consistency of style and subject-matter which drew down considerable critical scorn. His work ventures occasionally into derivative Gothic, as in *The Ruined City* (1828) and *The Castle of Ehrenstein* (1847), the latter a Radcliffean tale of the explained supernatural, but apart from these rare excursions, the rest of his fiction is in a slightly different area, chivalric romance, for which his name became a byword in the mid-nineteenth century.

Politically, James was, to quote Longfellow's raised-eyebrow comment, 'a Tory, and very conservative'.[17] In later life, he took up a diplomatic post in America, and his son, writing of those years, alludes to the origins of James's politics, pointing out that his parents' minds 'had been formed in the reaction against the French Revolution, and the democracy of America continually recalled to them the terrors of their childhood',[18] which suggests an important comparison with Lytton, and indeed an important factor in the whole range of mid-century historical and Gothic fiction. James was also a professional historian of some contemporary repute, and managed to secure for himself the post of Historiographer Royal to William IV and later to Victoria. The combination of historical and fictional purposes behind his writing can be seen in some comments he made about the reception of his history of the Black Prince (1836):

> two or three reviews written by ignorant blockheads upon a subject they do not understand, for the purpose of damning a work which throws some new light upon English History. I am very much out of spirits in regard to historical literature, and though I would willingly devote my time and even my money to elucidate the dark points of our own history, yet encouragement from the public is small and from the Government does not exist, so that I lay down the pen in despair of ever seeing English History anything but what it is – a farrago of falsehoods and hypotheses covered over with the tinsel of specious reasoning from wrong data.[19]

Since he produced an average of three novels a year for several decades, his promise to lay down the pen was clearly soon broken, but he did come to concentrate on presenting the fruits of his historical researches largely in fictional form, producing a seemingly endless series of cumbersome, monotonous historical narratives decked out in gorgeous costumes.

What made them so immensely popular is not now easy to perceive. The most interesting suggestions are those made by Fleishman, who says that James 'aimed to satisfy the growing public reverence for the chivalric ideal as a standard of gentility in an increasingly middle-class, industrial-commercial society' (Fleishman, p. 32), which places his work in a curious kind of parallelism with Lytton's. Much of the Victorian idealisation of the great man, Fleishman goes on, is anticipated in James, who, by maintaining a constant distinction between the spirit and the institution of chivalry, was able, despite his professional pretensions, to 'ignore the damaging historical facts about the institution and to portray his heroes not in the light of their historical situation but in the eternal light of quasi-religious sanctions for aristocratic norms'.

To test the adequacy of this version of James's project, and to see its relation to Gothic, we can turn to almost any of the novels: one of the less tedious is *Corse de Leon, or, The Brigand* (1841), which is reasonably gripping in terms of character and plot, although spoiled by simple lapses in continuity and unbearable authorial pomposity. It has two central figures, the nobleman Bernard de Rohan and the brigand Corse de Leon, and it is in the relations between them and the author that the ideological accent of the book can be found. De Rohan certainly exemplifies the chivalric qualities which James sees as typical of the mid-sixteenth century, but his courtesy and general affability are rarely adequate as a response to the villainies practised upon him. It is the brigand who provides us with a sterner outlook on the world:

> It is because man's law is not God's law that I stand here upon the mountain. Were laws equal and just, there would be few found to resist them. While they are unequal and unjust, the poor-hearted may submit and tremble; the powerless may yield and suffer: the bold, the free, the strong, and the determined fall back upon the law of God, and wage war against the injustice of man. If you and I, baron, . . . were to stand before a court of human justice, as it is called, pleading the same cause, accused of the same acts, would our trial be the same, our sentence, our punishment? No! all would be different: and why? Because you are Bernard de Rohan, a wealthy baron of the land, and I am none. A name would make the difference. A mere name would bring the sword on my head and leave yours unwounded. If so it be, I say – if such be the world's equity, I set up a retribution for myself. . . . ask [the poor] if there is not retribution to be found in the midnight court of Corse de Leon, if there is not punishment and justice poured forth even upon the privileged heads above.[20]

Now, as a writer of historical fiction, James saw himself, and was seen, as very much in the school of Scott: he even goes so far as to announce in *The Brigand* that he is a writer of history, not romance, and therefore presumably considered himself some kind of realist. Yet it is remarkable how even here the dream is shadowed by the nightmare: James's age of gentility is also one of almost metaphysical brutality. The knight in shining armour is conjured from the past but is overpowered almost instantly by the robber king. In terms of narrative, reasonably satisfactory justice is achieved not by de Rohan's manners but by the brigand's sword.

What one is therefore given by James is a paradoxical vision of an admired feudal society which nevertheless exists only by the grace of those who move outside the law. The brigands are not very distant from Lytton's Rosicrucians: certainly they are equally given to dashing philosophical speculation. Even so conservative a writer cannot escape domination by the Gothic criminal and his thirst for violent justice. And it is domination which is at stake: alongside his nostalgia, we can find in James a quivering, half-welcoming, half-fearful attitude to brutality. Although Corse de Leon is in himself only a minor example of the Gothic hero/villain, he is impressive in context because he continually oversteps the boundaries laid down for him, and reduces the lawful world to papier mâché. It is he who rails against man's use of chains and fetters:

> Ah, ah, accursed implements of tyranny! . . . When, when will the time come that ye shall be no longer known? God of heaven! even then it

must be remembered that such things have been. It must be written in books. It must be told in tradition, that men were found to chain their fellow-creatures with heavy bars of iron, to make them linger out the bright space given them for activity and enjoyment in dungeons and in fetters, till the dull flame was extinguished, and dust returned to dust. Would to heaven that there were no such thing as history, to perpetuate, even unto times when man shall have purified his heart from the filthy baseness of these days, the memory of such enormous deeds as fetters like that record!   (*Brigand*, I, 253–4)

There are Godwinian echoes here again (which the respectable James would only dare permit himself in the thrilling guise of Corse de Leon), but the crucial question concerns the contemporary applicability of the argument. What James thought was probably contradictory, although it seems doubtful that he would want to regard his beloved Middle Ages as any bloodier than the present; but what is important is that it is this rhetoric of social injustice, derived from Schiller, from Byron, even in a way from Lewis, which in the work of Reynolds and Dickens among others came to figure as a political weapon in a contemporary context. The process of rehabilitating chivalry is, as James discovers, double-edged; the model which one can dredge up from history is encrusted with barnacles and fraught with the monstrous, because the depths from which it comes are ones which are necessarily taboo to the middle classes. James's brigand heroes commit a kind of cultural violence; but it was clearly a violence which the reading-public thoroughly (and repeatedly) enjoyed.

Rivalling James for popularity in the field of so-called 'historical fiction' during the 1830s and 1840s was William Harrison Ainsworth, a writer with considerably less respect for historical fact than James, and much more obviously indebted to the Gothic tradition. His early work, mostly in the form of contributions to magazines, clearly shows his literary origins: a play called *Ghiotto, or The Fatal Revenge* (1821), which is a melodrama after Maturin; graveyard reveries, including 'The Churchyard' (1823); and various tales, including 'The Pirate' (1822), 'Adventure in the South Seas' (1822) and 'The Fortress of Saguntum' (1825), all of which are deeply indebted to Lewis. A further story, 'The Spectre Bride' (1821), again after Lewis, is particularly memorable for its luxuriant descriptions of brutality and the corruption of innocence. Like Chatterton, the young Ainsworth claimed at one point to have 'discovered' a seventeenth-century dramatist; and to complete his Gothic credentials, he wrote an early tragedy on the subject of the Foscari which has been compared to Byron's.

The most important influences, apart from the ever-present Lewis, were Radcliffe, Byron and, of course, Scott. *Ovingdean Grange* (1860), for instance, was suggested by Scott's *Woodstock* (1826), while *Crichton* (1837) and various other of Ainsworth's novels show the influence of Radcliffe's *Gaston de Blondeville*. It is the direct absorption of Gothic tradition which conditions most of his later fiction; as Ernest Baker says, 'it was the Gothic, or rather a neo-Gothic, mania that led him into pseudo-historical romancing',[21] and Ainsworth offers us in his major novels a curious blend of factual detail with Gothic atmospherics and emotions. The paradox of his work is that, unlike James, he actually *does* produce real places within his novels, but his touch transforms them all into modifications of Udolpho. Also, despite eventual moralism, Ainsworth's fiction is much darker than James's: it is, in fact, more in-door, but it also dwells to a far greater extent on evil, cruelty, torture.

He was a Tory, despite a Noncomformist Whig upbringing, and an emotional sympathiser with the Jacobite cause from youth; like Scott, he knew old Jacobites, and it was Scott – again as with James – who approved Ainsworth's first novel, *Sir John Chiverton* (1826), and supported its publication.[22] But he did not discover success through historical fiction but alongside Lytton in the Newgate controversy, which centred on two of his novels, *Rookwood* (1834) and *Jack Sheppard* (1839), and on their tendency both to horrify and also to encourage sympathy for subverters of law and order. Ainsworth spoke of *Rookwood*, which contains the famous account of Dick Turpin's imaginary ride to York, as 'a story by Mrs Radcliffe transplanted', and added:

> Romance, if I mistake not, is destined shortly to undergo an important change. Modified by the German and French writers, – by Hoffmann, Tieck, Hugo, Dumas, Balzac, and Paul Lacroix – the structure, commenced in our own land by Horace Walpole, Monk Lewis, Mrs Radcliffe, and Maturin, but left imperfect and inharmonious, requires, now that the rubbish, which choked up its approach, is removed, only the hand of the skilful architect to its entire renovation and perfection.[23]

Undoubtedly *Rookwood* owed its success, like Lytton's *Paul Clifford*, to its distinctness from 'tales of fashionable life': it offered a palatable account of history as a matter of highwaymen, desperate deeds and portentous omens. *Jack Sheppard* appears to have worried contemporaries rather more: S. M. Ellis, the biographer, cites a comment by Mary Russell Mitford:

> I have been reading *Jack Sheppard*, and have been struck by the great

danger, in these times, of representing authorities so constantly and fearfully in the wrong; so tyrannous, so devilish, as the author has been pleased to portray it in *Jack Sheppard*, for he does not seem so much a man or even an incarnate fiend, as a representation of power – government or law, call it as you may – the ruling power. Of course, Mr Ainsworth had no such design, but such is the effect; and as the millions who see it represented at the minor theatres will not distinguish between now and a hundred years back, all the Chartists in the land are less dangerous than this nightmare of a book, and I, Radical as I am, lament any additional temptations to outbreak, with all its train of horrors.[24]

We need not go into detail about *Rookwood* or *Jack Sheppard*, except to point out that they were naturally susceptible to the double reading which attends on any work with a romanticised criminal protagonist; they are important only as another link in the uneven chain which leads from Godwin, via Lytton, on to Reynolds and Dickens, and which thus produces a form of Gothic connected with the proletarian and the contemporary.

The kind of Gothic for which Ainsworth is best known is that represented in his most popular book, *Tower of London* (1840). This is an account of the brief reign of Lady Jane Grey and its consequences, and rather resembles Lee's production of 'personalised' patterns from political events: an interesting feature is the way in which it is centred on the Tower itself as chief focus of attention. In the course of the book, Ainsworth takes us on a carefully guided tour, showing us every dungeon and gateway, and describing in great detail this archetypal Gothic setting. His style, here and elsewhere, is more readable than James's, but he is much less competent at structuring plots: *Tower of London* relies in this respect entirely on history, and when Ainsworth tries to add sub-plots he usually forgets what he is doing.

In fact, when he relies on architecture to supply him with themes and Gothic resonance, the result is predictably disappointing; a far more attractive exercise in Gothic is *The Lancashire Witches* (1849), which Ellis rightly refers to as Ainsworth's best book.[25] Here he takes as a theme the actual Lancashire witch-trials of 1613, already dramatised by Thomas Shadwell and others and referred to in some detail by Scott in the *Letters on Demonology and Witchcraft*,[26] and weaves around them a copious and gripping world. The book's weaknesses are those habitual to Ainsworth: poor dialogue, an overreliance on costume details and a lack of narrative clarity. But its strengths are considerable: there are various descriptive passages as effective as many of Radcliffe's, and given an extra conviction by Ainsworth's familiarity with and love for the country he is describing. A similar familiarity enables him to be witty about the aspirations of country gentry towards the Court, and to describe well the impact of a visit to Lancashire by the witch-hunting James I.

Ainsworth's reliance on history to supply him with plots, however, leads again to problems. There is a suspension of moral judgement throughout *The Lancashire Witches*; on the one hand, this gives the book a kind of tragic grandeur, the stateliness of a death march, in which fate works itself out without much interference from human agents; on the other, it confuses the apparent point of the story. This point appears to be to demonstrate, after Scott, the evils consequent upon persecution: one is reminded of some lines in Shelley's *Charles I* (1818–22) which could well have served as an epigraph:

> *Without delay*
> *An army must be sent into the north;*
> *Followed by a Commission of the Church,*
> *With amplest power to quench in fire and blood,*
> *And tears and terror, and the pity of hell,*
> *The intenser wrath of Heresy.*
>
> *(Works, IV, 156)*

In accordance with this point, the good liberals are all on the side of the witches, and try to defend them against harassment; unfortunately, however, Ainsworth also seems to claim that the witches really *are* witches, which makes the good liberals appear rather foolish.

Where James's *Castle of Ehrenstein* is Radcliffean in its attempt to set up and explain away the supernatural, Ainsworth's novels are less vacillating: elements of the supernatural are quite often introduced simply because a historical record mentions them, without regard to whether they can be cogently connected to the plot. With Ainsworth, history is merely the ground of the marvellous; and although he is able, by means of archaisms and costume details, to introduce a sense of distance, the distance is the same regardless of the historical period to which he is referring. In the end, his purpose is quite different from James's: where James is attempting to produce from the past models that his readers might seek to emulate, Ainsworth is concentrating on the distinctness of the past from the present and demonstrating how far society has progressed since the days of execution, torture and belief in the supernatural. And this, of course, permits of a far greater degree of sensationalism, for he can show us all the lurid details of the past while holding up his own hands in horror.

In terms of the lurid, however, the distance between Lytton, James, Ainsworth on the one hand, and G. W. M. Reynolds on the other, is considerable, as is the political distance to be traversed; and the two matters are connected. When Reynolds died, he received almost no obituaries, and it is far from clear whether this was due to his political radicalism or to the nature of his writing, in which the sadistic and sexual elements always implicit in Gothic are developed to an unprecedented level. The connection is through Reynolds's lifelong obsession with the actual horrors incident to his own society, and his lifelong attempt to expose these horrors as consequent upon a hierarchical social organisation. Varma, in perhaps his most unpalatable critical aside, claims that the 'lower' forms of Gothic catered to 'the perverted taste for excitement among degenerate readers' (Varma, p. 189); Reynolds's point would be that this perversion and degeneracy is precisely the result of the models of behaviour demonstrated by the upper classes. 'The gorgeous robe and elegant dress of every high-born lady . . . is stained by the life-blood and infected by the pollution of the poor seamstresses who made them all',[27] says Reynolds; if the lower classes are corrupted, it is because of chronic poverty and oppression, and to convey a political message which will help to alleviate these circumstances it may be necessary to speak the language which they have been taught.

Reynolds – like Lytton, James, Ainsworth – was from a wealthy family; he spent much of his money on his associations with various political causes. In addition to his involvement with the Chartists, he campaigned, mainly in his various newspapers, for the recognition of women's rights, the rejection of anti-Semitism, the abolition of private property, the disestablishing of the state Church and against capital punishment and the powers of the peerage. It is a tribute to the power and honesty of his political arguments that, despite the element of sensationalism in his work, he finds an admirer in Q. D. Leavis: 'the constant insistence on open-mindedness in politics and non-material standards in living without any appeals to religious sentiment or anything cheap in the radicalism for which Reynolds stood, is a considerable achievement'.[28] Sensationalism, however, there certainly is, derived partly from the Gothic and particularly Lewis, and partly from French writers like Eugène Sue and Victor Hugo, with whom Reynolds was especially familiar.

It is true that apart from Gothic fiction Reynolds wrote a colossal amount of other work: popular imitations of Dickens, dramatisations of contemporary events, historical romances, even social novels like

The Seamstress (1850). But he was best known as the author of three supernatural novels, *Faust* (1845–6), *Wagner, the Wehr-wolf* (1846–7) and *The Necromancer* (1852) and, even more, of two immensely long works, *The Mysteries of London* (1844–8) and *The Mysteries of the Courts of London* (1848–56). All of these appeared originally in serialised form, and the latter two are between them almost as long as the complete works of Dickens.

The *Mysteries*, modelled of course on Sue's *Les Mystères de Paris* (1842–3), are fictional running indictments of the corruption of the British aristocracy, 'the most loathsomely corrupt, demoralised and profligate class of persons that ever scandalised a country'.[29] Interspersed with this theme is much practical advice to the lower classes about how to survive the horrors into which they are plunged by injustice and cruelty. The 'hook' is obvious: virulent anti-clericalism, descriptions of torture and a strong trace of pornography. Dalziel makes the point that elsewhere in mid-Victorian fiction there are few examples of a member of the middle or upper classes 'deliberately wronging his dependents or employees' (Dalziel, p. 140); this occurs in virtually every subplot of the *Mysteries* as Reynolds probes further and further into 'the great moral dung-heap'[30] of contemporary London. Crimes like sadism and incest, previously near the heart of Gothic anxieties about the aristocracy, are now also portrayed in the proletariat, but only because of the singular consistency of Reynolds's argument, which is that if one wishes to justify one's accusation of the aristocracy as utterly corrupting and tyrannical, then it only makes sense to portray their victims as utterly depraved and oppressed. Another point about the *Mysteries* which is worth making is that after reading Ainsworth and others, and despite the contemporary world in which much of Reynolds's fiction is set, his style appears deeply eighteenth-century, and this seems only appropriate if we suggest that, among English writers, it was only in Lewis and his 'confrères' that Reynolds was able to find a style appropriate to carrying the degree of violence which he wished to express.

Wagner, the Wehr-wolf is a good example of Reynolds's work. It would be pointless to try to give a plot summary, because the most remarkable thing about it is its extraordinary narrative complexity. Starting from a scene in which Faust appears and grants long life to the old shepherd Fernand Wagner at the cost of monthly bestial transformation, the book diverges into a host of apparently separate stories which are nonetheless brought together with complete precision by the end. E. F. Bleiler refers to 'one of the most remarkable structural abilities in English letters' (*Wagner*, p. xvii), and this is no exaggeration; Reynolds apologises at one point for narrative prolixity, but in fact there is almost no superfluous material in *Wagner*: the author is almost winking at us when in the very final scene he takes care to mention the explanation for a single puzzling glance which occurred hundreds of pages – and a year, in the serial form – earlier.

The central thematic preoccupation, like many other aspects of the book, is close to that of *Frankenstein* and *The Monk:* essentially, Reynolds is concerned with the power of corruption exercised by environment and social convention. Nisida, a lady who causes much of the evil in the story, is nevertheless transformed into a kind of nature goddess when she is shipwrecked on the statutory uninhabited island; but much is also made of the fact that her conditioning goes too deep for this to be a lasting state, and she has to return to the scenes of her previous machinations. This theme produces certain odd consequences in terms of characterisation. Reynolds has been accused of weakness in this respect, but the point is surely that he actually has little faith in the cogency of individual character. Nobody in *Wagner* is consistently good or evil: Wagner himself turns into a saint. Since individuals are in the end not seen as fully responsible for their actions, there is a remarkable degree of moral generosity: death-bed repentance is enough to obliterate a lifetime of murder and lust, for it signifies that one has become aware of one's previous capitulation in social evils, a capitulation which could not easily have been avoided.

The evil in the characters is caused by the fact that they live in a social world impregnated with horror, pain, torture. The most hideous scene occurs when a jealous husband, convinced of his wife's infidelity, has the suspected lover killed. The wife is then bound and gagged and led to the corpse, which is dismembered down to the skeleton before her eyes. It turns out later, when she has understandably died of shock, that the 'lover' was in fact her brother; their relation had been perfectly innocent, its secrecy having been caused by his social unacceptability. Reynolds carries further Lewis's emphasis on the role of the spectator of torture and cruelty, and thus brings to the fore the passive helplessness of those overborne by the power of a violent state.

For it is the state and its subsidiary institutions which are the source of cruelty in Reynolds, symbolised in the conventional Gothic motifs of convent, Inquisition and prison: his convent, for instance, is

> an institution recognised by the State as a means of punishing
> immorality, upholding the interests of the Catholic religion –
> persuading the sceptical – confirming the waverer – and exercising a
> salutary terror over the ladies of the upper class, at that time
> renowned for their dissolute morals.   (*Wagner*, p. 28a)

In his portrait of sixteenth-century Florence, he manages to combine
two critiques of the aristocracy and flagellate them for moral abandon on the one hand and violent repression on the other. These
are linked in the unbearable plight of Reynolds's women, who are
precisely caught in that double-bind. The spendthrift and gambler
Orsini shrinks from committing the crime of theft, but

> The seduction of the Countess of Arestino was not a crime in his
> estimation; – Oh! no – because a man may seduce, and yet not be
> dishonoured in the eyes of the world. It is his victim, or the partner
> of his guilty pleasure, only who is dishonoured. Such is the law written
> in society's conventional code. Vile – detestable – unjust law!
>   (*Wagner*, p. 43a-b)

And because it is the law which is to blame, Orsini is in the end
allowed to escape punishment.

Reynolds is also much concerned with the problems of prisons,
although less in *Wagner* than in the *Mysteries*, where his critique of
the degrading effect of imprisonment follows directly from those in
Godwin, in Shelley's *Rosalind and Helen*, and in Byron's meditations
on incarceration, *The Prisoner of Chillon*, *The Lament of Tasso* and *The
Prophecy of Dante*. The question which remains, however, is whether
these apparently humanitarian concerns are served or hindered by
sensationalism and Gothic apparatus. In answering it, one must
remember that there are two rather different kinds of sensationalism
in Reynolds, his dwelling on torture and cruelty, and his explicitness
about sex. Considering his work in the context of contemporaneous
popular fiction, it would surely have been the latter which stood
out most strongly: Lytton, Ainsworth and Dickens, quite apart from
many lesser writers, were quite profligate with scenes of physical and
mental hardship, and in this respect Reynolds was only marginally
developing an extant convention.

The situation is different with regard to sexuality, but here Reynolds's attitude is by no means exploitative. Where Lewis gloated over
frailty and its just deserts, Reynolds harps constantly on the extreme
difficulty of dealing reasonably with passion within the confines of
a repressive code: Dalziel comments that what must have seemed
really surprising to his readers was that 'lovers, the women as well
as the men, *enjoy* themselves' (Dalziel, p. 38), and 'lapses' are treated

with sympathy. When Nisida and her lover find themselves together away from civilisation and proceed lovingly in a natural direction, he puts the question to his readers: *dare* we call them man and wife? It is hard to see in this the moral degeneracy of which Reynolds's fiction was so consistently accused.

As for the element of exaggeration in his work, this is a question relevant to the whole of the Gothic. The point that needs to be made again, surely, is that Reynolds was a popular writer, and there is a kind of popular writing which, despite certain critical assumptions, has never been realistic. Ballad, broadsheet and melodrama, to say nothing of modern romantic fiction, deal not in realism but in excitement: it is the purpose for which this excitement is employed that determines the exploitativeness of a genre or of a text. The reason Reynolds appears so odd is not because he crudifies a previous literature, but because he sophisticates one: the debts to Lewis are to Lewis as *already* crudified by popular versions, and it is into this form that Reynolds injects explicit political and social concerns, although admittedly he complicates the issue by claiming that his obviously Gothicised world picture is in fact a realistic account of social relations. And despite his use of Gothic, if one places Reynolds alongside Lytton, James and Ainsworth he looks in some ways very contemporary: for the first time the working class is intruding significantly into the system of class relations characteristic of the Gothic, and things are said in the genre which are explicitly, even didactically, relevant to them. The upper classes are seen as posing threats not so much to the morality and power of the middle classes as to the actual lives of the people. The writer, of course, to whom this development points is Dickens, who effects similar changes in previous class assumptions: but before looking at Dickens's relation to Gothic, we need to turn aside and examine the early development of Gothic in America, where it produced some of its most remarkable fruits.

Notes and references

1. See **Anna Laetitia Barbauld**, 'Sir Bertrand', and **Nathan Drake**, 'The Abbey of Clunedale', in Haining, pp. 32–6, 55–67.
2. Scott, *Letters on Demonology and Witchcraft*, introd. R. L. Brown (Ardsley, 1968), pp. 61, 90, 94, 311, 174.
3. Scott, *Waverley Novels* (48 vols, Edinburgh, 1901), XIV, 482–3. All subsequent references are to *WN*.
4. See William Beckford, 'The Nymph of the Fountain', in Haining, pp. 117–50.
5. See **Daniel Defoe**, 'A True Relation of the Apparition of One Mrs Veal', in *Selected Writings of Daniel Defoe*, ed. J. T. Boulton (London, 1975), pp. 132–41.

6. On the 'Newgate Novel', see particularly **Keith Hollingsworth,** *The Newgate Novel 1830–1847: Bulwer, Ainsworth, Dickens, and Thackeray* (Detroit, 1963).
7. See Summers, p. 379; and **Avrom Fleishman,** *The English Historical Novel: Walter Scott to Virginia Woolf* (Baltimore, 1971), p. 31.
8. See **Margaret Dalziel,** *Popular Fiction 100 Years Ago* (London, 1957), p. 81, n. 1.
9. See **Michael Sadleir,** *Bulwer and his Wife: A Panorama 1803–1836* (London, 1933), pp. 121–4.
10. **Sir Edward Bulwer Lytton,** *England and the English* (London, 1874), p. 251.
11. See *Bulwer*, p. 315, n. 1.
12. 'Sir Bulwer Lytton's Lucretia' (anon. rev.), *Spectator*, 12 Dec. 1846, p. 1190.
13. **Lytton,** *The Caxtons; Zicci; The Haunted and the Haunters* (Boston and New York, 1849), pp. 313–14.
14. **Lytton,** *Paul Clifford* (Edinburgh, 1862), pp. ix-x.
15. In connection with Lytton and the 'aristocratic', I am indebted to conversations with John Oakley of Portsmouth Polytechnic.
16. See **S. M. Ellis,** *The Solitary Horseman, or, The Life and Adventures of G. P. R. James* (London, 1927), pp. 44–5.
17. See *Solitary Horseman*, p. 132.
18. See *Solitary Horseman*, p. 166.
19. See *Solitary Horseman*, p. 69.
20. **G. P. R. James,** *Corse de Leon, or, The Brigand* (3 vols, London, 1841), I, 78–80.
21. **Ernest A. Baker,** *The History of the English Novel* (10 vols, London, 1924–39), VII, 93.
22. See *The Journal of Sir Walter Scott,* ed. W. E. K. Anderson (Oxford, 1972), p. 213.
23. See **S. M. Ellis,** *William Harrison Ainsworth and his Friends* (2 vols, London, 1911),I, 286–7.
24. See *Ainsworth,* I. 376 n. 1.
25. See *Ainsworth,* II, 140 ff.
26. See *The Lancashire Witches* (1682), in *The Complete Works of Thomas Shadwell,* ed. Summers (5 vols, London, 1927), IV, 87–189; and *Letters on Demonology and Witchcraft,* pp. 202–5.
27. See Dalziel, p. 140.
28. **Q. D. Leavis,** *Fiction and the Reading Public* (London, 1968), p. 177.
29. See **G. W. M. Reynolds,** *Wagner, the Wehr-wolf,* ed. E. F. Bleiler (New York, 1975), p. xvi.
30. **Reynolds,** *The Mysteries of London* (London, 1844–8), First Series, I, 21.

CHAPTER 7

Early American Gothic

Charles Brockden Brown, Nathaniel Hawthorne, Edgar Allan Poe

American Gothic is, as it were, a *refraction* of English: where English Gothic has a direct past to deal with, American has a level interposed between present and past, the level represented by a vague historical 'Europe', an often already mythologised 'Old World'. Washington Irving described Europe as being

> rich in the accumulated treasures of age. Her very ruins told the history of times gone by, and every mouldering stone was a chronicle. I longed to wander over the scenes of renowned achievement – to tread, as it were, in the footsteps of antiquity – to loiter about the ruined castle – to meditate on the falling tower – to escape, in short, from the common-place realities of the present, and lose myself among the shadowy grandeurs of the past.[1]

This kind of sensibility is familiar in the Gothic tradition from Walpole to Ainsworth, but the British writers did not have far to go to seek sites for their meditations; the fact that the Americans did, that the effort of imagining a distant past from the perspective of the early nineteenth century was incomparably greater in the New World, may go some way to explaining the distinctive features of American Gothic: its darkness, its tendency towards obsession, its absorption with powerful and evil Europeans. Why American Gothic should also be intensely preoccupied with the pathology of guilt, perhaps the most important link between its three principal early protagonists, Charles Brockden Brown, Nathaniel Hawthorne and Edgar Allan Poe, is more problematic: but one factor has to be Puritanism and its legacy, which is the point at which the work of

165

these Americans connects emotionally with the historical reinterpretations of the British writers.

Charles Brockden Brown, renowned as America's first professional man of letters, was born in 1771 in Philadelphia, at that time a city of great importance. His family was Quaker but liberal, his father a reader of Godwin, Mary Wollstonecraft and Bage. Brown's letters and other writings reveal a curious intellectual mixture: his accounts of his early poetical ambitions and his reveries about natural objects read as romantic in the Keatsian sense, yet in most other ways he was very much a child of the eighteenth century, a rationalist and a formal stylist whose cultural heroes were Addison, Steele and Johnson. In his early *Rhapsodist* essays are conjoined emotional eulogy and a worship of the supreme power of reason, and perhaps this is the key: that Brown, a radical from youth and an avid reader of the *Encyclopédie*, belongs intellectually with the Jacobins, and was of that cast of mind which could derive emotional satisfaction and uplift from regarding the semi-divine operations of the Goddess Reason.

His early reading included most of the Enlightenment thinkers, Montesquieu, Helvétius, d'Holbach, Rousseau and of course Paine; on the literary side a major influence was Richardson, but he was also unusually well read in German literature and in the work of Madeleine de Scudery and the other French romanticists, and one can find plot-structures from Richardson and the French writers recurring in his novels. But in both political and literary terms, it has always been claimed that Brown's biggest debt was to the ubiquitous Godwin, whose *Political Justice* appeared in America in 1793 and echoes from whose novels can be found throughout his writings. This is a judgement which needs some probing, if only because of the critical contradictions within it: in 1858, the *Edinburgh Review* was likening Godwin and Brown to Poe in terms of their having 'the same love of the morbid and the improbable; the same frequent straining of the interest; the same tracing, step by step, logically as it were and elaborately, through all its complicated relations, a terrible mystery to its source',[2] whereas in 1878 the *Fortnightly* was referring to Brown's 'soft and childlike disposition' and his 'moments of high poetic exaltation',[3] not qualities we normally associate with Godwin. Politically, the position is even more complex, since Brown's charismatic villains tend to embody the evil consequences of Godwinism; however, this is a matter to which we will return.

Brown's influence on British writers was considerable, even

though he never achieved a sizeable British reading public. Keats, Scott and Hazlitt read his work; Mary Shelley, as we have mentioned, had been doing so immediately before embarking on *Frankenstein*. Peacock claimed that Brown was one of the deepest influences on Shelley, that 'nothing so blended itself with the structure of his interior mind as the creations of Brown', and his list of Shelley's six favourite books includes, alongside *Faust* and *Die Räuber*, four of Brown's novels: *Wieland* (1798), *Ormond* (1799), *Edgar Huntly* (1799) and *Arthur Mervyn* (1800).[4]

The book that Peacock singles out in *Gryll Grange* for particular mention is *Wieland*.[5] The novel begins by recounting the fate of the elder Wieland, who, as the result of early hardship, becomes a religious enthusiast. He builds himself a temple to nature, but one night while he is worshipping in it his family hear an explosion and see flame coming from the building. They discover him dying, scorched and bruised, and apparently believing that supernatural agents have been at work. The main story now begins: it concerns Theodore, Wieland's son, who becomes himself melancholy and religious, partly through brooding on his father's strange death. He eventually begins to hear voices, and these voices prompt him to the most terrible actions, including the slaughter of his family and eventually his own suicide. After several chapters of extraordinary suspense, the 'voices' are revealed to be the work of one Carwin, a rationalist friend of the family who claims to have been trying to teach Wieland a lesson in religious credulity, a lesson which has gone somewhat amiss. The death of Wieland's father, incidentally, is put down to spontaneous combustion.

It is an epistolary novel, recounted in the letters of Theodore's sister Clara. Brown has often been attacked on grounds of style: Birkhead talks of him 'reducing us to a mood of awestruck gravity by the sonority of his pompous periods' (Birkhead, p. 200), but by the standards of 1798 this seems an odd judgement. That Brown was capable of infusing into his first-person narrative a strong sense of immediacy and an unusual degree of realism in terms of the consciousness of his characters could be seen by comparing a passage from, say, *The Italian*, written only a year earlier, with this moment in *Wieland* when Clara experiences a crisis of terror:

> Alas! my heart droops, and my fingers are enervated; my ideas are vivid, but my language is faint; now know I what it is to entertain incommunicable sentiments. The chain of subsequent incidents is drawn through my mind, and being linked with those which forewent, by turns rouse up agonies and sink me into hopelessness.

> Yet I will persist to the end. My narrative may be invaded by
> inaccuracy and confusion; but if I live no longer, I will, at least, live
> to complete it. What but ambiguities, abruptnesses, and dark
> transitions, can be expected from the historian who is, at the same
> time, the sufferer of these disasters?[6]

This, of course, is one of the central questions of Gothic, and
Brown answers it admirably: Clara's character comes over very fully,
possessed of great dignity and an iron will, her occasional shrinkings
before horror far more reasonable and sympathetic than the multiple collapses of Radcliffe's heroines. There is a succinctness and a
psychological accuracy to *Wieland* which contrasts strongly with the
melodramatic tendencies in Radcliffe.

The principal reason for locating *Wieland* within a Gothic tradition is that it is a novel of persecution and terror, the depth of
which is made evident to Clara herself when she realises the extent
and effect of her brother's religious mania:

> What a tale had thus been unfolded! I was hunted to death, not by
> one whom my misconduct had exasperated, who was conscious of
> illicit motives, and who sought his end by circumvention and surprise;
> but by one who deemed himself commissioned for this act by heaven;
> who regarded this career of horror as the last refinement of virtue;
> whose implacability was proportioned to the reverence and love which
> he felt for me, and who was inaccessible to the fear of punishment
> and ignominy!   (*Wieland*, p. 213)

The most obvious comparison is the pursuit in Hogg's *Confessions*,
which is again motivated by religious delusion, a delusion strongly
supported by widely held beliefs, and Brown's purpose is ostensibly
very similar to Hogg's. The critic in the *Fortnightly* summed it up
well: 'man is rebuked for his proneness to believe that he is worked
upon by supernatural powers, and the crimes of Wieland are a
protest against those hysterical religious feelings which may not
always result in such dire calamities, but which – when cherished
and brooded over – inevitably lead to the dethronement of reason'.[7]
It is this dethronement of reason which is the main source of terror
in *Wieland*; and it is Brown's peculiar contribution to the Gothic
that he manages to portray the machinations of superstition and
delusion, not in distant castles or remote countries but in a contemporary and recognisable American world.

In other ways too, Brown moves beyond Radcliffe in his adap-
tation of conventional terror-motifs, particularly in his handling of
the social and psychological vulnerability of women, which is again
a principal theme of *Wieland*. Again one could compare the difficul-

ties of Ellena or Emily with those of Clara, who is capable of offering a much more rational account of the reasons for her terrors:

> My frame shook, and my knees were unable to support me. I gazed alternately at the closet door and at the door of my room. At one of these avenues would enter the exterminator of my honour and my life. I was prepared for defence; but now that danger was imminent, my means of defence, and my power to use them were gone. I was not qualified, by education and experience, to encounter perils like these: or, perhaps, I was powerless because I was again assaulted by surprise, and had not fortified my mind by foresight and previous reflection against a scene like this.   (*Wieland*, pp. 170–1)

As befits an early feminist who was well read in feminist literature and whose first novel, *Alcuin* (1798), had been subtitled *The Rights of Women*, Brown pursues his analysis of Clara's plight with honesty and rigour: the dangers she encounters enter the more vividly on our memory because she is no weeping heroine but a determined 'new woman', who is herself able to give account of her own feelings without false modesty. At one point she confesses her affection for her lover Pleyel, and comments thus on this confession:

> I feel no reluctance, my friends to be thus explicit. Time was, when these emotions would be hidden with immeasurable solicitude from every human eye. Alas! these airy and fleeting impulses of shame are gone. My scruples were preposterous and criminal. They are bred in all hearts, by a perverse and vicious education, and they would still have maintained their place in my heart, had not my portion been set in misery. My errors have taught me thus much wisdom; that those sentiments which we ought not to disclose, it is criminal to harbour.
> (*Wieland*, p. 90)

In the decade of *Wieland*, we would have to look far in British writing for such a poised account of the miseries and lessons of the division of the sexes: Clara's argument is impressive in itself, but what is even more impressive is the undertone of regret for an inevitably lost but nonetheless stable system of social relations, her awareness of the harshness of the transition from repression to comparative freedom.

Wieland could be called a work of the 'explained supernatural'; the persistent question, as G. R. Thompson puts it, is 'whether the younger Wieland acts under the influence of a demonic agent when he murdered his family or whether this was merely the act of a madman influenced by environmental forces'.[8] Brown's mode of explanation is sophisticated, and works at three levels. In the first place, Wieland's actions are the result of uncomprehended but supposedly scientifically valid phenomena: the remarkable death of

169

his father, but, more importantly, Carwin's gift of ventriloquism, which understandably confuses everyone. At another level, however, Brown's explanations are psychological: he goes into detail over the set of religious attitudes which renders Wieland a fitting prey for Carwin's machinations, hinting that they would have been ineffective were it not for Wieland's 'gloomy' and credulous disposition. And this, in turn, is the result of environmental and social forces: Wieland's family background and social isolation is the eventual cause of his downfall, and this returns us again to questions about the influence of Godwin and the political complexion of *Wieland*.

Birkhead claims that Brown sought to embody Godwin's political theory in his novels,[9] but this is at best only partially true. Wieland himself, certainly, is the victim of his environment, but he is also the victim of Godwinism itself, both in that his own ideology is not flexible enough to handle the apparently irrational, and also in that the demonic Carwin is himself an eminently Godwinian figure who works by cold logic to disillusion Wieland, and yet ends by causing murder and mayhem. Godwin's influence on Brown was contradictory: on the one hand, Brown was consistently fascinated by the *problems* of Godwin's theory, but on the other his principal effort is to separate off the beneficial aspects of that theory from certain others. *Wieland* is at one and the same time a Godwinian condemnation of superstition and vindication of the theory of social conditioning, and an anti-Godwinian warning against blind adherence to logic and against the Rosicrucian implications of Godwin's work, which seemed to Brown to imply the possibility that certain men might, because of the power of their intellect, be permitted to operate beyond human law and regulation. This is what Carwin does, and the consequences are disastrous, as they would not be, of course, in Lytton. This warning is quite deliberate on Brown's part:

> In the selection of subjects for a useful history, the chief point is not the virtue of a character. The prime regard is to be paid to the genius and force of mind that is displayed. Great energy employed in the promotion of vicious purposes, constitutes a very useful spectacle. Give me a tale of lofty crimes, rather than of honest folly.[10]

Thus we have Carwin: and Carwin, unlike many another Gothic hero/villain, at least tries to repent. 'I cannot justify my conduct', he says, 'yet my only crime was curiosity.' As events moved on,

> I saw in a stronger light than ever, the dangerousness of that instrument which I employed, and renewed my resolutions to abstain from the use of it in future; but I was destined perpetually to violate my resolutions. By some perverse fate, I was led into circumstances in

which the exertion of my powers was the sole or the best means of
escape.   (*Wieland*, p. 231)

Although Carwin is in himself a charismatic character, Brown does
not go the way of many other Gothic novelists and allow him to
dominate the stage; he is no robber-king or man of destiny, but the
fool of fate as much as is Wieland. In this as in other ways Brown
manages to remain in control of his material, and to bend his
depiction of terror to his social purpose. Extreme rationalism, like
superstition, results in personal aggrandisement and loss of perspective: the pretension of standing outside the law is the same as
the pretension of personally hearing the voice of God. Whether the
result is Falkland, Zanoni or the Wringhims, damage ensues, damage
to the gradual democratic progress which was Brown's ideal.

Brown, as is well known, held in low regard the 'puerile superstitions and exploded manners' of original Gothic.[11] He follows
Radcliffe in his attitude towards the power of nature and in his use
of terror, but 'romance' was to him an altogether serious business.
His most important definition of it occurs in an essay of 1800, where
he distinguishes it from history on the grounds that romance is
principally an enquiry into motives and causes, whereas history
contents itself with the display of facts.[12] Brown's major works conduct this enquiry on a supra-historical level: that is, they do not set
out to provide reinterpretations of specific historical conjunctures,
but to enquire into the question of social psychology in general.
But in other work, like the *Sketches of the History of Carsol* and the
Sketches of the History of the Carrils and the Ormes (both of uncertain
date), Brown does apply his investigative technique to real history,
albeit a history transmuted by the deliberate insertion of fictional
characters, events, subplots, a mode which recalls to mind the work
of Lee and her school. Early in his life Brown 'confessed' his 'attach-
ment to fictitious history',[13] and he was generally interested in fostering American historical writing.

Thus he saw in romance a way of laying bare the springs of
human action and thereby of understanding the past, although this
concern is less clearly manifested than in the case of Hawthorne.
His attempts at understanding the interrelations of society and ideology were formative in terms of American Gothic: they look towards
both Hawthorne's obsession with religious dogmatism and its social
effects, and Poe's minute analyses of situations of terror. Already
with Brown one sees a degree of explicitness of purpose in advance
of his British Gothic contemporaries, although this explicitness per-

171

haps decreases the symbolic force of his writings. The fact that Carwin *teaches* us more than Schedoni is bound up with the other fact that Carwin is a far less potently tragic figure than Schedoni; but then, Schedoni reaches back into depths of historical and religious terror which were hardly available to a writer in Brown's position. The rational strength and emotional thinness of Brown's writing are distinctive to his America, his ability to explore mental worlds with precision peculiar to a situation in which those worlds were not submerged beneath the pressure of a fearsome past.

Brown needs to be 'introduced' because his writings have suffered from the neglect of time, which is not true of Hawthorne or Poe, two of the best known of all Gothic writers. It would be presumptuous to attempt any kind of general survey of figures of such stature: instead, I want to make one or two general points, and then to look at three of their works in detail: Hawthorne's *House of the Seven Gables*, and two of Poe's short stories, 'The Fall of the House of Usher' and 'The Cask of Amontillado'. Each of these works has a huge critical literature devoted to it: I want only to concentrate on certain features of the texts which relate to British Gothic, in order to bring out crucial modifications which Hawthorne and Poe make in the texture of Gothic writing.

Nathaniel Hawthorne and Edgar Allan Poe were contemporaries, born within five years of one another, and both were influenced by British Gothic. Hawthorne read Godwin and also Scott when young, and his early poetry shows traces of the graveyard writers. Poe knew Beckford, Radcliffe, Lewis, Maturin, although most of his Gothic reading was done in the pages of *Blackwood's*, which, in the years between 1821 and 1827, carried stories like 'The Man in the Bell', 'The Buried Alive', 'The Suicide', 'The Murderer's Last Night', 'The Iron Shroud', and many other examples of Gothic genre writing. Perhaps a more potent though less clear-cut influence on both Hawthorne and Poe was the cult of 'Byronism', the romantic cultivation of the heroic and tragic self which underlies much of their private writing and carries over at least into Poe's stories. In Poe's case, Byronic self-conception was mediated through Lytton, the 'latter-day Byron', and he justified his interest in Gothic by appealing to the authoritative models of Lytton and Coleridge.[14] Both Hawthorne and Poe, again, were influenced by Hoffmann, whose story 'Das Majorat' (1817) – which Poe may have first known through a summary in Scott's article 'On the supernatural in fictitious composition' (1827)[15] – has strong resemblances to 'House of Usher'.

This is not, of course, to say that these were the only influences on either Hawthorne or Poe: nor is it to claim that the entire works of either writer can or should be summarised as Gothic. But it is as well to point out that American Gothic cannot be considered wholly as a native growth, for this leads to critical distortion. Poe, for instance, is heralded as the first investigator of 'morbid' psychological situations, which is not true, or as the writer who introduced the Gothic short story, which is farcical; Hawthorne as the original exposer of the evils of Puritanism and the witch-trials, which had been a topic of British Gothic for fifty years when *House of the Seven Gables* and *The Scarlet Letter* (1850) were written. In both writers, Americanness obviously makes a vast difference to the way in which Gothic methods and approaches are handled, but this can only be appreciated against a background which includes British writing.

To take Hawthorne first – purely for the sake of thematic argument, since *House of the Seven Gables* was written in 1851, five years after 'Amontillado' and twelve years after 'Usher' – the British resonances are principally from Scott and Byron rather than from the Gothic novelists as such – Scott, for instance, in *Fanshawe* (1828) and in the early 'Alice Doane', Byron particularly in *The Marble Faun* (1860). But *House of the Seven Gables* stands out as the most claustrophobic and obsessive of his romances, and also as the one which follows through most closely the arguments about class relations which characterise so much of the British writing.

The house in question is that which belongs to the family of Pyncheon, which at the time of the narrative is in a state of decaying gentility. Its principal members are Hepzibah, the old maid who tries to keep the house up, even to the extent of indulging, forlornly and unsuccessfully, in trade; her brother Clifford, who is supposedly weak-minded and whose return from incarceration sparks off the story; Phoebe, the young relative whose innocence of the dark secrets in the family history enables her to become an instrument of rejuvenation; and Judge Jaffrey, the solidly successful man of affairs, who has left the old house for a modern residence, and the unfolding and punishment of whose past crimes form the main plot development. There is also a lodger, Holgrave, a young radical whose affection for Phoebe eventually provides the Pyncheon family with a necessary infusion of new blood.

In a sense, there is almost no story to *House of the Seven Gables*, and there is certainly no suspense. Once Hawthorne has set up his characters, such is the extent of his narrative presence that the conclusion of the story is foregone. The house is the site of an ancient curse, pronounced by one Maule on the founding father of

173

the family, and this curse is duly visited on the stately and unpleasant figure of Judge Jaffrey; Jaffrey's death has 'a permanently invigorating and ultimately beneficial effect on Clifford',[16] whereupon he and Hepzibah, also invigorated by inheriting Jaffrey's fortune, ride rather slowly off into the sunset of a rural idyll, while Phoebe marries Holgrave, having already suitably tempered his fiery radicalism with sweetness and light.

The power of the book, however, is by no means in the narrative, but in the intensity with which Hawthorne concentrates his and our attention on his themes. The principal one, obviously, is the house, in the double sense so usefully summarised in the Greek *oikos*. The best description is that of H. H. Hoeltje, even though he is not describing the House of the Seven Gables but the remarkably similar house in *Doctor Grimshawe's Secret* (*c.* 1861):

> This old mansion had that delightful intricacy that can never be contrived, never be attained by design, but is the happy result of many builders, many designs, many ages – a house to go astray in, as in a city, and come to unexpected places, a house of dark passages and antique stairways where one might meet someone who might have a word of destiny to say to the wanderer. It was a dim, twilight place, where one felt as if he were on the point of penetrating rare mysteries, such as man's thoughts are always hovering round, and always returning from, as if some strange, vast, mysterious truth, long searched for, was about to be revealed; a sense of something to come; an opening of doors, a drawing away of veils; a lifting of heavy, magnificent curtains, whose dark folds hang before a spectacle of awe.[17]

What is particularly valuable in this description is that it brings out the fact that the Gothic mansion or castle is always without a total plan: Udolpho and the House of the Seven Gables are equally of doubtful extent and shape, no matter how solid their details might appear. And this, of course, reflects their metaphorical nature; the secret of the house is the secret of the family of Pyncheon. When Maule cursed the original Pyncheon, he told him he should 'have blood to drink',[18] and this is reflected in the literal level in the apoplexy which is hereditary in the family and which carries off the Judge; but metaphorically also, the blood which the Pyncheons drink is their own blood, as the line, enfeebled by time, turns back upon itself. The Pyncheons have to drink their own blood because they will suffer nothing else to happen to it, they will allow no intermixture between their 'gentle' stock and lesser mortals, and they thus perish of a kind of inverted haemophilia, mythically the hereditary disease of the proud and isolated.

Yet there are other aspects of the imagery which demonstrate the difference between Hawthorne's tangentially vampiristic argument and that of, say, Polidori, for the Pyncheons are not European aristocrats. Judge Jaffrey does not die of the airy weightlessness which might, as deathlessness and unlimited mobility, symbolically represent the condition of a powerless aristocracy, but of an excess of weight and solidity: he belongs to that class of men whose

> field of action lies among the external phenomena of life. They possess vast ability in grasping, and arranging, and appropriating to themselves the big, heavy, solid unrealities, such as gold, landed estate, offices of trust and emolument, and public honours. With these materials, and with deeds of goodly aspect, done in the public eye, an individual of this class builds up, as it were, a tall and stately edifice, which, in the view of other people, and ultimately in his own view, is no other than the man's character, or the man himself. Behold, therefore, a palace! (*Seven Gables*, p. 201)

Hawthorne goes on to describe the palace which is Judge Jaffrey in detail, and here the metaphor gets complicated, for Jaffrey dies of intensive bourgeoisification, while the effete Clifford remains blameless and harmless. Jaffrey is crushed under his own weight, which is the weight of the edifice of respectability around his rotten core; but is this the weight of the edifice with the seven gables?

The answer lies in the fact that Hawthorne is not talking about a past aristocracy, but about a present and prosperous upper middle class, for whom the House of the Seven Gables is not an accurate symbol. That house, and its occupants Hepzibah and Clifford, are dying blamelessly of isolation and atrophy; the building which topples on Jaffrey is a structure of hypocrisy of his own devising. The house which the Pyncheons' ancestor built was an aping of European style; it carries a fate with it, but not automatically. Jaffrey encounters it only when he robes himself in temporal power.

The House of the Seven Gables is not a middle-class myth of the aristocracy, but a lower-middle-class myth of an overpowerful *haute bourgeoisie* which has tried to usurp democratic privileges, decked in a Gothic mode which is not entirely appropriate to it, which might also be said of some of Dickens's work. It also recounts a much shorter history than British Gothic, and this must account in part for Hawthorne's knowing style: there is no suspense because there is no moral doubt, the author is fully in command of both the beginning and the end of history. The supernatural in the book is not important, because it is chronic materialism which is the source of fear: Maule does not lay his curse because of an ancient blood-feud, but very pragmatically, because he was cheated out of his land.

175

The centre-piece is the extraordinary chapter 'Governor Pyncheon', in which Hawthorne mercilessly taunts Jaffrey, already dead, with not going about his business on the very day when he was to achieve his ambition and be nominated for the Governorship:

> Make haste, then! Do your part! The meed for which you have toiled, and fought, and climbed, and crept, is ready for your grasp! Be present at this dinner – drink a glass or two of that noble wine – make your pledges in as low a whisper as you will – and you rise up from table virtually governor of the glorious old State! Governor Pyncheon of Massachusetts!
> *(Seven Gables,* p. 239)

The extent to which Hawthorne dominates his characters is remarkable: apart from Jaffrey, Hepzibah is treated with condescension, Clifford with tolerant benevolence, like a beautiful but retarded child, Holgrave with that wisdom of age which knows that he will grow out of his radical principles. The future belongs to Phoebe, but Phoebe is unreal, the only one of the major characters on whom Hawthorne's considerable dissecting skill makes no impression, because there is nothing of interest in her to dissect. It is this, surely, which justifies those critics, beginning with Melville, who speak of the 'blackness' in Hawthorne:[19] not his dealings in the dark places of the mind, but his scorn for aspiration, which means that his characters, here but even more in *The Scarlet Letter,* remain locked in their circles of guilt. In Hawthorne, the vision has been decisively betrayed, the corner-stone of the house is stained with blood, the blood of the persecuted, and nothing can clean it; it is symbolically appropriate that he spent so much time near the end of his life trying to write a story around the Bloody Footstep of Smithell's Hall, for that footstep walks through each of his 'romances', a sullying of innocence from which there is no escape. Even though, as in Phoebe, one may try to create a symbol which is free from taint, the curse is visited back upon the writer, for there is not even any blood in Phoebe's veins.

One of the many things which is remarkable about Poe is that he instantly upsets any such generalisations as one might go on to make about American Gothic. His contribution to Gothic is enormous and varied: the story of the split personality which was to produce Stevenson's *Dr Jekyll and Mr Hyde* is prefigured in 'William Wilson' (1839); the development of the detective thriller from Godwin through to Conan Doyle and others has two of its most important manifestations in 'The Murders in the Rue Morgue' (1841) and 'The Gold Bug' (1843); and the theme of premature burial received definitive statements in 'The Cask of Amontillado' and elsewhere. Yet Poe's greatest contribution was in terms not of themes but of structure and tone, in the evolution of a variety of symbolist terror in which he has never been surpassed, but which seems in most ways more European than American. Although Poe did not invent the Gothic short story, he invented something within it, a kind of story which does not move by simple narrative but by spiralling intensification: and this technique is at its most perfect in 'The Fall of the House of Usher', in which are summarised many of the themes to which we have already alluded, and in 'The Cask of Amontillado', which Birkhead refers to as 'the most terrible and the most perfectly executed of all Poe's tales'.[20] To wonder whether the pun on 'executed' is intentional is perhaps itself the legacy of reading Poe, and of the awareness of psychological complexity which this engenders: popular consciousness of psychology probably owes as much to him as to Freud and Jung together.

'Usher' – published in England, incidentally, by Ainsworth – cannot be summarised in terms of plot: Thompson mentions the most important thing about it when he comments that, by the end of the story, 'we do not know that anything the narrator has told us is "real", the whole tale and its structures may be the fabrication of the completely deranged mind of the narrator. Nothing at all may have happened in a conventional sense in the outside world – only in the inner world of the narrator's mind' (*Poe's Fiction*, pp. 96–7). The problem here is that this could be said in one sense about any work of fiction: it is specifically important in 'Usher' because of the degree of sensitivity with which Poe leads us to doubt the narrator's veracity and competence. Confronted with a fiction which may well be written by an insane pseudo-author, criticism tends to come full circle.

To begin with a crude statement, 'Usher' is a mounting spiral of terror in which the narrator, visiting his dying old friend Roderick Usher, perhaps witnesses certain supernatural events in his company; or becomes involved in his private but powerful fantasies; or, conceivably, himself visits the products of his dubious imagination on Roderick. At all events, it appears that Roderick's sister dies, and then returns to life:

> For a moment she remained trembling and reeling to and fro upon the threshold – then, with a low moaning cry, fell heavily inward upon the person of her brother, and in her violent and now final death agonies, bore him to the floor a corpse, and a victim to the terrors he had anticipated.

177

Subsequently the house itself, which Roderick has been blaming for exercising a malign influence over the lives of himself and his family, sinks into the surrounding lake.

One way of investigating the complexity of the prism through which we view these events is by looking at the opening and closing passages of the story. At the beginning, the narrator arrives at the house, whither Roderick has summoned him:

> I know not how it was – but, with the first glimpse of the building, a sense of insufferable gloom pervaded my spirit. I say insufferable: for the feeling was unrelieved by any of that half-pleasurable, because poetic, sentiment with which the mind usually receives even the sternest natural images of the desolate or terrible. I looked upon the scene before me – upon the mere house, and the simple landscape features of the domain – upon the bleak walls – upon the vacant eye-like windows – upon a few rank sedges – and upon a few white trunks of decayed trees – with an utter depression of soul, which I can compare to no earthly sensation more properly than to the after-dream of the reveller upon opium – the bitter lapse into every-day life – the hideous dropping off of the veil.

Already, everything is doubtful. Poe is deliberately dissociating the scene from any connotations of sublimity, substituting for Radcliffe's divine nature Coleridge's 'grief without a pang',[21] but thereby raising the question of whether this is a movement towards or away from reality. The after-dream of opium is no more 'real' than the revelry itself, and the narrator may already be suffering from a causeless melancholy. He appears given to extremes – 'insufferable', 'utter', 'bitter', 'hideous' – and the victim of incomprehensible feelings: 'it was a mystery all insoluble; nor could I grapple with the shadowy fancies that crowded upon me as I pondered'. But if he cannot grasp his own condition, what chance does he stand of perceiving aright the roots of Roderick's 'sickness unto death'?

He goes on to speculate on the possibility that in some way the arrangement of the features of the house might be producing this effect, but this only adds to the difficulty, because when Roderick comes round to suggesting something similar it is impossible to know whether the narrator has put it into his mind. What is especially frightening about the development of the relationship between the narrator and Roderick is that Roderick *knows* he is neurasthenic, whereas the narrator makes confessions of his own susceptibility while maintaining an apparently rational discourse. When he looks down into the tarn, his first impression of the house deepens:

There can be no doubt that the consciousness of the rapid increase of my superstition – for why should I not so term it? – served mainly to accelerate the increase itself. Such, I have long known, is the paradoxical law of all sentiments having terror as a basis.

He thus acknowledges his own tendency to inflate situations of fear, which is also an ironic comment on the writer's self-defeating ability to vest the most mundane of circumstances in a shroud of terror. For a psychological reading of the tale, there is already a problem, about *whose* psychological constitution is to be probed: Roderick's, the narrator's, the writer's? All three, of course, are intertwined in the text: it generates its own psychological structure which envelops the interlocking individual consciousnesses within it in a way which, after all, is only a development from the interlocking of perspectives which characterises Gothic as a whole, but which proceeds here to a point at which the psychology of persons becomes overshadowed by the evolution of the multiple symbol.

At the end of the story the narrator, to 'pass away this terrible night together', reads to Roderick one of his 'favourite romances', the imaginary *Mad Trist*. It is a story hardly calculated to allay Roderick's fears: during it, various sounds occur in the subtext which become 'real' in terms of the actual story, being transmuted into the sounds of the perhaps prematurely buried sister rising from her tomb, until Roderick, crazed with terror at her imminent appearance, bursts out:

> 'Oh! whither shall I fly? Will she not be here anon? Is she not hurrying to upbraid me for my haste? Have I not heard her footstep on the stair? Do I not distinguish that heavy and horrible beating of her heart? Madman!' – here he sprang furiously to his feet, and shrieked out his syllables, as if in the effort he were giving up his soul – '*Madman! I tell you that she now stands without the door!*'

Here is the crux of the story in a single word: 'Madman'. In a sense the whole action of the tale has been a movement towards the production of this one word, with its multiple interpretations. Roderick, at least, has seen the madness in his companion; or, Roderick has finally seen his own insanity in its full colours; or, the narrator is giving vicarious vent to his psychological triumph over the dying Roderick; or, the writer is celebrating his victory over the now disorganised perceptions of his readers. 'Madman' is the magic word on which the story has throughout hinged, the repressed term which underlies the arabesques of deflection. Once it is admitted and uttered, once the disorientation is no longer displaced, the lady appears; she and Roderick go down to death together; the house sinks; and the narrator flees 'aghast' – from the site of the destruction in which he has participated, perhaps as murderer, perhaps as agent of a kind of terrible catharsis. His pseudo-rational discourse and the neurotic discourse of Roderick are buried under the ruins when this unitary and paradoxically unifying primal scream breaks up the webs of reason and superstition which, in their interlocking, have sustained the house's apparent coherence; consciousness and the unconscious fuse under the pressure of the released energy, and house and tarn, pattern and depth, cancel each other out.

Most obviously, 'Usher' is yet another variation on the old ambiguity of the 'house' as building and as family, another attempt to deal with the problem of the blood-line. It is, in the end, a vampire story: Roderick perhaps takes the blood of his sister, the house takes the blood of both of them (as the aristocratic family demands the suppression of individual lives in its service), the narrator appears to feed on the general carnage. The by now familiar connotations are there: hints of incest, hints of infection ('It was no wonder that his condition terrified – that it infected me'), the physical and psychological atrophy of a class too specialised to survive in unrarefied air. Poe's story points both forward and back: back to Walpole and Radcliffe, forward to another whole constellation of Gothic at the end of the nineteenth century, exemplified particularly in Wilde and in Bram Stoker, when decadence, engaged in picking over the bones of aristocratic modes of life, starts to travel again in vampiristic circles, but with the benefit of the kind of supra-narrative symbolism which Poe himself inaugurated.

The reflexive symbolism of the word is even more pure in 'The Cask of Amontillado'. Here the narrator, Montresor, wreaks vengeance upon an apparent enemy, Fortunato (splendid irony); he takes him down to his wine-cellar on the pretence of tasting a vintage, takes advantage of his drunkenness and immures him alive. The story is conducted very largely in dialogue, and the atmosphere is the result of a very complicated play of language. The opening paragraph is this:

> The thousand injuries of Fortunato I had borne as I best could, but when he ventured upon insult, I vowed revenge. You, who so well know the nature of my soul, will not suppose, however, that I gave utterance to a threat. *At length* I would be avenged; this was a point definitely settled – but the very definitiveness with which it was resolved, precluded the idea of risk. I must not only punish, but punish with impunity. A wrong is unredressed when retribution overtakes its redresser. It is equally unredressed when the avenger fails to make himself felt as such to him who has done the wrong.

Thus Poe draws his readers into close intimacy with a man whose code of honour is an unspeakable parody of an aristocratic code, founded on the most unpleasant elements of Jacobean tragedy. Throughout the story, Montresor is breathing in our ear, gloating, perhaps much later, even on his death-bed, over the perfect execution of his plan. Yet by the same token, Poe precludes us from enquiring into the reasonableness of his case against Fortunato: precisely because we are *presumed* to know Montresor so well, Poe can place an apparent monster precisely at our unwilling shoulder. The 'thousand injuries' sound a mere poeticised invention, yet Montresor as narrator appears to experience no doubts that we are on his side.

'Amontillado' is more obviously ironic than 'Usher'. When Montresor at last encounters Fortunato, he is 'so pleased to see him, that I thought I should never have done wringing his hand'; he tempts him with the tasting of an Amontillado, upon which it is Fortunato who hurries *him* towards the vaults; he tells Fortunato of his coat of arms, a foot crushing a serpent with the motto 'Nemo me impune lacessit'; and all the while he invites the reader to join him in jeering at his enemy's obliviousness. He warns him of the danger to be expected from the damp in the cellar, but Fortunato goes on, and Montresor chains him to a wall.

It is at this point that Poe's technique is at its most remarkable. Fettered to the wall, Fortunato exclaims in bewilderment, 'The Amontillado!', to which Montresor replies 'True, the Amontillado'. The Amontillado has become many things: the goal of Montresor's efforts, the symbol of Fortunato's pride and of the inner sanctum of value which is now to be Fortunato's living tomb. Montresor is doing his 'friend' the honour of locking him away in his own heart. Fortunato falls silent for a while, but then begins to rattle his chains. Montresor, who wishes to relish his victory to the full and whose triumph seems increasingly to depend on savouring Fortunato's verbal and other protests, pauses in his building of the wall which will incarcerate him in order to enjoy the sound.

Fortunato starts screaming as the walls gets higher; Montresor 'replied to the yells of him who clamoured. I re-echoed – I aided – I surpassed them in volume and in strength. I did this, and the clamourer grew still'. What is unique in Poe's style is well expressed in the reference to 'him who clamoured'. In that phrase, Fortunato has ceased to be an individual, has become merely an effect, and a rather pleasing one, on Montresor's senses. He has also become

181

generalised; Montresor is the god silencing and placating troubled waters. When the last brick is about to be laid, Fortunato laughs:

> Ha! ha! ha! . . . a very good joke indeed – an excellent jest . . . But is it not getting late? Will not they be awaiting us at the palazzo, the Lady Fortunato and the rest? Let us be gone.

'Yes,' replies Montresor, 'let us be gone'; his repetition of Fortunato's words has itself become a subsidiary means of annihilation. Montresor denies his enemy's self by appropriating the attribution of meanings. Fortunato can say what he likes, but such is the skill and complexity of Montresor's revenge that everything he says can be perverted into a kind of complicity with the plan.

Under the pressure of this annihilation, Fortunato, like Roderick Usher, bursts the barriers of repression with a scream: '*For the love of God, Montresor!*' But whereas in 'Usher' the scream in a sense works, by calling down the unnaturally withheld disaster, here it is powerless to break the circle, for Montresor has 'foreseen everything': 'Yes', he says, 'for the love of God!' This is the twist of the knife: honour, carried to the point of insanity, knows no God other than itself, and Montresor, engaged in the operation of absolute power, is performing a final act of love – for himself, but also for Fortunato, who is liberated by this scream into silence. Thereafter he says nothing as Montresor inserts the last stone:

> I plastered it up. Against the new masonry I re-erected the old rampart of bones. For the half of a century no mortal has disturbed them. 'In pace requiescat!' The peace of God, indeed, passeth all understanding.

The play of symbolism is endless. The cask of Amontillado is the living heart within the dead body, within the vault of bones. Montresor has 'done Fortunato the honour' of giving him 'pride of place' in the wine-vault which symbolises his own family pride. He has buried his fortune, his treasure. Yet the completeness of his victory is doubtful: as he inserts the last stone, his heart 'grew sick – on account of the dampness of the catacombs'; perhaps the false explanations which he has enjoyed imposing on his enemy have now grown upon himself, yet if so they have apparently not disturbed his fifty years of peace, for the story is not a death-bed repentance but a final triumph. In its onanistic self-regard, 'The Cask of Amontillado' perhaps resembles most of all Genet's hymns to the self; but where Genet spins endless fabric out of the ego, Poe offers the ego as an enclosed capsule, echoing and reverberating with deathly desire.

In his essay on the supernatural in fiction, Scott comments on its tendency to be 'exhausted by coarse handling and repeated pressure. It is also of a character which it is extremely difficult to sustain, and of which a very small proportion may be said to be better than the whole'.[22] He is talking of the 'supernatural' as a recognisable entity, but Poe takes the argument one stage further and uses the brevity of his tales as a way of withholding judgement on even the existence of the supernatural, which after all may not be present in either 'Usher' or 'Amontillado'. In works like 'Usher' and 'Amontillado', 'supernatural' and 'natural' are equally unusable terms for the unnatural is their constant theme – not in the sense that either represent particularly strange perversions of the psyche, but in that the roots of the mind do not in any case accord with conventional versions of the natural.

A comment of Marcuse's is useful in considering not only Poe but also Hawthorne and, to a lesser extent, Brown; he is talking about the psychological role of the perversions as liberations from the domination of convention, from the rule of the socially domi-nant 'performance principle', whereby activity is organised into soci-ally useful channels:

> By virtue of their revolt against the performance principle in the name of the pleasure principle, the perversions show a deep affinity to fantasy as that mental activity which 'was kept free from reality-testing and remained subordinated to the pleasure principle alone'. Fantasy not only plays a constitutive role in the perverse manifestations of sexuality; as artistic imagination, it also links the perversions with the images of integral freedom and gratification. In a repressive order, which enforces the equation between normal, socially useful, and good, the manifestations of pleasure for its own sake must appear as 'fleurs du mal'.[23]

Every society has to insist on repression in order to function without excessive disruption; therefore the only vocabulary in which to express resistance to that insistence will involve that which is socially categorised as evil or guilt. Hoeltje talks of Hawthorne's 'descent into the spiritual charnel house' (Hoeltje, p. 110) but has a difficult time explaining that, in the end, Hawthorne stands for the light and the good. It is not surprising that he finds this difficult, for it is not true: what Hawthorne offers, in *Seven Gables* and elsewhere, is a revelation of psychological roots and drives which society can never accept as 'good' without breaking down. Similarly, Brown's villains cannot be fully 'saved' by thinking rationally about their misdeeds, for consciousness can have only one attitude towards the repressed unconscious: fear.

This is one aspect of the fear which pervades the whole of Gothic, but one can distinguish between types of Gothic in terms of the degree to which reason is allowed, in the end, to wield power over psychological villainy. In Poe, it barely does so at all: the elaborate and hideous gargoyles which adorn Gothic cathedrals are allowed their own life, for the creator is as 'insane' in social terms as his creations. That is to say, he does not regard himself as different in kind from those creations, but recognises that those hidden powers of the mind which 'infect' his characters also infect him. This is the source of Poe's multiple irony: as critics have said, his stories are ironic about the Gothic mode itself, but not in that Gothic is an invalid method of exposing hidden forces, rather in that its conclusion is reflexive, it reveals as much about the audience as about writer or characters.

When Hawthorne spent time in Europe, two features struck him particularly: the grandeur of Gothic art and architecture, and the strength of persisting class relations, in Britain in particular, although he felt that, at last, 'aristocratic institutions' were about to give way before the onset of republicanism.[24] Clearly, he connected the two things: precisely because the legacy of the European past was so awe-inspiring, it appeared to help to keep going a social system which would otherwise have been unthinkably unjust. The weight of the past signified both beauty and terror, and it was a weight under which Europe was in danger of suffocating. It is that suffocation which runs through Hawthorne and Poe, from Jaffrey Pyncheon crushed beneath his own power to the prematurely buried in 'Usher', 'Ligeia' (1838), 'The Black Cat' (1843) and elsewhere.

It could be said that Poe writes of American obsessions, provided we accept that the major American obsession is Europe. In Brown, Hawthorne and Poe, evil has in one sense or another to do with the European: Brown's villains generally come out of the Old World; the guilt which haunts Hawthorne's characters is associated with infection by European intolerance; Poe creates an artificial version of a European environment in which to set his tales. Europe stands in all three cases as a weighty impediment in the path of progress, but of course the attitudes of the three writers towards this are radically different. For Brown, it is a problem to be dealt with rationally in the process of social development; for Hawthorne, a continuing stain on American society; for Poe, evidence of and metaphor for the fundamental irony in human striving, a vocabulary in which to express the persistence of inadmissible desires.

For Hawthorne, romance was 'that pensive influence over the

mind which follows from brooding upon hoar antiquity, or which may be created by throwing a subdued tinge of the wild and wonderful over the homely aspects of familiar things'.[25] Perhaps, in retrospect, the most important part of that definition is the phrase 'influence over the mind' for it is these influences which Brown, Hawthorne, Poe describe: Brown the influences of superstition and its scientific counterparts, Hawthorne the influence of guilt and the past, Poe the influence of repressed desire. What Hawthorne's definition does is offer a connection between the sense of wonder or terror and the sense of history, a connection which takes us back to the not dissimilar definitions of the imagination made by Coleridge and Wordsworth.

American Gothic seems to be a refraction of British Gothic in that it can only *attempt* to transplant the British themes into American soil: in Hawthorne, the European legacy holds it spellbound. Yet perhaps it is this very problem which occasions Poe's sudden and dramatic breakthrough into new territory. His stories are noted as remarkable precisely for a certain kind of artificiality, of which he himself was proud; his very distance from the mainspring of Gothic brought him an added degree of self-consciousness, the appearance of which was to herald alterations in the entire tradition. In Britain in the mid-century, however, it is not principally through the short story that the history of Gothic can best be pursued, but through the extended narrative and particularly that most quintessentially Victorian of forms, the sensation novel.

Notes and references

1. **Washington Irving**, *Sketch Book of Geoffrey Crayon, Gent.* (2 vols, London, 1894), I, 20–1.
2. '*The Works of the Late Edgar Allan Poe*' (anon. rev.), *The Edinburgh Review*, CVII (Apr. 1858), 426.
3. **George Barnett Smith**, 'Brockden Brown', *The Fortnightly Review*, New Series, XXIV (Sept. 1878), 409.
4. See *The Works of Thomas Love Peacock*, ed. H. F. B. Brett-Smith and C. E. Jones (10 vols, New York, 1967), VIII, 77–8.
5. See *Works*, V. 358.
6. **Charles Brockden Brown**, *Wieland, or, The Transformation*, ed. F. L. Pattee (New York, 1926), p. 166.
7. *Fortnightly Review*, XXIV, 414.
8. **G. R. Thompson**, *Poe's Fiction: Romantic Irony in the Gothic Tales* (Madison, Wisc., 1973), p. 76.
9. See Birkhead, p. 197.
10. See **Brown**, *Ormond*, ed. Ernest Marchand (New York and London, 1962), p. xxviii (Introduction).
11. See *Ormond*, p. xxv (Introduction).

12. See **Brown**, *Arthur Mervyn, or, Memoirs of the Year 1793*, ed. Warner Berthoff (New York, 1962), p. xi (Introduction).
13. See **David Lee Clark**, *Charles Brockden Brown: Pioneer Voice of America* (New York, 1952), p. 105.
14. For Poe's view of Lytton, see especially his review of Lytton, *Rienzi, The Last of the Tribunes*, in *The Complete Works of Edgar Allan Poe*, ed. James A. Harrison (17 vols, New York, 1965), VIII, 222–9.
15. See *On Novelists and Fiction*, pp. 336–48.
16. **Nathaniel Hawthorne**, *The House of the Seven Gables*, Afterword by E. C. Sampson (New York, 1961), p. 273.
17. **Hubert H. Hoeltje**, *Inward Sky: The Mind and Heart of Nathaniel Hawthorne* (Durham, N.C., 1962), pp. 549–50.
18. See, e.g. *Seven Gables*, pp. 24–7.
19. For Melville's view, see particularly *Hawthorne: The Critical Heritage*, ed. J. Donald Crowley (London, 1970), pp. 115–16.
20. Birkhead, p. 217. For 'Usher' and 'Amontillado', see Poe, *Complete Works*, III, 273–97; VI, 167–75.
21. 'Dejection: an Ode', *Poems*, p. 364.
22. *On Novelists and Fiction*, p. 314.
23. *Eros and Civilisation*, pp. 53–4.
24. See Hoeltje, pp. 396–402.
25. See Hoeltje, p. 184.

CHAPTER 8

Gothic and the sensation novel

Dickens, Wilkie Collins, Sheridan LeFanu

In looking at the major developments in English Gothic fiction in the 1830s and 1840s in the hands of Lytton, James, Ainsworth and Reynolds, we have already set the scene for the emergence of the towering figure of Charles Dickens.[1] Like Hawthorne and Poe, he is of far too great a stature to be bounded by genres: the various modes of writing which he took up he fused and moulded into a style utterly distinctive, a style in which a certain kind of social realism and the grotesquerie of melodrama enter into a seemingly impossible alliance.

This style, and indeed this fusion of interests, would indeed have been unthinkable were it not for certain earlier developments in fictional style and structure. In the first place, Dickens's early work, *Oliver Twist* (1838) and *Barnaby Rudge* (1841) in particular, is heavily influenced by the Newgate novels of Lytton and Ainsworth. Dickens was personally acquainted with both men and his endeavour in much of his early fiction was to take up the 'novel of demons, housebreakers, hangmen, highwaymen, and murderers'[2] and, while continuing to use these motifs, to charge them with a depth of social commentary which in books like *Eugene Aram* and *Rookwood* had been undercut by that dangerous romanticisation of the criminal against which the middle-class press unceasingly railed. In doing so, and in trying to portray an underworld in colours which were lurid yet not rosy, Dickens returned in a sense full circle to the dark, bitter world of Smollett, whose descriptions of cut-throat heroes had been another strong influence in his reading. The connection with Lytton, indeed, emerged also in many other ways: in a mutual interest in the pseudo-science of mesmerism, in a mutual use of the ever-potent topic of Swedenborgianism and its societal implications, and of course in the shared determination to provide a genuinely popular fiction by taking up precisely those topics, whether or not they were 'approved', which excited wide-ranging public interest.

Dickens was conscious, as was Lytton, that the Newgate novel was only 'the descendant of the diabolical in earlier romance' (Phillips, p. 181), a particular contemporary modification of the tradition of terror. In this connection, he was well aware of the work of Radcliffe, and A. C. Coolidge mentions two specific ways in which Dickens was influenced by her; first, in choosing to emphasise narratives 'in which the protagonist was persecuted in a series of sensational incidents', in which respect Radcliffe had herself taken up the ambiguously sadistic inheritance of Richardson; second, in terms of narrative technique. In general, says Coolidge, 'Mrs Radcliffe's novels aroused anxiety and curiosity by systematic developments of the passive, reacting protagonist, the static situation of danger, and the externally manipulated plot. The chief means of development was exaggeration of the number and nature of the stimuli'.[3] One thinks in this connection of *The Old Curiosity Shop* (1841), and again of *Barnaby Rudge*, in which Dickens's suspense techniques are clearly derived from Radcliffe's.

And there was one very obvious reason why Dickens should look to Radcliffe for technical assistance: namely, that he was writing serial tales for magazines. Radcliffe herself, of course, had not been, but when Dickens looked around at the models of the popular available in contemporary magazines, what he would have found – as Poe found – was an enormous emphasis on terror, at least nominally derived from the Radcliffean school. Many of the interpolated tales in *Pickwick Papers* (1837) are modifications of the standard *Blackwood's* product, with the addition, again as in Poe, of an ironic self-consciousness which shows Dickens's awareness of the crudity of the magazine material while in no way dissuading him from using this crudity to serve his own purposes.

The Newgate novel, Radcliffean romance and the magazine tales and serials were among the most popular literary forms of the 1830s, and Dickens, like Reynolds, recognised that to reach a mass audience meant taking advantage of the hold which these forms had over the public imagination. The contemporary press saw the connection quite clearly, for instance when the *Spectator*, reviewing *Bleak House* (1853), commented that the story was 'both meagre and melodramatic, and disagreeably reminiscent of that vilest of modern books Reynolds's *Mysteries of London*'.[4] Dickens from the outset was a novelist of sensation, and the taste for terror runs right through his work. It is perhaps at its most obvious in his role, as writer but more importantly as editor, in the fostering of the short ghost story: he used *All the Year Round* partly as a means of commissioning tales of the supernatural, from Wilkie Collins and Elizabeth Gaskell among many others, and his own stories, 'The Trial for Murder' (1865) and 'The Signalman' (1866), are noted examples of the genre. Importantly, however, these stories are set in the present and derive their impact from the eruption of the supernatural into everyday scenes: 'The Trial for Murder' concerns spiritual intrusion into a murder trial, reminding one forcibly of Horace Walpole's already-quoted comments on Clara Reeve.[5] Dickens precisely takes up the mundane and, either by addition of the supernatural or more usually by habitual grotesquerie and caricature, converts it into a subject for terror.

The short stories are, of course, a very minor part of Dickens's achievement and it is to the novels themselves that we have to look for a fuller understanding of what he owed to the single tradition which he saw as underlying the novel of terror from Walpole and Radcliffe to Ainsworth and Lytton. Chiefly, it seems, he recognised that fear is the quickest and most effective way of commanding continuous audience attention, and that the evolution of the tale of terror had produced sophisticated narrative techniques which could be used to ensure this heightened interest on the part of the audience in the continuing serial. Coolidge, again, mentions as ingredients in Radcliffean narrative 'alternation of story threads, constant interruption, continual defeat of expectation, advancement of the plot in rigidly limited pieces, and virtually regular use of "curtains" or "cliffhangers" ', and says that this set of techniques was 'apparently adopted by Dickens with little change' (Coolidge, p. 106). Its appropriateness to serialisation is obvious, as is the advantage which these relatively complex structures have over the languid style of much other fiction in the earlier decades of the nineteenth century.

There are many examples from Dickens's novels which one could choose to demonstrate the Gothic element in his work: I have chosen *Oliver Twist*, less because it is a particularly blatant instance of fictional terror than because of the extraordinary hold which it still retains over the popular imagination. Probably its characters and settings have turned out to be the most memorable Dickens ever created, although the fact that this novel of crime, murder and all manner of melodramatic contrivance has been turned, among other things, into a jolly West End musical makes one wonder how accurate popular recollection is in terms of the text itself.

For *Oliver Twist* is a hideously violent book, more disturbing than even Reynolds's stories. This is partly because of its contemporaneity, but there are other factors too. Dickens etches in his backgrounds very much more strongly than Reynolds, which severely reduces the space which the audience might want to be able to draw back from the scene: even in the racking scene in *Wagner*, we are less present in the room than watching, thrilled, through a rather large keyhole, with Reynolds himself at our elbow holding up his hands in mock horror. The case is very different in Fagin's den, which appears metaphorically to have no door once we are inside. And this has to do, again, with the fact that Dickens has a heightened sense of squalor: where Reynolds portrays a scene in terms of the most significant and melodramatic elements, the tortured heroine, the grimly smiling executioner and so forth, Dickens adds the rats and directs our attention to the wreaths of cobwebs in the corners.

Again to pursue the important comparison with Reynolds – important because, however different their reputations now, they were at the time the principal contenders for a single crown of yew – Reynolds's sense of structure is radically different from Dickens's. Reynolds's power comes from endlessly repeating scenes of violence, so that we are sickened by the general inhumanity of man – and woman – whereas Dickens prefers to build from one horror to another in an ascending series. In *Oliver Twist*, he finally 'goes for broke' in Sikes's murder of Nancy. It is prepared for in the scene where Fagin, inciting him to the killing, asks what he would do to an informer, positing himself as an example:

> 'I don't know,' replied Sikes, clenching his teeth and turning white at the mere suggestion. 'I'd do something in the jail that 'ud get me put in irons; and if I was tried along with you, I'd fall upon you with them in the open court, and beat your brains out afore the people. I should have such strength', muttered the robber, poising his brawny arm, 'that I could smash your head as if a loaded waggon had gone over it.'[6]

When Sikes then actually commits the murder, Dickens is not content merely to recount its brutality:

> Of all bad deeds that, under cover of the darkness, had been committed within wide London's bounds since night hung over it, that was the worst. Of all the horrors that rose with an ill scent upon the morning air, that was the foulest and most cruel.   (*Twist*, p. 423)

In passages like this Dickens moves well beyond even such boundaries of the permissible as the Gothic had previously set itself and
attempts the portrayal of the one incarnate crime, a crime not
committed for grandeur or even justifiable vengeance, a sordid and
brutal crime which summarises a sordid and brutal world. Earlier
on, Oliver has a book placed in his hands by Fagin, a record of the
history of crime which he rather ill-advisedly supposes will convert
Oliver to his own cause, and one wonders to what extent Dickens
is vicariously describing, not only Oliver's horrified reaction, but
also his own designs on the public – not, of course, to convert them
to criminals, but to bring home to them the depths of infamy to
which the criminal mind can – for whatever social reason – sink.
Here, he says, Oliver

> read of men who, lying in their beds at dead of night, had been
> tempted (as they said) and led on, by their own bad thoughts, to
> such dreadful bloodshed as it made the flesh creep, and the limbs
> quail, to think of. The terrible descriptions were so real and vivid, that
> the sallow pages seemed to turn red with gore; and the words upon
> them, to be sounded in his ears, as if they were whispered, in hollow
> murmurs, by the spirits of the dead. (*Twist*, pp. 196–7)

Like Smollett and Reynolds, Dickens professes belief in the reforma-
tory value of the depiction of evil: like Richardson, Radcliffe and
Reynolds, but less like Smollett or the Newgate novelists, his principal means of enacting this moral lesson is by presenting innocence
in distress. 'I had it always in my fancy', he says of Little Nell in *The
Old Curiosity Shop*, 'to surround the lonely figure of the child with
grotesque and wild, but not impossible companions, and to gather
about her innocent face and pure intentions, associates as strange
and uncongenial as the grim objects that are about her bed when
her history is first foreshadowed.'[7] How Oliver manages to retain
his innocence despite his inauspicious circumstances is one of the
major problems of *Oliver Twist*, but there is no doubting the distress,
as in the scene where he is recaptured by Sikes and Nancy:

> Weak with recent illness; stupefied by the blows and the suddenness of
> the attack; terrified by the fierce growling of the dog, and the brutality
> of the man; overpowered by the conviction of the bystanders that he
> really was the hardened little wretch he was described to be; what
> could one poor child do? Darkness had set in; it was a low
> neighbourhood; no help was near; resistance was useless. In another
> moment he was dragged into a labyrinth of dark narrow courts, and
> was forced along them at a pace which rendered the few cries he
> dared to give utterance to, unintelligible. It was of little moment,

indeed, whether they were intelligible or no; for there was nobody
to care for them, had they been ever so plain.   (*Twist*, p. 158)

One feature of Oliver's innocence which is similar to Emily's or
Ellena's is that it is so profound that even the audience finds it
difficult to believe, as when Oliver fails completely to realise the
purposes for which Sikes wants him until they are at the very doors
of the house they are about to burgle: for this is not psychological
realism, with its half-shades of knowledge and acquiescence, but
Radcliffean sensationalism, in which both innocence and evil are
spread as thick as the public palate will allow.

Part of Dickens's great originality, of course, lies in his location of
these scenes of persecution and corruption in a richly recognisable
contemporary London. Both Brown, in *Arthur Mervyn*, and Ainsworth, in *Auriol* (1865), had attempted to create a 'Gothicised' city,
but it was only with Reynolds and Dickens that the expression on
the face of London became transformed into an evil grin. When
midnight comes in *Oliver Twist*, it falls upon 'the palace, the night-
cellar, the jail, the madhouse; the chambers of birth and death, of
health and sickness; the rigid face of the corpse and the calm sleep
of the child' (*Twist*, p. 407). And this structure of contradictions is
an index of one of the most interesting features of Dickens's
London: that it is two cities in one, an overworld superimposed on
an underworld. Beside, intertwined with, yet somehow in a different
physical dimension from the great streets and thoroughfares lie the
alleys and dark courts where Fagin and his kind slink and slide; and
it is surely not too fanciful to compare this 'double geography' with
that of the haunted castle, where the solid walls of rooms of state
conceal a network of hidden passages. And they are not merely
different geographical worlds, but different social realms; indeed,
the former is an extended metaphor for the latter. When Fagin goes
abroad of a night, he keeps within his own world, only crossing
open streets as a fox might cross a road; he glides 'stealthily along,
creeping beneath the shelter of the walls and doorways'; he seems
'like some loathsome reptile, engendered in the slime and darkness
through which he moved: crawling forth, by night, in search of
some rich offal for a meal' (*Twist*, p. 186). There is, perhaps, a
strange lack of real pity in *Oliver Twist*; pity certainly there is for
Oliver, in overripe abundance, but precious little for the spawn of
such admittedly deadly and poisoning localities as the notorious
Jacob's Island, where the denouement of Sikes's suicide is played
out against a background of mud and terminal poverty.

This partiality derives again from the heritage of the Newgate novel, which had been pilloried for showing evil people with 'good sides': there is little question of that in *Oliver Twist*. Nancy is perhaps the closest example, but she is martyred precisely as she fears: 'Horrible thoughts of death, and shrouds with blood upon them, and a fear that has made me burn as if I was on fire, have been upon me all day' (*Twist*, p. 409), she says, with dire foreboding, but the audience is not cheated of its prey. Even in the descriptions of interactions between the 'overworld' characters, it is allowed full measure of terror and mental torture, as when Rose lies at death's door, to the despair of her friends and relations:

> The suspense, the fearful, acute suspense, of standing idly by while the life of one we dearly love, is trembling in the balance! Oh! the racking thoughts that crowd upon the mind, and make the heart beat violently, and the breath come thick, by the force of the images they conjure up before it; the desperate anxiety *to be doing something* to relieve the pain, or lessen the danger, which we have no power to alleviate; the sinking of soul and spirit, which the sad remembrance of our helplessness produces; what tortures can equal these; what reflections or endeavours can, in the full tide and fever of the time, allay them!
>
> (*Twist*, pp. 298–9)

This is not a question but an exclamation: not an enquiry addressed to the sensibilities of the reader, but a rhetorical outburst designed to underline the melodramatic power of the scene.

Melodrama is a key term: one is reminded of it in the hideous description of Oliver's first night at the undertaker's, in the effect of thunder on Monks's nerves and on his face, in the death of Sikes with its attendant apparatus of the apparition of the eyes and the ensuing violent demise of his dog. And one is reminded of it more forcefully and deliberately in the chapter where Dickens begins by pointing out the theatrical taste for alternation between scenes of calm and scenes of violence, only to go on, not to castigate the practice, but to make the surprising argument that in that respect at least melodrama is a permissibly faithful representation of real life. But melodrama itself has its roots deep in the Gothic, in the plays of Walpole and Lewis, and in the endless adaptations of other Gothic fictions: its language of gesture and expression reproduces the postures of the Radcliffean villain, whether the setting be haunted castle or Victorian drawing-room. There would, however, be few besides Dickens who would choose to justify melodrama in terms of realism, rather than of some kind of necessary exaggeration. John Bayley writes that his main feat, in *Oliver Twist* in particular, is in 'combining the genre of Gothic nightmare with that of social denunciation',[8] which is true, but the combination is of a distinctive kind; the Gothic is permissible, not merely as an enhancement of interest, but also because the power and bitterness of the social denunciation is so strong that he really wishes his readers to see contemporary Britain in those terms. His idea is that the continuation and development of popular literature in his time depends essentially on 'fanciful' treatment, but this fanciful element needs to be seen in conjunction with his convictions about the 'dark age' in which he lived, about the actual prevalence of criminal and circumstantial terror in the Victorian city.[9]

Oliver Twist I have taken only as an example. As W. C. Phillips says, 'from the scene in which Sikes brutally murders his mistress through the opium-tainted atmosphere of *Edwin Drood*, there is no full-length story of his without its generous reliance upon the most brutal stimulants to fear' (Phillips, p. 11). One can find the Gothic debt in his manipulation of the passive protagonist, as with Florence Dombey; in the 'criminal Gothic' of *Sketches by Boz* (1836) and *The Pickwick Papers*; in the bitter Marshalsea chapters of *Little Dorrit* (1857). Poe could see it very clearly in *Barnaby Rudge*; in an otherwise rather scornful review, he nonetheless paid tribute to Dickens's power of economically invoking terror:

> What . . . could more vividly enhance our impression of the unknown horror enacted, than the deep and enduring gloom of Haredale – than the idiot's inborn awe of blood – or, especially, than the expression of countenance so imaginatively attributed to Mrs Rudge – 'the capacity for expressing terror – something only dimly seen, but never absent for a moment – the shadow of some look to which an instant of intense and most unutterable horror only could have given rise?'[10]

And, of course, a section of the bourgeois press was as duly scandalised by Dickens's popular sensationalism as it had been by Lytton's aristocratic blood-tragedies; if the terms in which they chose to express their anger were designed to suggest that all this violence was pointless or socially evil, history has adequately demonstrated that this can be regarded only as a comment on the press. For the reception of Victorian sensationalism shows a wilful confusion of moral and formal categories: what is really at stake, in the campaigns against both Lytton and Dickens, and equally in the conspiracy of silent disgust which greeted Reynolds, is the validity and power of forms of writing which do not acquiesce in an established definition of realism. Dickens's world undeniably has to do with reality, but not in terms of the formal categories which the critics chose to recognise. Even an utterly conventional approach to the actual reward of virtue and punishment of vice, which is absolutely central to *Oliver Twist*, was not initially enough to overcome this deep-seated, class-based antipathy.

In talking of Victorian sensationalism in connection with Dickens, however, one is only talking about one of the genres from which he formed his complexly original novels; for a representative master of the mode itself, one does better to turn to Dickens's 'disciple' and close friend, Wilkie Collins. The two writers shared many interests: in collaboration and an atmosphere of mutual admiration they composed melodramas; in common they located stories of violence and mystery in the heart of the contemporary world; in common they refused to allow the business of psychological intricacy to hold up the essential task of telling a story – in which latter respect Collins certainly surpassed his master, albeit at the expense of a gallery of memorable characterisations on Dickensian lines. Collins could still be said to stand as one of the most obviously readable authors of the nineteenth century: his narrative flows with perfect fluency and ease through the pages of the three great novels, *The Woman in White* (1860), *Armadale* (1866) and *The Moonstone* (1868), in which his combination of melodramatic technique and superb manipulation of suspense earned him the title of 'Mrs Radcliffe brought down to date'. They also earned him a similar reception: on the one hand, massive sales, indicating the willingness of a wide range of readers to indulge in sensation, and on the other some critical annoyance, indicating the unwillingness of the Victorian literary establishment to admit to sensation as a valid source of literary enjoyment.

They had, in a sense, a far better case with Collins than with Dickens, for his more popular novels were largely unredeemed by overt moral thesis; yet the case was still weak, for they were nonetheless perfectly conventional in terms of moral outcome. It was, again, the means which were objectionable, means which we can see Collins employing at their best in *The Woman in White*. The most obvious strength of the book is its intricate story, which it would be impossible to recount here; but equally impressive is Collins's creation of a genuinely Victorian Gothic villain. Count Fosco is the traditional foreign nobleman with mysterious origins and equally mysterious sources of power. He turns out to be, not surprisingly, partly motivated by political intrigue and the need to escape the consequences of having betrayed a pseudo-Rosicrucian 'Brotherhood', but Collins invests this fat, foppish, grandiose and eloquent figure with a startling amount of life. He is a chemical experimenter, well versed in 'medical and magnetic science' and callous of other lives when carrying out his secret purposes, yet what imparts a unique level to his personality is his thoroughgoing enjoyment of his own melo-dramatic potential, which Collins brings to the fore in those parts of the book where Fosco himself takes over the narrative. He is enabled to come out with statements like, 'I accomplish my destiny with a calmness which is terrible to myself',[11] without any of the hesitation and agonising which accompany the machinations of a Montoni or an Ambrosio. He is also granted by Collins entire confi-dence in his own powers of persuasion: 'women can resist a man's love, a man's face, a man's personal appearance, and a man's money', it is pointed out, although Fosco manages to make full use of even these supposedly inferior gifts, 'but they cannot resist a man's tongue, when he knows how to talk to them' (*WW*, p. 232). He is even conscious of the inherently melodramatic power of the actions which he undertakes. At one point he recounts his abduction of Marian Halcombe with the panache which derives from total self-admiration: 'the scene', he says, of her removal, 'was picturesque, mysterious, dramatic, in the highest degree' (*WW*, p. 565); and, a little later, of another part of his deeply laid plan: 'What a situation! I suggest it to the rising romance writers of England. I offer it, as totally new, to the worn-out dramatists of France' (*WW*, p. 568).

Fosco is, in fact, himself a 'writer of romance', in the sense that he organises the raw material of his own and other people's lives into 'grand guignol'. The two occasions when he takes over the narrative are both connected with this. The first one is when he discovers the diary in which Marian has been recording her opinions of the mystery, and writes on its final page a commendation of her intellectual powers and of her skill in unfolding problems; the second is when the hero, Walter Hartright, exposes his schemes and forces him to write a confession, which he thoroughly enjoys: 'habits of literary composition', he says, 'are perfectly familiar to me. One of the rarest of all the intellectual accomplishments that a man can possess is the grand faculty of arranging his ideas. Immense privi-lege! I possess it. Do you?' (*WW*, p. 552).

This becoming modesty clearly suggests the extent to which Fosco is a 'projection' of Collins himself; although if this is so there are other aspects of Fosco's personality which, in a thorough psychologi-cal analysis, might well give pause for thought. One of the outstand-ing features of *The Woman in White* is its very curious sexual emphases. Almost all the characters are in one way or another deviant, even if only in appearance. When Walter is first introduced to Marian, he sees her from the back and admires the femininity of her figure, only to be sharply disappointed when she turns round, revealing a face that is dark, even 'swarthy', and 'masculine' (*WW,* p. 25). Her stepfather, on the other hand, is part of the line which runs from Roderick Usher to decadent transvestitism, a person of acute and 'feminine' sensibilities, and of a degree of fractiousness and petty irritability which, in the range of Victorian stereotypes, is normally associated only with women. Marian even sees Fosco himself on one occasion indulging in one of his odder habits, wandering through the woods singing Figaro's song from *The Barber of Seville,* and dressed for relaxation so curiously that she compares him to 'a fat St Cecilia masquerading in male attire' (*WW,* p. 205).

Fosco's political significance is perfectly clear: he is in the long line of aristocratic hero/villains portrayed by Radcliffe, Byron, Lytton and so many others, but Collins is even more explicit about his role than his predecessors had been. When he dies, his adoring wife writes an expurgated biography of him which concludes with the resounding judgement: 'His life was one long assertion of the rights of the aristocracy, and the sacred principles of Order – and he died a Martyr to his cause' (*WW,* p. 582). Collins even ironically underlines the 'tragedy' of the displaced aristocrat by having him die in a peasant's costume which he was using as a disguise. Sexually, it is almost unsurprising in terms of the coordinates which Collins sets up that Fosco, who combines in himself the dandy and the man of traditional privilege, should find himself attracted to Marian, the masculine 'new woman', resigned to spinsterhood and thus capable of real converse with males; it is also for the same reasons unsurprising that Marian feels nothing for Fosco but revulsion, for she really *is* a new woman, of a kind quite foreign to most previous British sensational fiction. One's sense of this derives partly from the extraordinary skill with which Collins impersonates her at those points when the narrative is told through her diary, partly from the fact that she has a role, as discoverer and rationalist, which had rarely been attached to women. The supposed heroine of the book, Marian's half-sister Laura, is 'sensibility' to her finger-tips, and in the figure of Fosco's English wife, the cowed but mutedly ferocious Madame Fosco, Collins repeats many of the features of Radcliffe's Madame Cheron, but Marian is different. Walter feels the onset of the paranoid uncertainties familiar to the Gothic hero: 'I began to doubt', he says in connection with the mysterious appearances of Anne Catherick, the woman in white herself, 'whether my own

197

faculties were not in danger of losing their balance. It seemed almost like a monomania to be tracing back everything strange that happened, everything unexpected that was said, always to the same hidden source and the same sinister influence' (*WW*, p. 69). But Marian is generally more clear-minded: when she speaks of the wicked Sir Percival's 'active persecution' (*WW*, p. 282) of herself and Laura, his wife, she is quite sure – and thus makes the reader quite sure – that real persecution is what is taking place, a certainty underlined by having her narrative contribution in the form of a day-to-day diary rather than of the remembered accounts which make up most of the rest of the book.

But, as with earlier Gothic fiction, the presence of rational characters and the absence of actually supernatural events is not allowed to cheat the audience of supernatural thrills, even if these are later explained. Most of these thrills centre around the early appearances of the woman in white, the wraithlike and disturbed Anne, and one can judge Collins's tone from Walter's reflections on her death:

> Through what mortal crime and horror, through what darkest windings of the way down to Death, the lost creature had wandered in God's leading to the last home that, living, she never hoped to reach! . . . *That* rest shall be sacred – that companionship always undisturbed! . . . So the ghostly figure which has haunted these pages as it haunted my life, goes down into the impenetrable Gloom. Like a Shadow she first came to me, in the loneliness of the night. Like a Shadow she passes away, in the loneliness of the dead.   (*WW*, p. 515)

It is only really in connection with Anne that Collins adopts this stance of high reflection which reminds one of Dickens and Hawthorne: normally he is by no means an intrusive narrator, as indeed is evident from the skill with which he allows the narrative to impersonate different characters' voices.

In terms of location, Collins takes the Gothic ideal of isolation and gloom and brings it to England in the lowering shape of Blackwater Park with its disused wings and dark lake, the house to which Sir Percival takes his less than willing bride, and also in the setting of the earlier part of the book, Limmeridge House. Limmeridge is situated in pure Brontë country, which seems to have had an effect on Marian's freedom from social constraint: 'in our wild moorland country', she says, 'and in this great lonely house, we may well claim to be beyond the reach of the trivial conventionalities which hamper people in other places' (*WW*, p. 168). But these locations are invested with a distinctive quality: they are drawn in with a firm hand, and the mysterious management of large households which appeared to provoke so many difficulties in the eighteenth century is depicted in naturalistic and convincing detail.

This partial domestication of Gothic is a major contribution which Victorian sensation fiction makes to the romance tradition, and in this connection it is worth quoting at length Phillips's comments on the origins of the form:

> Historically sensationalism clearly represents a popular development in fiction in which the novel of mystery is crossed with that of fashionable life. The appeal to fear and the delineation of society in a peculiarly ignorant and vulgar fashion were inherent in conditions, because the appeal to fear is even a more nearly universal appeal than that of love between the sexes and because none are so curious about Lady Audley and her boudoir or Strathmore and his perfumed beard as the bourgeois. The public of the sixties cared little for the castle in the Apennines. The adapting of its melodramatic terrors to local conditions and scenes, however, involved difficulties. The summary vengeance dealt out with the sword by a Byronic hero becomes stealthy murder, and the violence to her person always threatening Mrs Radcliffe's heroine becomes adultery. The themes are the same; but the portrayal in a community where police decently enforce the civil law made difficult the task of the sensationalist.
>
> (Phillips, p. 34)

This needs a little glossing: Phillips is not, of course, talking about Collins but about much less accomplished sensation writers. The specific references are to Mary Elizabeth Maxwell's *Lady Audley's Secret* (1862) and 'Ouida''s *Strathmore* (1865) and to the subgenre to which they belong, in which voyeuristic interest in the aristocracy is stronger and less clothed in irony; it is in this subgenre that 'stealthy murder' and 'adultery' actually occur, whereas Collins, in his more sophisticated treatment of the themes, manages to achieve a far more interesting atmosphere of doubt. 'There is,' Phillips writes, placing Collins and Dickens together, 'no want of continuity between the romance that Walpole and the Terrorists wrote at the end of the eighteenth century, and that which Dickens and his followers wrote in the middle of the nineteenth' (Phillips, p. 6); but although this is true, there are some complexities in the genealogy which we need to turn to, particularly in terms of public reception.

We have suggested that much of the original Gothic fiction was not 'popular' in any sense we might recognise now, because of the different organisation of the fiction market, but that it rather appealed to the mingled interest and fear which the middle classes felt in connection with the aristocracy. One might reasonably go on from this to infer that the mixed reception which that fiction got was due to the fact that, by dealing with things noble, it became infected with the taboo nature of its subjects. But class relations were very different by the 1860s. Bourgeois anxiety about the aristocracy was still there: the interests fostered by the tale of 'fashionable life' in the 1820s carried over into Lytton and then into the minor sensation novelists. But alongside this, very different kinds of anxiety are developing on the part of the dominant class, particularly about what is stirring at the lower social levels: Reynolds and Dickens clearly reflect this half-fascinated, half-horrified interest in working-class violence, and it is to the credit of both that they see the connections between this and the wider violence which the state practises upon its lesser members. What is important is that both these anxieties become elided in terms of form; it seems as if, Gothic having become implanted as the form in which the bourgeoisie expressed its anxieties, any new one naturally attracted the same techniques.

There are good reasons why this might be the case. One of the essential features of the Gothic is its habit of distortion, as if looking through a badly made window, and this presumably could be seen as reflecting the distance between various classes and social groups. The Gothic was and remained the dimension of the imperfectly perceived. But it would not, unfortunately, be true to say that the Gothic remained in as conveniently simple a category as this. Reynolds, Dickens and Collins reached an audience which was vastly wider than the previously established middle-class one, and the result of this was a change in form. Principally, Dickens and Collins partially democratised the Gothic novel, although in different ways, Dickens by means of humour and characterisation, Collins by means of excitement and fast narrative. The long-drawn-out terrors and complex literary allusions of Radcliffe might suit a leisured audience, but the 'conditions' of which Phillips speaks, the emergence of serial publication and increase in literacy, required greater clarity and heavier outline. Collins's kind of Gothic was transitional and short-lived, partly because it points the way towards other kinds of fiction altogether, the adventure story primarily, in which excitement remains but all the other distinguishing features of the Gothic have disappeared. That is to say, they disappear as the adjuncts of a popular genre: certainly they are, as we shall see, only too manifest in the later years of the nineteenth century, in some of the works of Stevenson and Wilde and of course in Stoker: but in all three of these writers, there is a conscious interest in decadence which makes their relation to a mass audience oblique. A further level is reached, of archaism within archaism, but the popularity of *Dr Jekyll and Mr Hyde, The Picture of Dorian Gray* and *Dracula* is the popularity of individually significant 'myths', rather than that of outstanding examples of a generally popular literary form.

Phillips's explanation of the popularity of Dickens, Collins and also Charles Reade seems not wholly convincing: he talks of their ability, because of the conditions of publication, to mount a 'direct appeal of writer to audience', and claims that 'just as direct appeal in the Elizabethan theatre called out the tragedy of blood which *Hamlet* or *The White Devil* glorified, so here among the Victorians it gave vogue to the sensationalism which *Great Expectations* and *The Moonstone* rendered memorable... both are democratic art' (Phillips, p. 108). Both types may be 'democratic art' but in the case of the Victorians this has to do not only with 'direct appeal' but also with a certain kind of craftsmanship and an intense awareness of the *different* requirements of different sections of the audience. To point out that Shakespeare was also well aware of that difficulty does not mean that the particular relations which Shakespeare had to comprehend were the same as those which confronted Collins, and even more to the point Shakespeare did not have at his back the kinds of traditional acceptance which Gothic had contributed to the literature of terror.[12]

These modifications of the Gothic do not, however, mean that the older kind of Gothic had disappeared by the 1860s: indeed, the year 1864 saw the publication of a novel which could fairly be regarded as the first properly Gothic masterpiece in Britain since *Melmoth the Wanderer*, Sheridan LeFanu's *Uncle Silas*. LeFanu came, like Maturin, of Irish Huguenot stock, and an early interest in Ireland's national legendary conditions much of his work. His two early novels, *The Cock and Anchor* (1845) and *Torlogh O'Brien* (1847), were historical works formed after the model of Scott but transferred to Ireland, and he talked of himself as a member of the 'legitimate school of tragic English romance, which has been ennobled, and in great measure founded, by the genius of Sir Walter Scott'.[13] As his work went on, however, Scott seems to have become less significant as an influence than the terror-writers, Ainsworth, Reynolds and of course Radcliffe. Already in *Torlogh O'Brien*, considerable prominence is given to scenes of violence, and this emphasis is extended in *The House by the Churchyard* (1861–2), the last of LeFanu's novels to be set in the past, in which historical depiction becomes decidedly secondary to a growing reliance on supernatural terror.

All his later work uses established Gothic motifs. *The Rose and the*

Key (1871) takes up Maturin's symbolic theme of the horrors of the private lunatic asylum; in *Wylder's Hand* (1864) a young lawyer, in his first encounter with the mad Uncle Lorne, describes himself as feeling like 'one of Mrs Ann Radcliffe's heroes – a nervous race of demigods';[14] while in *Checkmate* (1870) the tradition of the horrors of science is taken a step further in perhaps the first literary depiction of plastic surgery. Nelson Browne, one of LeFanu's few critics, claims that 'Mrs Radcliffe is the progenitrix of everything in him that may be termed romantic – his gloomy heroes, his intrepid heroines in perpetual flight from ruthless persecutors, his chivalrous conception of honour, his ancient houses and castles falling into ruin, his fondness for showing Nature in her sombre and threatening moods';[15] and it is in the much underrated *Uncle Silas* that these elements come together in their finest form.

LeFanu's habits of writing were curious, in that he worked in terms of short stories, novellas and novels and often used remarkably similar plot structures across the different genres. Many of the short stories are themselves masterly, from the jocular 'The Ghost and the Bone-Setter',[16] a dialect tale of a spirit that singularly fails to inspire real fear, and 'The Drunkard's Dream' (both 1838), in which LeFanu borrows and develops Beckford's description of the halls of Eblis, to the later tales. Five of the best of these, 'Green Tea,' 'The Familiar', 'Mr Justice Harbottle', 'The Room in the Dragon Volant' and 'Carmilla', are collected in the volume *In a Glass Darkly* (1872), which was also the birthplace of the linking figure of Dr Hesselius, a 'psychic doctor' who prefigures William Hope Hodgson's Carnacki the Ghost-Finder and Algernon Blackwood's Dr John Silence.[17] These stories are notable chiefly for their insight into the nature of the psyche: LeFanu's typical plot is one in which the protagonist, whether deliberately or otherwise, opens his mind in such a way as to become subject to haunting by a figure which is unmistakably part of his own self. These figures are truly imaginative, from the malignant monkey in 'Green Tea' to the vision of vengeance seen in 'Mr Justice Harbottle', and LeFanu also has a light and memorable touch in drawing more conventional phantoms, as in the novella *The Haunted Baronet* (1870):

> there passed . . . into the room a figure dressed, it seemed to him, in gray that was nearly white. It passed straight to the hearth . . . looked round, with large eyes that in the moonlight looked like melting snow, and stretching its long arms up the chimney, they and the figure itself seemed to blend with the smoke, and so pass up and away.[18]

Most of the best tales were written late in life, when Lefanu had become a creature of odd and irregular habits, living a largely nocturnal and reclusive life. Perhaps the most interesting of the stories is 'Carmilla', which concerns a female vampire and brings out very strongly the already present sexual content in the vampire legends; Browne reminds us of LeFanu's 'exorcist', Baron Vordenburg, who 'stresses the vehement passion of the vampire for its victim which, in some cases, will cause it "to protract its murderous enjoyment with the refinement of an epicure, and heighten it with the gradual approaches of an artful courtship" ' (Browne, p. 84). Carmilla is certainly very much more alarming than Polidori's vampire, and the story itself is told with an ease and fluency which makes it easy to see why LeFanu was referred to as an Irish Wilkie Collins.

Julia Briggs, in her book on the English ghost story, claims that LeFanu 'is at his weakest where sustained invention is required, tending to fall back on the stock melodramatic devices of his day, but at his best in a traditional and well-tried tale to which he can bring his own imaginative powers' (Briggs, p. 47). This seems to me not wholly true; many of LeFanu's short stories are good, but there are also some very doubtful ones, and much seems to depend on the intensity of his involvement with the particular hallucination he is describing; 'Carmilla' is narratively unusual in this respect. The force they have is that of a single psychological *aperçu*, sometimes well conveyed, sometimes not. There is a similar unreliability in the novels, but *Uncle Silas* at least demonstrates the mastery of suspense and fine perception which LeFanu could achieve when relatively freed from limitations of length.

Uncle Silas is the story, told by herself, of Maud Ruthyn, who, on the death of her father, finds that she is intended to go and live with Silas, her uncle. She is surprised by this because Silas has always been regarded within the family as taboo, having committed some dreadful disreputability in his youth, but she surmises that her father may have intended this as a final gesture of trust in his brother. Maud's stay under Silas's roof is not a pleasant one; she is terrified by the uncle himself, an ill and gloomy religious fanatic, and harassed by his brutal and underbred son Dudley; she is also victimised by a horrific governess named Madame de Rougierre, a creation worthy of Dickens. The house also contains within itself the riddle of an unexplained murder, which may or may not have been committed by, or at the instigation of, Uncle Silas. It is a measure of the skill of the book that events are few and far between: its power comes from the consistent brooding atmosphere of the house and the equally continual but largely offstage presence of Silas, and from the fineness with which LeFanu etches in the details of Maud's feelings as she oscillates between security, doubt and terror. It appears only at the very end that there has indeed been a plot afoot, which goes badly wrong; but as with Radcliffe, explanations count for very little, and during the actual course of the book there is not much of which we would not believe the deathly Silas and his minions capable.

Maud herself is a creation as well rounded as Marian in *The Woman in White*, and indeed LeFanu shares with Collins a gift for impersonating his heroines. The fact that he also shares with Collins a penchant for febrile males may be evidence of something in Le Fanu and Collins, or evidence of something amiss in Victorianism: be that as it may, Maud, with her mixture of innocence and snobbery, conscious virtue and condescension, stands not only with Marian but also with Jane Austen's Emma and, in certain ways, with Henry James's governess in *Turn of the Screw*. The tone of LeFanu's dealings with his characters can be gauged in the scene where Maud, still living a retired life with her father, first meets Captain Oakley, a dashing but rather untrustworthy distant relation:

> Just at that moment Captain Oakley joined us. He was my first actual vision of that awful and distant world of fashion, of whose splendours I had already read something in the three-volume gospel of the circulating library.
>
> Handsome, elegant, with features almost feminine, and soft, wavy, black hair, whiskers and moustache, he was altogether such a knight as I had never beheld, or even fancied, at Knowl – a hero of another species, and from the region of the demigods. I did not then perceive that coldness of the eye, and cruel curl of the voluptuous lip – only a suspicion, yet enough to indicate the profligate man, and savouring of death unto death.
>
> But I was young, and had not yet the direful knowledge of good and evil that comes with years; and he was so very handsome, and talked in a way that was so new to me, and was so much more charming than the well-bred converse of the hum-drum county families with whom I had occasionally sojourned for a week at a time.
>
> It came out incidentally that his leave of absence was to expire the day after to-morrow. A Lilliputian pang of disappointment followed this announcement. Already I was sorry to lose him. So soon we begin to make a property of what pleases us.
>
> I was shy, but not awkward. I was flattered by the attention of this amusing, perhaps rather fascinating, young man of the world; and he plainly addressed himself with diligence to amuse and please me. I dare say there was more effort than I fancied in bringing his talk down

to my humble level, and interesting me and making me laugh about people who I had never heard of before, than I then suspected.[19]

The contradictions in Maud's personality are well summarised here: she is innocent but attentive to experience, retiring but conscious of her own dignity, interested in her own feelings but half-deprecating about them. Partly these contradictions have to do with the fact that LeFanu gives us two Mauds: Maud at the time of the action, and a sadder, wiser Maud, who narrates the story and who is oddly *present* throughout, guiding us detachedly through the mistakes and misapprehensions of her younger self. This gives a certain density to the narrative, evidenced here in the use of 'Lilliputian' and in the small, offhand reflections which the present Maud offers us with a resigned smile: 'So soon we begin to make a property of what pleases us.' It also avoids the awkward problem in Radcliffean fiction as to how heroines so inundated with sensibility can nevertheless pen well-balanced and reasonable sentences about the horrors which they have undergone: Maud's pain is truly something 'recollected in tranquillity', and the clarity of the recollection is coherent in terms of the *developing* character which we are given.

Thus Maud's experiences can be seen to have formed her: her eighteenth-century admiration for Oakley and her circulating-library reading can find a place in the novel without making the reader impatient. Past innocence and present understanding form a composite whole. With Uncle Silas too, LeFanu takes up a Gothic stereotype and forms it afresh:

> A face like marble, with a fearful monumental look, and, for an old man, singularly vivid strange eyes . . . his eyebrows were still black, though his hair descended from his temples in long locks of the purest silver and fine as silk nearly to his shoulders . . . I can't convey in words an idea of this apparition, drawn as it seemed in black and white, venerable, bloodless, fiery-eyed, with its singular look of power, and an expression so bewildering – was it derision, or anguish, or cruelty, or patience?   (*Silas*, p. 192)

The light in Silas's eyes glares 'white and suddenly – almost fatuous . . . I never saw in any other eye the least glimmer of the same baleful effulgence. His fits, too – his hoverings between life and death – between intellect and insanity – a dubious, marsh-fire existence, horrible to look on!' (*Silas*, p. 261). In some ways LeFanu's technique of physical description here is similar to Poe's, but it has little of Poe's conscious extravagance and exaggeration; in general, the portraits are more similar in style to Collins's, who in for instance Fosco and Sir Percival also gives us pictures which depend more on intense actual description than on the collections of gestures and expressions which comprise Radcliffe's villains.

LeFanu also re-uses the old Gothic theme of religious fanaticism, both in connection with Silas, where it is both in some sense genuine and also a mask for conspiracy and evil, and in Maud's father, in whom is portrayed a tendency towards Swedenborgianism modelled on LeFanu's own life. In terms of settings, again, Knowl and Silas's house, Bartram-Haugh, are in the tradition of wild places which Collins and the Brontës also use, and the connection has been made, by Ellis among others, between LeFanu's insistence on anglicised Gothic settings and his own obsessions:

> Horrible dreams troubled him to the last, one of the most recurrent and persistent being a vision of a vast and direly foreboding old mansion (such as he had so often depicted in his romances), in a state of ruin and threatening imminently to fall upon and crush the dreamer rooted to the spot. (*Collins, LeFanu*, p. 177)

The further connection with the house of Usher is too obvious to need underlining.

LeFanu is a master of the old terror techniques of suspense and accumulation, and he uses them with subtlety. But there is something further in the tone of *Uncle Silas*, something which, more than the mere character of Maud, looks towards Henry James. There are two elements here: first, LeFanu's deliberate flatness of language. It is precisely the level of understatement, of disbelief by Maud in her own fears, throughout the earlier part of the book which makes the fast-moving denouement so effective. And second, there is the particular kind of prolixity: *Uncle Silas* is a long book and, as we have noted, very little happens but, just as in *Turn of the Screw*, the author is able to fill up space with minutiae which have at least symbolic relation to the plot in such a way that all seems invested with potential significance. In this respect at least, LeFanu has nothing to do with Collins and the sensationalists, and this might partly account for his failure to reach a large audience. LeFanu, in his novels at least, did not compromise with the mass audience but continued to turn out tales appropriate to leisured reading habits, books to 'stroll around in'.

Yet alongside this old-fashioned tendency LeFanu is also oddly modern, calling to mind in the density of his symbols the Brontës certainly but also later terror-writers like Blackwood and Arthur Machen, in whom the insistence on the power of the repressed becomes more explicit. And this, clearly, needs a further comment:

how can it be that a writer who is working, almost deliberately, in an outmoded form, can nonetheless look forward to a more consciously psychological fiction? It seems to me that there are two possibilities. The first lies in the nature of Gothic itself: insofar as Gothic had become the primary mode in which to explore terror and other extreme feelings, it was naturally invested with a psychological content which LeFanu continued to probe. The second possibility, though, is perhaps the more interesting: that in LeFanu's work, precisely *because* it was being bypassed by sensationalism, the Gothic is pared down to psychological essentials. There is very little historical or political interest in his 'supernatural' novels, for they are consciously and almost resignedly archaic: they are exercises on a preestablished theme or set of themes, and for this very reason LeFanu is able to use his skill on refinement, on taking up Gothic settings, characters, themes and moulding them into those exquisite shapes which can result when wider kinds of literary purpose have temporarily atrophied. And this, of course, is a procedure which already suggests one form of decadence, and prepares us for the decadent transmutations which Gothic was to undergo at the end of the century.

Notes and references

1. It should be said at this point that tracing Gothic traditions through the middle years of the nineteenth century requires considerable selectivity. I have chosen to concentrate here on Dickens, Collins, LeFanu: certainly because they are important, but also because they demonstrate very different tendencies and possibilities within the Gothic. This has entailed omissions, the Brontës most obviously, but also a host of revealing minor figures. The alternative would have been, as it would with the early period, compendious and unwieldy.
2. **Walter C. Phillips**, *Dickens, Reade and Collins: Sensation Novelists* (New York, 1919), p. 179.
3. **Archibald C. Coolidge**, Jr., *Charles Dickens as a Serial Novelist* (Ames, Iowa, 1967), pp. 148–50.
4. 'Dickens's *Bleak House*' (anon. rev.), *Spectator*, 24 Sept. 1853, p. 924.
5. See above, p. 48.
6. **Charles Dickens**, *Oliver Twist*, ed. Peter Fairclough (Harmondsworth, Middx., 1966), p. 419.
7. **Dickens**, *The Old Curiosity Shop*, ed. Angus Easson (Harmondsworth, Middx., 1972), p. 42.
8. **John Bayley**, '*Oliver Twist*: "Things as they really are",' in *Dickens and the Twentieth Century*, ed. John Gross and Gabriel Pearson (London, 1962), p. 64.
9. On this argument, see Phillips, pp. 99–100; and **Joseph Gold**, *Charles Dickens: Radical Moralist* (Minneapolis, 1972), pp. 25–30.
10. See *Dickens: The Critical Heritage*, ed. Phillip Collins (London, 1971), p. 109.
11. **William Wilkie Collins**, *The Woman in White*, ed. H. P. Sucksmith (London, 1975), p. 308. All subsequent references are to *WW*.
12. What is curious about contemporaneous reactions to Dickens and Collins is

connected with the ambiguous class status of the texts themselves which, while indeed in some sense treating the enemies of the bourgeoisie *as* enemies, nonetheless depict them with such fascination that actual middle-class characters end up as blanched as their audience. The animal that the sensation novelists tried to domesticate would have been less dangerous left outside the parlour.

13. See **S. M. Ellis**, *Wilkie Collins, LeFanu and Others* (London, 1931), p. 165.
14. **Sheridan LeFanu**, *Wylder's Hand* (London, 1963), p. 51.
15. **Nelson Browne**, *Sheridan LeFanu* (London, 1951), p. 105.
16. In Haining, pp. 523–33.
17. On the genealogy of the 'psychic doctor', see **Julia Briggs**, *Night Visitors: The Rise and Fall of the English Ghost Story* (London, 1977), pp. 59ff.
18. See **LeFanu**, *Best Ghost Stories*, ed. E. F. Bleiler (New York, 1964), p. 89.
19. **LeFanu**, *Uncle Silas; A Tale of Bartram-Haugh*, ed. Frederick Shroyer (New York, 1966), pp. 41–2.

Appendix on Criticism

It seems useful, since fifteen years have elapsed since the first publication of *The Literature of Terror*, and also in view of the vast amount of critical material that has appeared during those years, to append at this point a brief survey of recent criticism of Gothic. What I have chosen to include is criticism which pays attention to what we are perhaps by now beginning to call 'classic' or 'traditional' Gothic; in other words, roughly speaking the tradition(s) discussed in this first volume. For reasons of space, I have excluded all works devoted to single authors, or even focused *towards* a single author, however far they may help our study of Gothic; for similar reasons, but perhaps even less justifiably, I have restricted myself to monographs, although the reader will find details of recent essay collections included in the updated Bibliography. I have provided no footnotes, because again details of all texts mentioned are in the Bibliography.

I cannot attempt to provide a critique even of the works mentioned, but merely to allude to them and to try to set up some kind of useful map of the main lines of criticism being followed; and even this, of course, is bound to prove contentious. I have identified three principal tendencies within the field, and have had perforce to group other, no less interesting but very diverse, readings under a general heading at the end.

1. READINGS CENTRED ON QUESTIONS OF FORM AND GENRE

Elizabeth MacAndrew's *The Gothic Tradition in Fiction* (1979) is a highly general survey of the field, running from eighteenth-century origins through to a brief Epilogue on the twentieth century, paying considerable attention along the way to Victorian Gothic in particular. Eclectic in her ideas, MacAndrew sees Gothic mainly as a set of conventions, modified through time, but centred on her opening assertion that 'Gothic fiction is a literature of nightmare'.

Judith Wilt, in *Ghosts of the Gothic: Austen, Eliot and Lawrence* (1980), adopts a more systematic concept of the Gothic, taking into account theological, formal and sociological determinants but centring ultimately on 'the birthplace of . . . the trace of the imagination – dread'. The first half of her book is devoted to the Gothic tradition, the second to a detailed exploration of the further 'trace' of Gothic in her three title authors.

Although I have classified MacAndrew and Wilt as 'centred' on questions on form and genre, the formal arguments in both are quite loose; much tighter is the proposed argument of Margaret Carter's *Specter or Delusion? The Supernatural in Gothic Fiction* (1987), which is essentially about the complexities of mediated narrative as viewed through the prism of the classic Gothic. It is, however, open to doubt as to whether such criticism can really escape from the traditional, and flawed, distinction between the 'explained' and the 'unexplained' supernatural.

Elizabeth R. Napier's *The Failure of Gothic: Problems of Disjunction in an Eighteenth-Century Literary Form* (1987) has attracted a good deal of criticism – from Robert Miles and Michelle A. Massé among others – for adopting a 'normative' approach to Gothic and essentially mounting a judgement of it based on inappropriate criteria. Can we, the question could be put, fairly judge a form a 'failure' – if indeed at all – for producing within itself what might otherwise be seen as materials which are fractured precisely in accordance with the fracturing of the subject which runs through it?

Joseph Wiesenfarth's *Gothic Manners and the Classic English Novel* (1988) is a more subtle and scholarly book, which adopts a broadly Bakhtinian approach to Gothic traces in a number of authors normally regarded as tangential to the tradition, including Austen, Trollope, George Eliot and Hardy. His avowed aim is to introduce a substantial new genre definition, the 'novel of Gothic manners', to help us to see how manners themselves in certain canonical fictions 'become horrors'; the question here for the reader would be whether anything much is left of the original Gothic in the new definition Wiesenfarth proposes.

George E. Haggerty's *Gothic Fiction/Gothic Form* (1989) addresses the question of the 'manner in which Gothicists managed to satisfy the demands of form while at the same time releasing their expressive inclination toward formal instability and fragmentation', specifically through looking at the nature of the 'Gothic tale' as it emerges within the Gothic novel (Mary Shelley, Emily Bronte) and then continues as a form in its own right (Poe, Hawthorne, James). The argument is tight and suggestive, leading to a view of a 'ghostliness' through which we are 'led into a more direct and a more horrifying knowledge of ourselves'.

Neil Cornwell's extremely interesting *The Literary Fantastic: From Gothic to Postmodernism* (1990) is the only book mentioned so far to attempt a setting of Gothic within a broader European context. Beginning from, but moving substantially beyond, Todorov's famous distinctions within the fantastic, Cornwell advances a rigorous argument and backs it with a wealth of material, culminating in a chapter on figures as apparently diverse as Bulgakov, Banville, Rushdie and Morrison.

Ian Duncan's *Modern Romance and Transformations of the Novel: the Gothic, Scott, Dickens* (1992) is an extremely well written and suggestive account of the formal relations between novel and romance. While this might seem an old problem, Duncan brings a new vision to it, and although the Gothic is hardly the end point of his complex argument, nevertheless there is a continuing engagement with the formal characteristics of Gothic, even when Scott or Dickens are the ostensible focus of enquiry.

2. READINGS CENTRED ON GENDER

Perhaps the most energetic of current fields of enquiry into the Gothic arose initially from Ellen Moers's influential essay on the female Gothic and also from Sandra Gilbert and Susan Gubar's equally influential *The Madwoman in the Attic: The Woman Writer and the Nineteenth-Century Literary Imagination* (1979), which includes work on Mary Shelley and the Brontes as well as on *Northanger Abbey*. Gilbert and Gubar's general arguments are too well known to be worthy of rehearsal here, but clearly underpin a whole series of attempts to look more closely at Gothic as a gendered form.

The Female Gothic (1983), edited by Juliann E. Fleenor, is an essay collection but I have included it here because it also advances a substantial series of linked arguments. Fleenor acknowledges debts to Moers, Showalter, Gilbert and Gubar, and MacAndrew, and brings before us a wide variety of feminist approaches to both classic and popular Gothic texts. 'Mystique: The Popular Gothic', 'Madness: Apocalypse and Transcendence', 'Monsters: Sexuality and Terror' and 'Maternity: The Body as Literary Metaphor', the titles of the book's four sections, perhaps give a glimpse of the range of issues addressed.

Kate Ellis takes up and develops one of the key areas, the relation between Gothic and 'domestic space', in *The Contested Castle: Gothic Novels and the Subversion of Domestic Ideology* (1989). The Gothic, Ellis claims, is concerned with the 'failed home' and her book centres on the relationship between two 'epiphenomena of middle-class culture: the idealisation of the home and the popularity of the Gothic', with 'the point of connection between them' being the woman novel reader. The theme is powerfully and convincingly developed.

Ellis writes of 'danger and imprisonment'; Eugenia C. Delamotte in her, to my mind, even more remarkable *Perils of the Night: A Feminist Study of Nineteenth-Century Gothic* (1990) speaks of 'domestic entrapment' and specifically of the way in which a masculist fascination with a rhetoric of the 'boundaries of the self' may have served to divert our attention from the all too present reality (to women) of the dangers of the Other: 'the evil Other the Gothic heroine confronts is not a hidden self at all but is just what it appears to be: an Other that is profoundly alien, and hostile, to women and their concerns'.

Elisabeth Bronfen's *Over Her Dead Body: Death, Femininity and the Aesthetic* (1992) also needs to be noted at this point: its argument, about the fascination in Western culture with images of dead, tortured and suffering women, is far broader than the Gothic, but many classic Gothic texts, as we might expect, do figure in it. Michelle A. Massé, in *In the Name of Love: Women, Masochism and the Gothic* (1992) could be seen – although no doubt, in view of the datings, by common interest rather than influence – to be developing Bronfen's thesis in a more specifically Gothic direction. In tune also with Delamotte, she emphasises that masochism, 'the intertwining of love and pain, is not natural and does not originate in the self: women are taught masochism through fiction and culture, and masochism's causes are external and real'.

Keri J. Winter, in *Subjects of Slavery, Agents of Change: Women and Power in Gothic Novels and Slave Narratives, 1790–1865* (1992) proposes an entirely new and challenging context for Gothic by placing Gothic texts, and the role of women within them, alongside the narratives of slaves in the nineteenth century, extending the Western cultural collocation of women and slaves which runs from Aristotle to Wollstonecraft and beyond. There are, of course, substantial differences of form, ideology and reader relations between the two genres; but Winter acknowledges these and still proceeds to weave a complex, fascinating and highly disturbing argument.

In her *Gothic (Re)Visions: Writing Women as Readers* (1993) Susan Wolstenholme, in a book which follows directly from some of the issues opened out in the Fleenor collection, writes – and in doing so perhaps provides a useful statement of at least one point to which gendered reading of the Gothic has now come – that 'in its double movement, what the Gothic mode provides is a structure that not only (within the text) meditates on the problem of women writers' double status *as* women and writers; it also redramatises this relationship in its particular mode of inscribing readers; it tends obsessively to repeat deliberately staged scenes which additionally reconfigure this relationship; and it consequently mirrors within itself the relationship it invites between the text and its reader'.

3. READINGS HISTORICAL, SOCIOLOGICAL, POLITICAL

Within my first two classifications, I believe it is possible to trace some commonalty of concern; less so here. Donald A. Ringe's *American Gothic: Imagination and Reason in Nineteenth-Century Fiction* (1982), the only general monograph wholly on classic American Gothic to emerge within the period, is a wide-ranging but under-theorised survey of Gothic reading and writing in nineteenth-century America, focusing on Brown, Irving, Poe and Hawthorne, which is still addressing what is perceived by Ringe as a need to assert the claims of Gothic as a 'serious' form of fiction.

Class, family and other sociohistorical constructs form the basis of William Patrick Day's *In the Circles of Fear and Desire: A Study of Gothic Fantasy* (1985). He looks at the classic canon, and adds to this with some exploration of film and a section on *Heart of Darkness*; he also pays some attention to the birth of the detective story, but the general lines of the argument seem hardly original, with more interest attaching to asides – on bondage, for instance, or on the underworld – which do not seem fully integrated into the book's structure.

Chris Baldick's *In Frankenstein's Shadow: Myth, Monstrosity and Nineteenth-Century Writing* (1987) is an altogether more interesting book, which could be seen to mark the beginnings of the encounter of the new historicism with Gothic studies. Baldick takes the Frankenstein 'myth' and traces it through a wealth of mainly nineteenth-century contexts – industry and galvanism, mad scientists, Carlyle, Marx, Conrad and Lawrence – addressing himself not merely to historical phenomena as such, but also to, as it were, the trajectory of a rhetoric and its many transmutations.

Victor Sage's views on the nature of history, as expressed in his *Horror Fiction in the Protestant Tradition* (1988), are more conventional, but the argument he advances is nonetheless an extremely important one. Forcefully rejecting Freud and all his works in favour of a historical reading, Sage goes on to contend that the primary determinant which previous studies of Gothic have largely omitted is the religious one: the sense in which, although the French Revolution may be important to Gothic, more important was the Glorious Revolution and the formation of an (admittedly diverse) Protestant orthodoxy which essentially generates all the major symbols of the Gothic tradition.

In the course of tracing these primarily historical accounts, it would be wrong not to mention once more, if only in passing, Delamotte's study, which raises issues to do with Gothic and history with force and vigour. Marie Roberts' *Gothic Immortals: The Fiction of the Brotherhood of the Rosy Cross* (1990) also falls broadly under the historical heading, although Roberts' concerns are with the history of ideas, the development of science and more particularly, as the title suggests, with Rosicrucianism as it appears in the work of, for example, Godwin, the Shelleys, Maturin and Lytton.

Robert Miles' *Gothic Writing 1750–1820: A Genealogy* (1993) returns us to a more theorised view of history. In this excellent book, Miles makes use of an essentially Foucauldian framework to approach the relation between Gothic and the notion of the fragmented subject, also making use of Bakhtinian and deconstructive ideas. His central concern is with the internal development of a 'tradition', with the ways in which we can read the key texts as commentaries on other texts and so forth; and from this he constructs one of the most satisfyingly articulated pictures of classic Gothic to date.

4. OTHER READINGS

It is surprising to find that there has been so little recent work on Gothic from a psychoanalytic viewpoint. It is of course true that most gendered readings either presuppose or actively contend with some kind of psychoanalytic framework; but of the works mentioned so far, only those by Bronfen and Massé develop substantial points from an analytic base.

There has been no full-scale Freudian study during the period; but there has been one from a post-Jungian perspective, Joseph Andriano's *Our Ladies of Darkness: Feminine Daemonology in Male Gothic Fiction* (1993). In this book – which is also the only study of an explicitly 'male' tradition, although Miles also alludes to masculine Gothic – Andriano takes care to distance himself from 'essentialist Jungianism' and produces a somewhat eclectic but never less than interesting series of readings of the Gothic canon, in the course of which he also provides some valuable starting-points for further work.

The question of deconstruction is similarly vexed; one reason for this, of course, is that deconstruction is never fully at home when trying to deal with genre rather than text, but even so few of the studies mentioned above could be found to owe a great deal to Derrida or even to the work of the Yale School. One exception, which integrates deconstructive procedures into a historical framework, is Miles; another is Eve Kosofsky Sedgwick's *The Coherence of Gothic Conventions* (1980) which, although it could in some ways be seen as a formal study, is deeply marked by Yale School presuppositions. The textual readings themselves are often brilliant, and centre on an argument about language and silence, the said and the unsaid, which cuts straight to the heart of several of the Gothic problems.

Terry Heller's *The Delights of Terror: An Aesthetics of the Tale of Terror* (1987) fits into none of the above categories, and is essentially a philosophical and aesthetic enquiry, taking as its starting-points the reader relations theory of Iser and the phenomenology of Ingarden and moving towards the end to Freudian and Lacanian approaches, into where we as readers are in the tale of terror. This excellent book provides us with a series of extremely close readings centred on the *effects* of the tale of terror, a topic which has otherwise been consistently undertreated.

S. L. Varnado's *Haunted Presence: The Numinous in Gothic Fiction* (1987) is a short book which similarly evades classification; Varnado's master is the theologian Rudolf Otto, and Varnado seeks to apply Otto's ideas, particularly of the numinous, the *mysterium tremendum et fascinans* (a concept Andriano also picks up) to a range of Gothic, producing in the course of the book a series of perhaps quirky but certainly stimulating readings, whose closeness to the presumed 'spirit' of Gothic may be an attraction for some readers, a source of irritation to others.

Bibliography

This bibliography does not claim to act as a reading-list in respect of any of the individual authors under discussion; it does, however, mention every work referred to in the text, along with a selection of others, and is divided into 'Primary' and 'Secondary' sections. In the latter section I have mentioned additional critical material where it seems to me to open up interesting lines of investigation into the Gothic; I have also consistently tended to include material on lesser known texts and writers at the expense of the more mainstream. As pointed out in the Preface, I have in many cases cited the most available edition; where important, however, I have also included reference to the original date of publication.

Primary

Aikin, John and Anna Laetitia. *Miscellaneous Pieces, in Prose*. London, 1773.

Ainsworth, William Harrison. *Auriol: or, The Elixir of Life*. London, 1865.

———. *Crichton*. 3 vols. London, 1837.

———. *Jack Sheppard; A Romance*. 3 vols. London, 1839.

———. *The Lancashire Witches*. 3 vols. London, 1849.

———. *Ovingdean Grange*. London, 1860.

———. *Rookwood; a Romance*. 3 vols. London, 1834.

———. *Sir John Chiverton; a Romance*. London, 1826.

———. *The Tower of London*. London, 1840.

Aristotle. *The Poetics*; 'Longinus'. *On the Sublime*, trans. W. Hamilton Fyfe; Demetrius. *On Style*, trans. W. R. Roberts. London, 1927.

Austen, Jane. *Northanger Abbey* (1818), ed. A. H. Ehrenpreis. Pbk edn, Harmondsworth, Middx., 1972.

Bage, Robert. *Hermsprong: or, Man As He Is Not.* 3 vols. London, 1796.

Baring-Gould, Sabine. *Curious Myths of the Middle Ages.* London, 1866.

Barrett, Francis. *The Magus, or Celestial Intelligencer: Being a Complete System of Occult Philosophy.* London, 1801.

Beckford, William. *Vathek* (1786), ed. R. Lonsdale. London, 1970.

——. *The Vision* (1777), ed. G. Chapman. London, 1930.

Blair, Robert. *The Poetical Works of Robert Blair,* introd. W. Gardiner. London, 1802.

Blake, William. *The Poetry and Prose of William Blake,* ed. David V. Erdman. New York, 1965.

Bleiler, E. F., ed. *Three Supernatural Novels of the Victorian Period.* Pbk edn, New York, 1975.

Brontë, Emily. *Wuthering Heights* (1847), ed. David Daiches. Pbk edn, Harmondsworth, Middx., 1968.

Brown, Charles Brockden. *Alcuin: or, The Rights of Women.* New York, 1798.

——. *Arthur Mervyn: or, Memoirs of the Year 1793* (1798), ed. Warner Berthoff. New York, 1962.

——. *Edgar Huntly: or, The Sleep Walker* (1799). London, 1931.

——. *Ormond: or, The Secret Witness* (1799), ed. Ernest Marchand. New York and London, 1962.

——. *Weiland: or, The Transformation; together with Memoirs of Carwin the Biloquist, a Fragment,* ed. F. L. Pattee. New York, 1926.

Burke, Edmund. *A Philosophical Enquiry into the Origin of Our Ideas of the Sublime and Beautiful* (1756), ed. J. T. Boulton. London, 1958.

Byron, George Gordon, Lord. *The Works of Lord Byron: Poetry,* ed. Ernest H. Coleridge. 7 vols. New York, 1966.

Campbell, Margaret. *The Spectral Bride* (Joseph Shearing. *The Fetch*) (1942). London, 1973.

Carter, John. *Specimens of the Ancient Sculpture and Painting now Remaining in England, from the Earliest Period to the Reign of Henry VIII* (1780–94), ed. S. R. Meyrick. London, 1838.

Coleridge, Samuel Taylor. *Biographia Literaria* (1817), ed. J. Shawcross. 2 vols. London, 1907.

——. *Coleridge's Miscellaneous Criticism,* ed. T. M. Raysor. London, 1936.

——. *The Poems of Samuel Taylor Coleridge,* ed. Ernest H. Coleridge. London, 1912.

Collins, William Wilkie. *Armadale.* 2 vols. London, 1866.

——. *The Haunted Hotel, and My Lady's Money*. 2 vols. London, 1879.

——. *The Moonstone* (1868), ed. J. I. M. Stewart. Pbk edn, Harmondsworth, Middx., 1966.

——. *The Woman in White* (1860), ed. H. P. Sucksmith. London, 1975.

Dacre, Charlotte. *Zofloya: or, The Moor* (1806), introd. Montague Summers. London, 1928.

Defoe, Daniel. *The Fortunes and Misfortunes of the Famous Moll Flanders* (1722), ed. G. A. Starr. London, 1971.

——. *Selected Writings of Daniel Defoe*, ed. J. T. Boulton. London, 1975.

Dickens, Charles. *Barnaby Rudge* (1841), ed. G. Spence. Pbk edn, Harmondsworth, Middx., 1973.

——. *Bleak House* (1853), ed. N. Page, introd. J. H. Miller. Pbk edn, Harmondsworth, Middx., 1971.

——. *Great Expectations* (1861), ed. A. Calder. Pbk edn, Harmondsworth, Middx., 1965.

——. *Little Dorrit* (1857), ed. J. Holloway. Pbk edn, Harmondsworth, Middx., 1967.

——. *The Mystery of Edwin Drood* (1870), ed. A. J. Cox, introd. Angus Wilson. Pbk edn, Harmondsworth, Middx., 1974.

——. *The Old Curiosity Shop* (1841), ed. A. Easson, introd. M. Andrews. Pbk edn, Harmondsworth, Middx., 1972.

——. *Oliver Twist* (1838), ed. Peter Fairclough, introd. Angus Wilson. Pbk edn, Harmondsworth, Middx., 1966.

——. *The Posthumous Papers of the Pickwick Club* (1837), ed. R. L. Patten. Pbk edn, Harmondsworth, Middx., 1972.

——. *Sketches by Boz* (1836), introd. G. K. Chesterton. London, 1968.

Fairclough, Peter, ed. *Three Gothic Novels*, introd. Mario Praz. Pbk edn, Harmondsworth, Middx., 1968.

Fielding, Henry. *The History of the Adventures of Joseph Andrews* (1742), ed. A. R. Humphreys. Pbk edn, London, 1968.

——. *The History of Tom Jones* (1749), ed. R. P. C. Mutter. Pbk edn, Harmondsworth, Middx., 1968.

——. *Jonathan Wild and Journal of a Voyage to Lisbon*, introd. A. R. Humphreys. Pbk edn, London, 1964.

——. *A Journey From This World to the Next* (1741–2), introd. C. Rawson. Pbk edn, London, 1973.

Fleming, Joan. *Too Late! Too Late! The Maiden Cried; a Gothick Novel*. London, 1975.

Godwin, William. *The Adventures of Caleb Williams: or, Things as They Are* (1794), ed. Herbert von Thal, introd. Walter Allen. Pbk edn, London, 1966.

———. *Enquiry Concerning the Principles of Political Justice, with Selections from Godwin's Other Writings*, ed. K. C. Carter. Oxford, 1971.

———. *St Leon; a Tale of the Sixteenth Century.* 4 vols. London, 1799.

Goethe, Johann Wolfgang von. *Faust*, trans. B. Taylor, introd. J. W. Smeed. London, 1969.

———. *Werke*, ed. E. Beutler. 24 vols. Zurich, 1948–54.

Grant, Joan. *Castle Cloud (The Laird and the Lady)*. London, 1949.

Grosse, Karl Friedrich August. *Horrid Mysteries*, trans. P. Will (1797). London, 1968.

Haining, Peter, ed. *Gothic Stories of Horror and Romance 1765–1840*, Vol. 1, *Great British Tales of Terror.* London, 1972.

Hawthorne, Nathaniel. *Doctor Grimshawe's Secret* (c. 1861), ed. E. H. Davidson. Cambridge, Mass., 1954.

———. *The House of the Seven Gables* (1851), Afterword by E. C. Sampson. Pbk edn, New York, 1961.

———. *The Scarlet Letter, and Selected Tales*, ed. T. E. Connolly. Pbk edn, Harmondsworth, Middx., 1970.

Hoffmann, Ernst Theodor Amadeus. *The Devil's Elixirs* (1816), trans. R. Taylor. London, 1963.

———. *Sämtliche Werke*, ed. C. G. von Maassen. 9 vols. München and Leipzig, 1908–28.

Hogg, James. *The Private Memoirs and Confessions of a Justified Sinner* (1824), ed. John Carey. Pbk edn, London, 1970.

Holcroft, Thomas. *The Adventures of Hugh Trevor* (1794–7), ed. S. Deane. London, 1973.

———. *Anna St Ives* (1792), ed. P. Faulkner. London, 1970.

Hurd, Richard. *Letters on Chivalry and Romance* (1762), ed. Hoyt Trowbridge. Los Angeles, 1963.

Irving, Washington. *Sketch Book of Geoffrey Crayon Gent.* (1819–20). 2 vols. London, 1894.

———. *Tales of a Traveller,* (1824) London, 1864.

James, George Payne Rainsford. *The Castle of Ehrenstein: its Lords Spiritual and Temporal; its Inhabitants Earthly and Unearthly.* 3 vols. London, 1847.

———. *Corse de Leon: or, The Brigand; a Romance.* 3 vols. London, 1841.

———. *A History of the Life of Edward the Black Prince.* 2 vols. London, 1836.

———. *Richelieu; a Tale of France.* 3 vols. London, 1829.

Keats, John. *The Poetical Works of John Keats*, ed. H. W. Garrod. Oxford, 1958.

Lathom, Francis. *The Castle of Ollada; a Romance.* 2 vols. London, 1794.

——. *The Midnight Bell; a German Story Founded on Incidents in Real Life* (1798). London, 1968.

Lee, Sophia. *The Recess: or, A Tale of Other Times.* 3 vols. London, 1785.

LeFanu, Joseph Sheridan. *Best Ghost Stories*, ed. E. F. Bleiler. Pbk edn, New York, 1964.

——. *The Cock and Anchor* (1845), ed. and introd. Herbert von Thal. Pbk edn, London, 1967.

——. *The Fortunes of Colonel Torlogh O'Brien.* Dublin, 1847.

——. *The House by the Churchyard.* Dublin, 1861–2.

——. *In a Glass Darkly.* 3 vols. London, 1872.

——. *The Rose and the Key.* 3 vols. London, 1871.

——. *Uncle Silas; a Tale of Bartram-Haugh* (1864), ed. Frederick Shroyer. Pbk edn, New York, 1966.

——. *Wylder's Hand* (1864). London, 1963.

Lewis, Matthew Gregory. *Alfonso, King of Castile; a Tragedy, in Five Acts.* London, 1801.

——. *The Castle Spectre; a Drama, in Five Acts.* London, 1797.

——. *Feudal Tyrants: or, The Counts of Carlsheim and Sargens. A Romance.* 4 vols. London, 1806.

——. *The Monk; a Romance* (1796). Pbk edn, London, 1973.

——. *Tales of Wonder.* 2 vols. London, 1801.

——. *Venoni: or, The Novice of St Mark's.* London, 1808.

Lytton, Edward G. E. L. Bulwer-Lytton, Lord. *The Caxtons; Zicci; The Haunted and the Haunters.* Boston and New York, 1849.

——. *England and the English* (1833). London, 1874.

——. *Miscellaneous Prose Works.* 3 vols. London, 1868.

——. *Paul Clifford* (1830). Edinburgh, 1862.

——. *Works.* 29 vols. London, 1895–8.

MacKenzie, Henry. *The Man of Feeling* (1771), ed. Brian Vickers. Pbk edn, London, 1970.

Mallet, Paul Henri. *Northern Antiquities*, trans. Thomas Percy. 2 vols. London, 1770.

Marryat, Frederick. *The Phantom Ship.* London, 1839.

Maturin, Charles Robert. *The Albigenses; a Romance.* 4 vols. London, 1824.

——. *The Fatal Revenge: or, The Family of Montorio.* 3 vols. London, 1807.

——. *Melmoth the Wanderer; a Tale* (1820), ed. Douglas Grant. London, 1968.

——. *The Milesian Chief; a Romance.* 4 vols. London, 1812.

Maxwell, Mary Elizabeth. *Lady Audley's Secret* (1862), introd. N. Donaldson. New York, 1974.

Moore, John. *Zeluco: Various Views of Human Nature, Taken from Life and Manners, Foreign and Domestic.* 2 vols. London, 1786.

Naubert, Christiane Benedikte Eugenie. *Alf von Deulmen: or, The History of the Emperor Philip, and his Daughters,* trans. A. E. Booth. 2 vols. London, 1794.

———. *Herman of Unna: A Series of Adventures of the Fifteenth Century, in which the Proceedings of the Secret Tribunal under the Emperors Wincaslaus and Sigismond, are Delineated* (1788). 3 vols. London, 1794.

'Ossian'. *The Poems of Ossian,* trans. James Macpherson, introd. W. Sharp. Edinburgh, 1926.

'Ouida'. *Strathmore; a Romance.* 3 vols. London, 1865.

Parnell, Thomas. *The Poetical Works of Thomas Parnell.* London, 1833.

Peacock, Thomas Love. *The Works of Thomas Love Peacock,* ed. H. F. B. Brett-Smith and C. E. Jones. 10 vols. New York, 1967.

Percy, Thomas, ed. *Reliques of Ancient English Poetry.* 3 vols. London, 1765.

Poe, Edgar Allan. *The Complete Works of Edgar Allan Poe,* ed. James A. Harrison. 17 vols. New York, 1965.

Pope, Alexander. *The Poems of Alexander Pope,* ed. John Butt. 10 vols. London, 1939–67.

Prest, Thomas Peckett. *The Black Monk: or, The Secret of the Grey Turret.* London, 1844.

Price, Uvedale. *Essays on the Picturesque, as Compared with the Sublime and the Beautiful* (1810). 3 vols. Farnborough, Hants., 1971.

Radcliffe, Ann. *The Castles of Athlin and Dunbayne; a Highland Story.* London, 1789.

———. *Gaston de Blondeville; a Romance. St Alban's Abbey; a Metrical Tale, With Some Other Pieces.* 4 vols. London, 1826.

———. *The Italian: or, The Confessional of the Black Penitents* (1797), ed. Frederick Garber. Pbk edn, London, 1971.

———. *The Mysteries of Udolpho; a Romance, interspersed with some Pieces of Poetry* (1794), ed. Bonamy Dobrée. Pbk edn, London, 1970.

———. *The Romance of the Forest: Interspersed With Some Pieces of Poetry.* 3 vols. London, 1791.

———. *A Sicilian Romance.* 2 vols. London, 1790.

Reeve, Clara. *The Old English Baron; a Gothic Story* (1777), ed. James Trainer. London, 1967.

———. *The Progress of Romance, through Times, Countries, and Manners.* 2 vols. Colchester, 1785.

Reynolds, George William MacArthur. *Faust.* London, 1845–6.
——. *The Mysteries of the Courts of London.* London, 1848–56.
——. *The Mysteries of London.* London, 1844–8.
——. *The Necromancer; a Romance.* London, 1852.
——. *The Seamstress; a Domestic Tale.* London, 1850.
——. *Wagner, the Wehr-wolf* (1846–7), ed. E. F. Bleiler. New York, 1975.
Richardson, Samuel. *Clarissa: or, The History of a Young Lady* (1748), introd. John Butt. 4 vols. London, 1962.
——. *The History of Sir Charles Grandison* (1754), ed. J. Harris. 3 vols. London, 1972.
Roche, Regina Maria. *The Children of the Abbey; a Tale.* 4 vols. London, 1796.
Sade, Marquis de. *Oeuvres Complètes du Marquis de Sade.* 16 vols. Paris, 1966.
Schiller, Johann Christoph Friedrich von. *The Ghost-Seer; or, Apparitionist* (1789), trans. D. Boileau. London, 1795.
——. *The Robbers; a Tragedy* (1777–80), trans. Lord Woodhouselee. London, 1792.
——. *Sämtliche Werke,* ed. E. von der Hellen. 16 vols. Stuttgart, 1904–5.
Scott, Sir Walter. *The Correspondence of Sir Walter Scott and Charles Robert Maturin,* ed. F. E. Ratchford and W. H. McCarthy, Jr. Austin, Texas, 1937.
——. *The Journal of Sir Walter Scott,* ed. W. E. K. Anderson. Oxford, 1972.
——. *Letters on Demonology and Witchcraft* (1830), introd. R. L. Brown. Ardsley, 1968.
——. *Lives of the Novelists* (1825), introd. Austin Dobson. London, 1907.
——. *Sir Walter Scott on Novelists and Fiction,* ed. Ioan Williams. London, 1968.
——. *Waverley Novels.* 48 vols. Edinburgh, 1901.
Shadwell, Thomas. *The Complete Works of Thomas Shadwell,* ed. Montague Summers. 5 vols. London, 1927.
Shelley, Mary Wollstonecraft. *Falkner.* 3 vols. London, 1837.
——. *The Fortunes of Perkin Warbeck, a Romance.* 3 vols. London, 1830.
——. *Frankenstein* (1818), introd. R. E. Dowse and D. J. Palmer. Pbk edn, London, 1963.
——. *The Last Man* (1826), ed. H. J. Luke, Jr. Lincoln, Nebr., 1965.
——. *Tales and Stories,* introd. Joanna Russ. Boston, Mass., 1975.

——. *Valperga: or, The Life and Adventures of Castruccio, Prince of Lucca.* 3 vols. London, 1823.

Shelley, Percy Bysshe. *The Complete Works of Percy Bysshe Shelley,* ed. Roger Ingpen and Walter E. Peck. 10 vols. New York, 1965.

——. *St Irvyne: or, The Rosicrucian; a Romance.* London, 1811.

——. *Zastrozzi, a Romance* (1810), introd. Phyllis Hartnoll, London, 1955.

Smith, Charlotte. *Celestina, a Novel.* 4 vols. London, 1791.

——. *Emmeline, the Orphan of the Castle* (1788), ed. A. H. Ehrenpreis. London, 1971.

——. *Ethelinde: or, The Recluse of the Lake.* 5 vols. London, 1789.

——. *The Old Manor House* (1793), ed. A. H. Ehrenpreis. London, 1969.

Smollett, Tobias George. *The Adventures of Ferdinand Count Fathom* (1753), ed. Damian Grant. London, 1971.

——. *The Adventures of Roderick Random* (1748), introd. H. W. Hodges. London, 1960.

Sterne, Laurence. *A Sentimental Journey through France and Italy* (1768), ed. G. Petrie, introd. A. Alvarez. Pbk edn, Harmondsworth, Middx., 1967.

Sue, Eugène. *Les Mystères de Paris* (1842–3). 4 vols. Brussels, 1844.

——. *The Mysteries of Paris,* trans. J. D. Smith. 3 vols. London, 1844.

Volney, Constantin François Chasseboeuf, Comte de. *Oeuvres.* 8 vols. Paris, 1825.

——. *The Ruins, or a Survey of the Revolutions of Empires.* London, 1795.

Vulpius, Christian August. *The History of Rinaldo Rinaldini, Captain of Banditti* (1798), trans. I. Hinckley. 3 vols. London, 1800.

Walpole, Horace. *The Castle of Otranto; a Gothic Story* (1764), ed. W. S. Lewis. London, 1969.

——. *Horace Walpole's Correspondence,* ed. W. S. Lewis. 34 vols. New Haven and London, 1937–71.

——. *The Mysterious Mother; a Tragedy.* London, 1781.

White, James. *The Adventures of John of Gaunt, Duke of Lancaster.* 3 vols. London, 1790.

——. *The Adventures of King Richard Coeur-de-lion, to which is added, The Death of Lord Falkland; a Poem.* 3 vols. London, 1791.

——. *Earl Strongbow: or, The History of Richard de Clare and the Beautiful Geralda.* 2 vols. London, 1789.

Wilkinson, Sarah. *The Ghost of Golini: or, the Malignant Relative; a Domestic Tale.* London, 1804.

——. *The Priory of St Clair: or, The Spectre of the Murdered Nun.* London, 1811.

Wordsworth, William. *The Prelude* (1805), ed. E. de Selincourt, corrected by Stephen Gill. Pbk edn, London, 1970.

—— and Samuel Taylor Coleridge. *Lyrical Ballads* (1798), ed. R. L. Brett and A. R. Jones. London, 1968.

Young, Edward. *Conjectures on Original Composition* (1759), ed. Edith J. Morley. Manchester, 1918.

——. *The Poetical Works of Edward Young.* 2 vols. London, 1834.

Zschokke, Heinrich. *Ausgewählte Novellen und Dichtungen.* 10 vols. Aarau, 1847.

——. *The Bravo of Venice* (1804), trans. Matthew Gregory Lewis. London, 1805.

Secondary

Allen, Michael. *Poe and the British Magazine Tradition.* New York, 1969.

Allen, Walter. *The English Novel: A Short Critical History.* London, 1954.

Altick, Richard D. *The English Common Reader: A Social History of the Mass Reading Public, 1800–1900.* Chicago, 1957.

Andriano, Joseph. *Our Ladies of Darkness: Feminine Daemonology in Male Gothic Fiction.* University Park, 1993.

Arvin, Newton. 'Melville and the Gothic novel', *New England Quarterly,* XXII (1949), 33–48.

Baker, Ernest Albert. *The History of the English Novel.* 10 vols. London, 1924–39.

Baldick, Chris. *In Frankenstein's Shadow: Myth, Monstrosity and Nineteenth-Century Writing.* Oxford, 1987.

Barclay, Glen St John. *Anatomy of Horror: The Masters of Occult Fiction.* London, 1978.

Bayer-Berenbaum, L. *The Gothic Imagination: Expression in Gothic Literature and Art.* Rutherford, N.J., 1982.

Beachcroft, Thomas Owen. *The Modest Art: A Survey of the Short Story in English.* London, 1968.

Birkhead, Edith. *The Tale of Terror: A Study of the Gothic Romance.* London, 1921.

Briggs, Julia. *Night Visitors: The Rise and Fall of the English Ghost Story.* London, 1977.

Brockman, Harold Alfred Nelson. *The Caliph of Fonthill.* London, 1956.

Bronfen, Elisabeth. *Over Her Dead Body: Death, Femininity and the Aesthetic.* Manchester, 1992.

Brooks, Peter. 'Godlike science/Unhallowed arts: Language and monstrosity in *Frankenstein*', *New Literary History*, IX (1978), 591–605.

——. 'Virtue and Terror: *The Monk*', *ELH*, XL (1973), 249–63.

Browne, Nelson. *Sheridan LeFanu.* London, 1951.

Buranelli, Vincent John. *Edgar Allan Poe.* New York, 1961.

Carpenter, Lynette and Wendy K. Kolmar, ed. *Haunting the House of Fiction: Feminist Perspectives on Ghost Stories by American Women.* Knoxville, Tenn., 1991.

Carroll, Noel. *The Philosophy of Horror.* London, 1990.

Carter, Margaret L. *Spectre or Delusion? The Supernatural in Gothic Fiction.* Ann Arbor, 1987.

Chapman, Guy Patterson. *Beckford.* London, 1937.

Clark, David Lee. *Charles Brockden Brown: Pioneer Voice of America.* New York, 1952.

Clark, Kenneth McKenzie, Lord. *The Gothic Revival: An Essay in the History of Taste.* London, 1928.

Collins, Philip, ed. *Dickens: The Critical Heritage.* London, 1971.

Conant, Martha Pike. *The Oriental Tale in England in the Eighteenth Century.* New York, 1908.

Coolidge, Archibald C., Jr. *Charles Dickens as Serial Novelist.* Ames, Iowa, 1967.

Cooper, David, ed. *The Dialectics of Liberation.* Pbk edn, Harmondsworth, Middx., 1968.

Cornwell, Neil. *The Literary Fantastic: From Gothic to Postmodernism.* New York, 1990.

Cottom, Daniel. *The Civilised Imagination: A Study of Ann Radcliffe, Jane Austen and Sir Walter Scott.* Cambridge, 1985.

Crowley, J. Donald, ed. *Hawthorne: The Critical Heritage.* London, 1970.

Dalziel, Margaret. *Popular Fiction 100 Years Ago: An Unexplored Tract of Literary History.* London, 1957.

Day, William Patrick. *In the Circles of Fear and Desire: A Study of Gothic Fantasy.* Chicago, 1985.

Delamotte, Eugenia C. *Perils of the Night: A Feminist Study of Nineteenth-Century Gothic.* New York, 1990.

Dobson, Austin. *Eighteenth Century Vignettes.* 3 vols. London, 1892–6.

Docherty, Brian, ed. *American Horror Fiction: From Brockden Brown to Stephen King.* New York, 1990.

Dowson, Leven M. '*Melmoth the Wanderer*: Paradox and the Gothic novel', *Studies in English Literature 1500–1900*, VIII (1968), 621–32.

Duncan, Ian. *Modern Romance and Transformations of the Novel: the Gothic, Scott, Dickens*. Cambridge, 1992.

Ellis, Kate. *The Contested Castle: Gothic Novels and the Subversion of Domestic Ideology*. Urbana, Ill., 1989.

Ellis, Stewart Marsh. *The Solitary Horseman: or, The Life and Adventures of G. P. R. James*. London, 1927.

——. *Wilkie Collins, LeFanu and Others*. London, 1931.

——. *William Harrison Ainsworth and His Friends*. 2 vols. London, 1911.

Fiedler, Leslie Aaron. *Love and Death in the American Novel*. New York, 1960.

Fleenor, Juliann E., ed. *The Female Gothic*. Montreal, 1983.

Fleishman, Avrom. *The English Historical Novel: Walter Scott to Virginia Woolf*. Baltimore, 1971.

Folsom, James K. 'Beckford's *Vathek* and the Tradition of Oriental satire', *Criticism*, VI (1964), 53–69.

Frank, Frederick S. *Gothic Fiction: A Master List of Twentieth-Century Criticism and Research*. Westport, Ct., 1987.

Frankl, Paul. *The Gothic: Literary Sources and Interpretations through Eight Centuries*. Princeton, N.J., 1960.

Freud, Sigmund. *The Standard Edition of the Complete Psychological Works of Sigmund Freud*, ed. James Strachey. 24 vols. London, 1953–74.

Furrow, Sharon. 'Psyche and setting: Poe's picturesque landscapes', *Criticism*, XV (1973), 16–27.

Gilbert, Sandra, and Susan Gubar. *The Madwoman in the Attic: The Woman Writer and the Nineteenth-Century Literary Imagination*. New Haven, 1979.

Gold, Alex, Jr. 'It's only love: The politics of passion in Godwin's *Caleb Williams*', *Texas Studies in Language and Literature*, XIX (1977), 135–60.

Gold, Joseph. *Charles Dickens: Radical Moralist*. Minneapolis, 1972.

Goldmann, Lucien. *Towards a Sociology of the Novel* (1964), trans. Alan Sheridan. London, 1975.

Gorer, Geoffrey. *The Life and Ideas of the Marquis de Sade*. London, 1953.

Gose, Elliott B., Jr. *Imagination Indulged: The Irrational in the Nineteenth Century Novel*. Montreal and London, 1972.

Graham, Kenneth W. 'Beckford's *Vathek*: A study in ironic dissonance', *Criticism*, XIV (1972), 243–52.

———, ed. *Gothic Fictions: Prohibition/Transgression.* New York, 1989.

Grixti, Joseph. *Terrors of Uncertainty.* London, 1989.

Gross, John, and Gabriel Pearson, ed. *Dickens and the Twentieth Century.* London, 1962.

Haggerty, George. *Gothic Fiction/Gothic Form.* University Park, 1989.

Hammond, Ray. *The Modern Frankenstein: Fiction becomes Fact.* Poole, 1986.

Harvey, A. D. 'The nightmare of *Caleb Williams*', *Essays in Criticism,* XXVI (1976), 236–49.

Hazlitt, William. *Lectures on the English Comic Writers, and Fugitive Writings,* introd. A. Johnston. London, 1963.

Heine, Maurice. 'Promenade a travers le Roman noir', *Minotaure,* No. 5 (May 1934), pp. 1–4.

Heller, Terry. *The Delights of Terror: An Aesthetics of the Tale of Terror.* Urbana, Ill., 1987.

Hennessy, Brendan. *The Gothic Novel.* Harlow, 1978.

Hill, Christopher. *Puritanism and Revolution: Studies in Interpretation of the English Revolution of the Seventeenth Century.* Pbk edn, London, 1968.

Hirsch, David H. 'The Pit and the Apocalypse', *Sewanee Review,* LXXVI (1968), 632–52.

Hoeltje, Hubert H. *Inward Sky: The Mind and Heart of Nathanial Hawthorne.* Durham, N.C., 1962.

Hollingsworth, Keith. *The Newgate Novel 1830–1847: Bulwer, Ainsworth, Dickens, and Thackeray.* Detroit, 1963.

Horkheimer, Max, and Theodor W. Adorno. *Dialectic of Enlightenment* (1947), trans. John Cumming. London, 1973.

Howells, Coral Ann. *Love, Mystery, and Misery: Feeling in Gothic Fiction.* London, 1978.

Hoyt, Charles A. *Minor British Novelists.* Carbondale, Ill., 1967.

Hume, Robert D. 'Gothic versus Romantic: a revaluation of the Gothic novel', *Publications of the Modern Language Association,* LXXXIV (1969), 282–90.

Idman, Niilo. *Charles Robert Maturin: His Life and Works.* London, 1923.

Jarrett, David. *The Gothic Form in Fiction and its Relation to History.* Winchester, 1980.

Joseph, Gerhard J. 'Poe and Tennyson', *Publications of the Modern Language Association,* LXXXVIII (1973), 418–28.

Kelly, Gary. *English Fiction of the Romantic Period, 1789–1830.* London, 1989.

Kerr, Howard. *The Haunted Dusk: American Supernatural Fiction 1820–1920.* Athens, Ga., 1983.

Kiely, Robert. *The Romantic Novel in England.* Cambridge, Mass., 1972.

Krafft-Ebing, Richard von. *Psychopathia Sexualis,* trans. and introd. F. S. Klaf. London, 1965.

Kristeva, Julia. *Powers of Horror: An Essay on Abjection.* New York, 1982.

Leavis, Queenie. *Fiction and the Reading Public.* London, 1968.

Levine, George, and U. C. Knoepflmacher, ed. *The Endurance of Frankenstein: Essays on Mary Shelley's Novel.* Berkeley, Calif., 1979.

Lévy, Maurice. *Le roman gothique anglais, 1764–1824.* Toulouse, 1968.

Lloyd Smith, Allan, and Victor Sage, ed. *Gothick: Origins and Innovations.* Amsterdam, 1994.

Longueil, Alfred, 'The word "Gothic" in eighteenth century criticism', *Modern Language Notes,* XXXVIII (1923), 453–60.

Lovecraft, Howard Phillips. *Supernatural Horror in Literature* (1945), introd. E. F. Bleiler. New York, 1973.

Lucas, John. *The Melancholy Man: A Study of Dickens's Novels.* London, 1970.

MacAndrew, Elizabeth. *The Gothic Tradition in Fiction.* New York, 1979.

Maier, Rosemarie. 'The Bitch and the Bloodhound: Generic Similarity in "Christabel" and "The Eve of St Agnes" ', *Journal of English and Germanic Philology,* LXX (1971), 62–75.

Mannheim, Karl. *Essays on Sociology and Social Psychology,* ed. Paul Kecskemeti. London, 1953.

Marcuse, Herbert. *Eros and Civilisation: A Philosophical Inquiry into Freud.* Pbk edn, London, 1969.

Marx, Karl. *Early Writings,* trans. R. Livingstone and G. Benton, introd. Lucio Colletti. Pbk edn, Harmondsworth, Middx., 1975.

——, and Frederick Engels. *Articles on Britain.* Moscow, 1971.

Massé, Michelle A. *In the Name of Love: Women, Masochism, and the Gothic.* Ithaca, N.Y., 1992.

Matthiesen, F. O. 'Poe', *Sewanee Review,* LIV (1946), 175–205.

Maxwell, Richard C., Jr. 'G. W. M. Reynolds, Dickens, and the mysteries of London', *Nineteenth-Century Fiction,* XXXII (1977), 188–213.

May, L. C. *Parodies of the Gothic Novel.* New York, 1980.

McIntyre, Clara Frances. *Ann Radcliffe in Relation to Her Time.* New Haven, 1920.

McNutt, Dan J. *The Eighteenth-Century Gothic Novel: An Annotated Bibliography.* Folkestone, 1975.

Meester, Marie E. de. *Oriental Influences in the English Literature of the Nineteenth Century.* Heidelberg, 1915.

Mehrotra, Kewal Krishna. *Horace Walpole and the English Novel: A Study of the Influence of* The Castle of Otranto, 1764–1820. Oxford, 1934.

Miles, Robert. *Gothic Writing 1750–1820: A Genealogy.* London, 1993.

Moers, Ellen. *Literary Women.* London, 1977.

Mogen, David, Scott P. Sanders and Joanne B. Karpinski, ed. *Frontier Gothic: Terror and Wonder at the Frontier in American Literature.* Rutherford, N.J., 1993.

Mooney, Stephen L. 'Poe's Gothic waste land', *Sewanee Review,* LXX (1962), 261–83.

Moretti, Franco. *Signs Taken for Wonders.* London, 1983.

Murphy, John V. *The Dark Angel: Gothic Elements in Shelley's Works.* Cranbury, N.J., and London, 1975.

Napier, Elizabeth R. *The Failure of Gothic: Problems of Disjunction in an Eighteenth-Century Literary Form.* Oxford, 1987.

Nelson, Lowry, Jr. 'Night thoughts on the Gothic novel', *Yale Review,* LII (1962), 236–57.

Oliver, John Walter. *The Life of William Beckford.* London, 1932.

Passage, Charles E. 'E. T. A. Hoffmann's *The Devil's Elixirs:* A flawed masterpiece', *Journal of English and Germanic Philology,* LXXV (1976), 531–45.

Phillips, Walter C. *Dickens, Reade and Collins: Sensation Novelists: A Study in the Conditions and Theories of Novel Writing in Victorian England.* New York, 1919.

Pollin, Burton R. 'Philosophical and literary sources of *Frankenstein*', *Comparative Literature,* XVII (1965), 97–108.

Porte, Joel. *The Romance in America: Studies in Cooper, Poe, Hawthorne.* Middletown, Ct., 1969.

Praz, Mario. 'Poe and psychoanalysis' (1933), *Sewanee Review,* LXVIII (1960), 375–89.

——. *The Romantic Agony* (1930), trans. A. Davidson, introd. F. Kermode. London, 1970.

Quinn, Arthur Hobson. *Edgar Allan Poe: A Critical Biography.* New York, 1941.

Railo, Eino. *The Haunted Castle: A Study of the Elements of English Romanticism.* London, 1927.

Rieger, James Henry. ' "Au Pied de la Lettre": Stylistic uncertainty in *Vathek*', *Criticism,* IV (1962), 302–12.

Ringe, Donald A. *American Gothic: Imagination and Reason in Nineteenth-Century Fiction.* Lexington, Ky., 1982.

Roberts, B. B. *The Gothic Romance: Its Appeal to Women Writers and Readers in Late Eighteenth-Century England.* New York, 1980.

Roberts, Marie. *Gothic Immortals: The Fiction of the Brotherhood of the Rosy Cross.* London, 1990.

Robertson, Fiona. *Legitimate Histories: Scott, Gothic and the Authorities of Fiction.* Oxford, 1994.

Rodway, Allan Edwin. *The Romantic Conflict.* London, 1963.

Rothstein, Eric. 'The lessons of *Northanger Abbey*', *University of Toronto Quarterly*, XLIII (1974), 14–30.

Rudwin, Maximilian Josef. *The Devil in Legend and Literature.* Chicago, 1931.

Sadleir, Michael. *Bulwer and his Wife: A Panorama 1803–1836.* London, 1933.

——. *The Northanger Novels: A Footnote to Jane Austen.* Oxford, 1927.

Sage, Victor. *Horror Fiction in the Protestant Tradition.* London, 1988.

Scarborough, Dorothy. *The Supernatural in Modern English Fiction.* New York, 1917.

Sedgwick, Eve Kosofsky. *Between Men: English Literature and Male Homosocial Desire.* New York, 1985.

——. *The Coherence of Gothic Conventions.* New York, 1980.

——. *Epistemology of the Closet.* London, 1990.

Small, Christopher. *Ariel like a Harpy: Shelley, Mary and Frankenstein.* London, 1972.

Sontag, Susan. *Against Interpretation and Other Essays.* New York and Toronto, 1966.

Spark, Muriel. *Child of Light: A Reassessment of Mary Shelley.* Hadleigh, Essex, 1951.

Sperry, Stuart M., Jr. 'Romance as wish-fulfilment: Keats's "The Eve of St Agnes" ', *Studies in Romanticism*, X (1971), 27–43.

St Armand, Barton Levi. 'Hawthorne's "Haunted Mind": A subterranean drama of the self', *Criticism*, XIII (1971), 1–25.

Steeves, Harrison R. *Before Jane Austen: The Shaping of the English Novel in the Eighteenth Century.* London, 1966.

Sterrenburg, Lee. 'The Last Man: Anatomy of failed revolutions', *Nineteenth-Century Fiction*, XXXIII (1978), 324–47.

Strachey, Giles Lytton. *Characters and Commentaries*, ed. J. Strachey. London, 1933.

Stuart, Dorothy Margaret. *Horace Walpole.* London, 1927.

Summers, Montague. *A Gothic Bibliography.* London, 1941.

——. *The Gothic Quest: A History of the Gothic Novel.* London, 1938.

Thompson, Gary Richard. *Poe's Fiction: Romantic Irony in Gothic Tales.* Madison, Wisc., 1973.

——, ed. *The Gothic Imagination: Essays in Dark Romanticism.* Pullman, 1974.

Thorslev, Peter L., Jr. 'Incest as Romantic symbol', *Comparative Literature Studies*, II (1965), 41–58.

Tompkins, Joyce Marjorie Sanxter. *The Popular Novel in England, 1770–1800*. London, 1932.

Tuan, Y. F. *Landscapes of Fear*. London, 1979.

Twitchell, J. B. *Dreadful Pleasures: An Anatomy of Modern Horror*. New York, 1985.

——. *The Living Dead: A Study of the Vampire in Romantic Literature*. Durham, N.C., 1981.

Tymm, Marshall. *Horror Literature: A Core Collection and Reference Guide*. New York, 1981.

Tymms, Ralph Vincent. *Doubles in Literary Psychology*. Cambridge, 1949.

Vanderbilt, Kermit. 'Art and nature in "The Masque of the Red Death" ', *Nineteenth-Century Fiction*, XXII (1968), 379–89.

Varma, Devendra Prasad. *The Gothic Flame: Being a History of the Gothic Novel in England: its Origins, Efflorescences, Disintegration, and Residuary Influences*. London, 1957.

Varnado, S. L. *Haunted Presence: The Numinous in Gothic Fiction*. Tuscaloosa, 1987.

Veeder, William. *Mary Shelley and Frankenstein: The Fate of Androgyny*. Chicago, 1986.

Walker, I. M. 'The "Legitimate Sources" of terror in "The Fall of the House of Usher" ', *Modern Language Review*, LXI (1966), 585–92.

Watt, Ian. *The Rise of the Novel: Studies in Defoe, Richardson and Fielding*. London, 1957.

Wiesenfarth, Joseph. *Gothic Manners and the Classic English Novel*. Madison, Wisc., 1988.

Wieten, Alida A. S. *Mrs Radcliffe: Her Relation towards Romanticism*. Amsterdam, 1926.

Williams, Raymond. *The Long Revolution*. London, 1961.

Wilson, Colin. *The Strength to Dream: Literature and the Imagination*. London, 1962.

Wilson, Edmund. *Patriotic Gore: Studies in the Literature of the American Civil War*. London, 1962.

Wilt, Judith. *Ghosts of the Gothic: Austen, Eliot and Lawrence*. Princeton, 1980.

Winter, Keri J. *Subjects of Slavery, Agents of Change: Women and Power in Gothic Novels and Slave Narratives, 1790–1865*. Athens, Ga., 1992.

Wolff, Robert Lee. *Strange Stories, and Other Explorations in Victorian Fiction.* Boston, Mass., 1971.

Wolstenholme, Susan. *Gothic (Re)Visions: Writing Women as Readers.* Albany, N.Y., 1993.

Index